UGLY

UGLY

A Bikie's Life

PHIL 'UGLY' MAWSON
WITH PAULY FENECH & JORDAN KING-LACROIX

The names of certain people and places have been changed to protect the innocent, the guilty, the living and the dead.

PENGUIN BOOKS

UK | USA | Canada | Ireland | Australia
India | New Zealand | South Africa | China

Penguin Books is part of the Penguin Random House group of companies whose addresses can be found at global.penguinrandomhouse.com

Penguin Random House Australia

First published by Penguin Books in 2021

Copyright © Paul Fenech and Jordan King-Lacroix 2021

The moral right of the authors has been asserted.

All rights reserved. No part of this publication may be reproduced, published, performed in public or communicated to the public in any form or by any means without prior written permission from Penguin Random House Australia Pty Ltd or its authorised licensees.

This book is a memoir. It reflects the author's present recollections of experiences over time. In some instances, events have been compressed and dialogue has been re-created. The names and identifying characteristics of some persons described in the book have been changed.

Cover design by Alex Ross © Penguin Random House Australia Pty Ltd
Typeset in 12.5/17 pt Bembo by Midland Typesetters, Australia
Printed and bound in Australia by Griffin Press, part of Ovato, an accredited ISO AS/NZS 14001 Environmental Management Systems printer

A catalogue record for this book is available from the National Library of Australia

ISBN 978 1 76104 372 7

penguin.com.au

*To my wife, Lyn, and to Leon Moon, David Cripps, Mick Evans,
Rick Pont, Paul Brooks and the Gypsy Jokers.*
Phil 'Ugly' Mawson

*To all the Australian soldiers who served in Vietnam.
Lest we forget.*
Paul Fenech

*To A.N.Y. and the W.N.H.C. Without them,
this book would not have been possible.*
Jordan King-Lacroix

Contents

Introduction by Paul Fenech   1
Preface by Jordan King-Lacroix   5

1   My Dad Was a Boxer   17
2   The Fighter   27
3   The Soldier   49
4   The Bikie   77
5   The Citizen   117
6   The Gypsy Joker   129
7   The One Percenter   155
8   The Killer   191
9   Strike Force Raptor   221
10   The Jaded Old-Timer   235

Afterword by Jordan King-Lacroix   263
Acknowledgements   267
Bibliography and Further Reading   269
About the Authors   275

Introduction

My name is Pauly Fenech. You might know me from cult Australian TV and cinema comedies like *Fat Pizza* and *Housos*, which I created, directed and performed in. Around 2010, we were casting the first season of *Housos* and needed people to fill out the ranks of a fictional bikie gang called the Sunnyvale Hunters MC.

That's where I first met Phil 'Ugly' Mawson.

Ugly was introduced to me by Greg King. At the time, both were members of a real-life outlaw motorcycle club called the Gypsy Jokers. When they walked into our casting office, I noticed a few things about Ugly straightaway.

The first was obvious – he had a strange tattoo that looked like barbed wire above his left eye. That wasn't something I'd seen before. Then I noticed his wild blue eyes. When Ugly looks at you, he has this cheeky expression. I could tell right away there was a bright fire inside him. Eyes never lie.

UGLY

We talked briefly. Ugly's a man of few words. In the end, because he looked the part, he was cast as one of the Hunters.

In all honesty, I was a little intimidated at the start. I knew that Greg and Ugly had been in jail together. I later found out Ugly was a Vietnam veteran; that he founded the Gypsy Jokers Motorcycle Club in New South Wales; and that he was the great-grandson of the famous Antarctic explorer Sir Douglas Mawson. From that early meeting I had no idea that, over the next ten years, he would trust me with his life story and we'd become good friends.

Ugly's like a real-life Clint Eastwood or Charles Bronson. Even in his seventies, he'll still stand up against any enemy, two fists raised, ready to fight for himself and the people he cares about. Some might consider him a very bad man given the violent details of his life. But I see him differently. I see a code of honour, an honesty and a toughness that I've never known in anyone else I've met.

Why did we become mates?

We share a wicked sense of humour. We love motorbikes and boxing. We have a healthy contempt for corrupt authority. We also both have military experience. Every year we catch up after marching on Anzac Day. We always get very drunk and I am always honoured by being allowed to drink with Ugly's old war buddies from Vietnam.

He and another friend of his, Rick Pont, had been trying to turn his life story into a TV series. Unfortunately, it was not to be. After many letdowns from various film production companies, I offered to try to turn it into a book. That was also not to be. I tried writing it myself many times, but realised I just wasn't doing the story justice. So I decided to team up with a great young writer, Jordan King-Lacroix. Jordan's done an excellent

Introduction

job of telling Ugly's story in Ugly's own voice. I'm pleased that an account of this man's wild life will finally be shared.

I'd like to thank Ugly for his trust and friendship. He's a great bloke and probably the toughest hard cunt I've ever met. I should also emphasise how rare it is for an outsider to gain the trust of an ex-president of an outlaw motorcycle club. I hope you enjoy reading about my friend Phil 'Ugly' Mawson. Boxer, soldier, biker.

This is the Ugly side of life.

Preface

More often than not, when you tell people you're a writer, they'll say something like, 'Oh, I've got a great idea for a story.' Unfortunately, and though it's rude to say so at the time, they rarely do. Most of the time – because we live in a society that demands politeness over honesty – you just nod and smile. But every now and then someone comes to you with a story so good you just have to write it down.

Paul Fenech came to me with Phillip Mawson's story in mid-2019. It was a tale of the founder of the Australian chapter of the Gypsy Jokers Motorcycle Club, a guy known affectionately to his friends as 'Ugly' (though not for the reason you might think). He may have been related to Sir Douglas Mawson,* at least according to his dad. Ugly said his dad had big fists and that 'although he could have been bullshit', he didn't question

---

* In response to being asked about his (alleged) great-grandfather, Ugly said, 'Yeah, but he ate dogs. I don't eat dogs.'

what he was told. In researching this book, we found out that Mawson only had two daughters, so the likelihood of his surname being passed down to Ugly was unlikely, or at the very least unusual. Also, given Ugly's age, it's more likely that Douglas Mawson would have been his grandfather, not his great-grandfather. Either way, it's a part of the Mawson family folklore.

I'll admit that when Paul first told me about Ugly, I had visions of writing my own version of Hunter S. Thompson's classic book, *Hell's Angels*, even though it was not the kind of project I normally took on. The danger of it appealed to me.

In reality, my experience with Ugly and the Jokers was very different to Thompson's with the Angels. The main difference was that, initially, Ugly wouldn't talk to me. And I had no way of being in touch with him or the Jokers. It had taken years of working with Paul on a variety of projects before he opened up about his experiences as a young fighter in Smithfield; as a soldier off to war in Vietnam; as a rebel biker founding the Gypsy Jokers; and as the man who went to prison for murder to protect his family.

So Paul came up with a compromise. He'd go over to Ugly's house with a video camera and talk to him, and then I'd watch the recordings. Details sometimes needed to be prompted, but over the course of the lengthy interviews, all the corners of Ugly's life started to take shape.

I'd never heard anything quite like it.

I've watched a lot of TV, so I had a superficial understanding of the life of bikies, but nothing could have prepared me for the gritty detail.

When I opened the first video file, I saw an older, heavy-set man; age indeterminate, but in that time of life where he could be anywhere from a hard forty-five to a young eighty. He was

Preface

sitting in a chair, wearing a black T-shirt that featured a white diamond with a '1%' in its centre, with curvy lettering above and below. This was the Norwegian Gypsy Jokers patch design. The '1%' signified it as an outlaw motorcycle club, not some civilian social club. Behind him, hanging on a dresser, was the leather back patch of the Australian Gypsy Jokers – a grinning white skull adorned with a gold earring superimposed over an inverted red triangle.

Above Ugly's left eyebrow was a tattoo of barbed wire, and on each earlobe were smaller tattoos that read 'GJ': Gypsy Jokers. He had a classic downturned handlebar moustache, the white of it contrasting with the dark silver of his thick head of hair.

His eyes were kind, laughing, but they looked like they'd seen a lot, like they were always in the process of remembering something far gone, something harrowing. His voice was husky and ocker, like that of the local storyteller down the pub. He spoke with the same intonation at all times, as if no piece of information was more important or more shocking than another. Some stories were punctuated by a hoarse laugh.

The specifics of his life were, at times, scant. Ugly would brush over something and my writer-brain would say, 'No, wait, please, more of that.' When that happened, I'd text Paul the question and he'd pass it on. It turned out Ugly was a hard man to get in touch with, though it maybe shouldn't have been all that surprising that a septuagenarian bikie wasn't an avid texter. Sometimes I got answers, sometimes I didn't.

As you might imagine, Ugly didn't really like talking about his feelings. And I don't mean in a therapeutic way, I mean in a way that tells you how he felt in any given moment. Was he scared? Was he having fun? It was hard getting that information out of him. He was always skipping around, jumping to new topics as his mind made connections between one event and another. For example:

[00:00:03.25] UGLY: When I shot that bloke up the road here in the street, I had the same feeling come out of there, of his spirit leaving his body. It was like I was back in Vietnam, you know?

[00:00:20.27] PAUL: So just explain that, describe that.

[00:00:25.24] UGLY: Well, I shot him twice in the car. He got out and kicked me in the head, of all fucking things. So I took perfect aim then and dropped him and straightaway I'm thinking I'm back in Vietnam. Straightaway I go *bang, bang,* then *bang* in the forehead and I just felt this, I don't know, sort of funny sense come over me. 'Oh, I shouldn't have done that.' But I already done it. I started cursing him in Vietnamese, you know?

[00:01:01.23] PAUL: So do you think you had – like, people talk about having flashbacks to Vietnam – was that a flashback to Vietnam?

[00:01:10.04] UGLY: Yeah, it was a flashback. When I shot him and dropped him I just ran over to him, finished him off. Yeah. It was like a flashback. A sad one. Brought a lot of, you know, grief, out.

[00:01:34.22] PAUL: Okay. Before we get into that, let's just start off with some basics. What's your name, date of birth and which part of Australia are you from?

Preface

Sometimes it was hard to understand the things Ugly *did* say because they were so foreign to me. How could I possibly comprehend what it had been like for him? How could I really grasp why he reacted to things the way he did? The world he grew up in – the world he actively created for himself – was a world far removed from my own. What your average Joe might do in any given situation is not necessarily what Ugly would do. But, then again, Ugly had the Gypsy Jokers with him.

At one point, I knew I was going to need more than the interviews could provide. I asked Paul what we could do.

'You know what?' he said. 'I'll just call Ugly tomorrow and see if he's all right speaking with you.'

'Really?' This would make everything much easier.

'Yeah. I'll give him a ring and let you know.'

The next day Paul called and said Ugly was willing to meet with me that Friday morning at his home in Padstow, in Sydney's south-west.

Great! But then I started worrying myself into a lather. I hadn't done many interviews like this. Would I be able to get the answers I wanted? Would he talk openly to me? Would he hate me?

The drive out to Padstow was uneventful. Green lights all the way. Google Maps led me to a small cul-de-sac with idyllic homes adorned with bright green lawns. Was this really where the notorious Phil 'Ugly' Mawson lived? On a quiet residential cul-de-sac? As I pulled up, a couple in the driveway next door were helping an elderly woman out of a car. It all just seemed so . . . normal.

Approaching Ugly's house, I could see a swing-seat on the front lawn. Sitting in it was the unmistakeable figure himself. He was staring at me as I drew closer, me in my T-shirt and sweatshirt and backpack. So I waved. It disarmed him immediately. A distant, familiar voice reached my ears.

'Hey there, mate,' he said.

'Hey hey,' I said back.

'How's it goin'?' He tried to stand up. This clearly wasn't easy for him. He had to rock back and forth a few times before he could swing himself into a standing position.

He reached out to shake my hand. Visions of accidentally giving Ugly COVID-19 flashed inside my head, but I knew I was healthy, and I was more or less certain he didn't go out enough to have caught it. I shook his hand. That handshake told me that, despite him getting on, he could absolutely still take me. No doubt. Since I'd last seen footage of him, he'd let the beard on his cheeks grow out. It looked like old-fashioned mutton chops. In another world Ugly might have been a wartime general.

'Wanna come in for a cup of coffee?' He gestured behind him at the two-storey family home.

'Yeah,' I said. 'Let's.'

I followed him inside. In the lounge room immediately to my right the TV was on and a bunch of kids were playing and screaming. Ugly's son-in-law, Dion, was sitting on the couch half-watching them and half-watching the TV. One of the little ones screeched something at Grandpa Ugly as he walked by, making direct eye contact with me. Ugly kept going and went into the hallway. Then he steered me left.

'This is my wife, Lyn,' he said.

'Oh, hello, dear,' Lyn said. She was seated in a chair in a small sewing room, hooked up to a dialysis machine and breathing oxygen through a tube in her nose. 'Pardon me not getting up.'

'The dialysis,' Ugly said.

'Yeah.' I didn't know what else to say. 'That does not look fun.'

Preface

Lyn chuckled and smiled softly. 'It is not, no.'

Ugly then took me through to the kitchen. The wallpaper was peeling. Dishes were piled in the sink and on the bench. A young woman stood behind the counter making sandwiches.

'This is my daughter, Skye,' Ugly said.

'Hello,' she said, smiling.

'Hi.' Again, not knowing exactly what to say, I said, 'I'm working on the book about your dad.'

'Oh, are you?' she said and laughed. 'That'll be one hell of a story. He's got a few good ones.'

'That he does.'

Ugly gestured for me to follow him to the room beyond the kitchen, which either used to be a garage or was an addition to the house. I recognised it immediately. This was where Paul had done the interviews – Ugly's room, the place he felt the most comfortable. Hung all around the walls were Gypsy Jokers artefacts, army memorabilia, an Elvis poster and the occasional piece displaying Batman's nemesis, the Joker, including one from his son, which had been inscribed, 'Dad, sometimes you're Batman, and sometimes you're the Joker', with a relief of the two characters. There were also photos of Ugly with various people I didn't know.

'How do you like your coffee?' he asked me.

'Black, thanks.'

'Black?' He sounded surprised. 'No milk or sugar?'

'Nope,' I said. 'Just black is fine.'

'You like it like me,' he said. 'And how I like my girlfriends.' He giggled like a kid at his own joke.

There was a small table set up with a chair, which he waved at and told me I could sit down. I did and he went out and dragged in a big cushioned office chair.

UGLY

'No sugar, you said, yeah?'

'No thanks,' I said, following up with the line from *Snatch* I always thought of in response to that question, 'I'm sweet enough.'

Ugly laughed. 'Me too.'

I set up the recorder and my notebook and started off by asking how old he was, just for reference.

'Seventy-five.'

'And you don't look a day over seventy.'

'Ah, you bastard,' he said, smiling.

It was then that I realised we'd actually met before. It all came rushing back to me.

'You were in *Fat Pizza vs Housos*, weren't you?' I said.

'Yeah, and *Dumb Criminals*.'

'We've met before. I played one of the junkies.'

'Oh, shit, yeah. We had that big brawl in the park.'

'That's right. You gave me a few hits.'

'You went down pretty good,' he said. 'Like a ragdoll. It was like you'd taken a hit before.'

'Luckily, just acting,' I said.

Suddenly, the awkwardness was gone.

As I'd sat down I noticed a set of handcuffs hanging on a cupboard door behind me.

'Are those real?' I asked.

'Yeah,' he said with a chuckle. 'My son, Brock, gave them to me when I got out of jail.'

'He's got a sense of humour.'

'He does, the little bastard,' he said, and laughed. 'Oh, I've got something for you.'

'You have?' This was unexpected.

'Look in that box next to you. You're about a medium, yeah?'

Preface

I pulled out a black T-shirt that looked like it had been self-screen-printed, with the slogan '1% UGLY' written on the arms and body.

'Yeah, I'm a medium,' I said. 'I love it.'

'Thought I'd eyeballed you right. Wear it when you see Paul, he'll get a kick out of it.'

And then the interview began.

•

The following has been written in the first person, in order to capture as much of Ugly's storytelling authenticity as possible. It wouldn't feel right or apt to write it in the third person. It'd lose its personality and feel too clinical, too much like some outside observer looking in. Phil 'Ugly' Mawson's life needs to be related as if he were talking to you at the pub or around a camp fire after a long ride down to Wollongong.

Always carry a mouthguard with you. If you're in a shit position, a bloke's looking at you and you're gonna have a go, and you put the mouthguard in, you're ready. It gives you a split second for him to be startled and think, 'Fuck, I'm in trouble', then you attack him straightaway and you've got the advantage.

—Phil 'Ugly' Mawson

1

My Dad Was a Boxer

I was born Phillip William Mawson on 9 February 1945 in Fairfield, a western suburb of Sydney. Life was much quieter back in those days. You didn't need to lock your doors. People trusted each other. You didn't have to watch your back. That all comes later, when you grow up. Back then, it was rock 'n' roll and leather jackets; that post-World War II kind of thing.

My dad, William Horace Mawson, was strict, but I loved him. William's a bit of a family name, which is why I ended up with it. Dad had it, and his dad had it, and so on. Mum was Violet May Tripp. She was a sweetheart, but if I didn't do as she said, Dad would whack me across the arse. He had a hand like cement. They were a good team. I respected them and did as I was told most of the time, but I was a cheeky little bugger, always starting trouble and making smart-arse comments.

Dad worked as a stonemason, but in his spare time he was an amateur heavyweight boxer. I had two big brothers, Neil and Peter, who were ten and eleven years older than me, respectively.

UGLY

Neil was a middleweight boxer. Our love of fighting came from Dad. It was like a family business. He used to train at a gym on Harris Street in Fairfield, around the back of the School of Arts. I'd sneak over and watch him spar without him knowing I was there. It was exciting. I admired the strength. Dad didn't want me watching because he didn't want me to get into fighting, but I was soon addicted. It's hard to not get into it as a young boy, when both your dad and your brother are into it too.

I guess it was inevitable that I'd get a fire in my belly about fighting.

Even at that early age, I knew strength was something that was respected.

My other brother, Peter, was a circuit pushbike rider. I used to go watch him race at Bankstown Velodrome. He ended up doing his national service with the army.

And there you have it, really: fighting, bikes and the army were all in the family from the very start. I was riding pushbikes at a young age, but I didn't get a taste of my first motorbike until I was fifteen.

But I'm getting ahead of myself.

Dad was a fighter in the tent. A tent fighter was like a circus act, a dodgy set-up, with a paid plant on the ground. They'd have someone go around with a big drum – *bonga bonga bonga* – and the ringleader would present a row of fighters – strapping, strong fellas – and then call for volunteers from the audience to step up and fight them.

My dad was the paid plant, the 'volunteer'. He'd put up his hand and yell, 'I'll fight him!'

And then off they'd go. They never really hurt each other, not seriously, but they could have if they wanted to. It was good to watch, pretty believable. And they fought properly, it wasn't

My Dad Was a Boxer

completely fake, but Dad was a trained boxer so he wasn't some chump stepping up and risking a full-on beating. He'd get up and fight and my brothers would egg him on.

At the time, I didn't know it was rigged.

'No, don't do it!' I'd yell at Dad. I was scared for him.

'It's all right,' he'd whisper, putting his hand on my shoulder. 'Just shut up and let me go up.'

When I found out later how everything worked – that he was the paid plant and was going to be okay – I egged him on as well. We looked just like three regular boys proud of their dad for taking a risk in the ring.

Once he got going, it was more or less like any other fight in that he'd either win, or he'd lose. Sometimes, though, he wouldn't even make it into the ring. Some local smart-arse would jump up and get in first, volunteering to fight, and barging right past Dad. Well, that fella would get tuned up pretty good by the main fighter. That usually taught him a lesson.

Dad had ten wins under his belt in the tent, but he only fought for about a year. At least, as far as I knew. I don't know how many fights he really had – I never tallied them up – but then and there I decided I wanted at least *eleven* wins.

I wanted to one-up him.

I ended up with more than that.

Dad fought for fun and for the exercise. Being a stonemason only made his hands even stronger. He wasn't tall, about five-foot-five, but he was solid. A real puncher. I get my build from him, although I'm definitely heavier now than he ever was.

My brother Neil, the middleweight, was a bit of a shit-stirrer. He got me my first punching bag, although that wasn't his intention. I was about twelve years old and Neil had just won the Australian Jitterbug championship. He was a hell of a dancer. When he wasn't fighting or dancing, he worked at a printer's shop. So he had a trade, too, like Dad and, later, me. Anyway, after winning the dancing championships, Neil brought me home his prize: this big fluffy teddy bear. It was about four foot high, same as me. He handed it over and said, 'You can cuddle right up to that, because *you're* a teddy bear.'

Well, I took that fucking thing and I went out and got some rope. I wrapped the rope around its neck and hung it up in the backyard, next to the chook pen.

I used that teddy as a punching bag.

Dad came out and gave me a whack on the arse for my trouble.

'What the hell are you doing?' he said.

'Just going to punch a bag of teddies!' I said, smart as can be.

He laughed. I ended up training on that bear for quite a while.

Later, I practised on a punching bag made out of Neil's army kit bag. He was in the national service – we called them nashos, but they're the army reserves now – and we filled his bag up with sawdust and paper. It was pretty solid. I also did karate, which I kept up for a long time. There was something about the pacing of it, the peace of it, the structure that I loved. It settles your mind as well as being really good for your body.

•

Mum and Dad didn't own a car – this was the 1940s and 50s – and I don't think Dad even had his driver's licence. We went everywhere by train or bus. Mum had her licence and could

My Dad Was a Boxer

drive because she needed to for her work as a Meals on Wheels volunteer. She'd spend all day cooking and then delivering the meals around town. As I got older, I'd sometimes go along for the ride, just to check that the people she was seeing were being good to her and weren't trying anything on. I didn't help her cook, though, I was never much good in the kitchen.

One time we were all coming back from a family outing to Bronte, in the eastern suburbs. We'd gone to do some shopping and spend time at the beach. To get home, we walked to Bondi Junction train station – a very different place then to what it is now – to catch the train home. In those days, the gap between the platform and the train was pretty big. Big enough for someone to fall into.

Dad was getting onto the train and must have missed his footing, because he slipped in between the train and the platform and got stuck. He told me to go for help so I ran off screaming for the guards.

'Stop the train!' I yelled. I was only about ten or twelve. 'Stop the train! My dad's stuck and can't get out!'

The guard quickly sent a signal up the line to the conductor and he stopped the train from leaving the platform. A crowd of people gathered, along with a few of the guards, and somehow pushed the carriage back so they could haul Dad out. They pulled his arms and he came sliding up and back onto the platform. He wasn't injured and must have felt lucky that he wasn't a big fella.

I didn't end up much bigger than Dad, and kids used to pick on me for it. That's one of the reasons why both Neil and I ended up getting into boxing. We didn't want to have to deal with that kind of nonsense, that kind of disrespect. The idea of being respected took root in my head at a pretty young age.

I saw the kind of respect Dad got at work and at the tent boxing shows, and how successful Neil was becoming.

Strength was the key to all of that.

Because my brothers were so much older than me, we didn't really have a close relationship. Peter and Neil were close, because they grew up together, but I was too young. They'd buy me things sometimes, because I was their kid brother, but that's about it. Neil showed me a few boxing moves here and there, got me started, but we didn't spend a lot of time together. He did some tent fighting for a while, just like Dad. And he gave me some good advice which has stuck with me ever since.

'You've got to be angry to fight,' he said. 'You've got to be angry and channel that.'

So I got angry. I was already angry because I wasn't tall, and a bunch of kids would be on me for that. I was also by myself a lot of the time, and that wasn't something I dealt with very well.

•

Every Friday night, Dad would come home with a big tub of ice cream and some cones. We'd all plonk down on the lounge and eat that as a treat. It was our favourite thing about the week. Dad would watch us with this huge smile on his face while he drank his Dirty Annie.* He wouldn't drink it out of the bottle, though, he'd always pour it into a glass. Two glasses and the whole thing was gone.

Home life was quiet. I spent a lot of time listening to *Night Watch* on the radio, a reality crime news program that gathered

---
* Resch's Dinner Ale.

up a bunch of stories from the week. In the 1950s I listened to the Larry Kent* program, which was a lot of fun, and we watched *Homicide* on TV.** I liked crime. As I got older, I didn't go in for fiction much. Not because it was bad, but because my patience for bullshit got pretty thin. I gravitated towards fair dinkum stuff. I liked learning about things that had really happened.

I never saw much of my extended family. Mum had one sister, but she lost the plot, got dementia. She stayed with us a few times, but she was always wandering around at night, not knowing what a toilet was. It was sad. They ended up having to put her in a nursing home, and I lost contact with her after that.

Dad had one brother who ended up setting himself alight. He was a smoker and he fell asleep in his lounge chair with a cigarette in his hand. The smoke probably – hopefully – got him before he felt anything.

That was 1972, the first time I ended up in jail.

•

I went to Fairfield Primary and then Fairfield High, but I left school at fourteen and a half. I couldn't wait to get out of there. Back then, you were allowed to leave at fifteen, but I didn't want to sit still for that long. I wanted to enjoy school, I wanted to learn, and so I went every day and never skipped class. There was a lot of sport on offer, too, which was great, but what bugged me was that the teachers couldn't be bothered giving us proper lessons. They'd give us a few things to do, but that was about it.

---

* Larry Kent, created by Ron Ingleby, was a series of pulp detective stories, novelettes and books published from the 1950s through to the 1970s. The Macquarie radio network aired 155 half-hour episodes of the Larry Kent radio show, with Ken Wayne as the titular character and all episodes written by Ingleby.
** An Australian procedural drama that aired from 1964–77 on Channel Seven.

Nothing like actual schooling. So of course I was always waiting to go outside and play sport.

I was in G class. You know, there's A class, B class, and so on. Well, I was in G class, which basically meant that they cared even less about trying to teach us. They didn't see the point. The teachers were slack. And that pissed me off. Going to school felt like a waste of time. Instead of English lessons, they took us out to the field to do emu-bobbing.* What's the point of that?

So I left.

Mum tried teaching me for a bit, doing a sort of home-schooling, but it didn't really stick. I found learning hard, especially as I didn't have any real grounding, thanks to the teachers at Fairfield. After about a year and a half had gone by and I'd turned sixteen, Mum decided that it was time for me to get out there and do something with myself. I'd been hanging around on the streets, getting into trouble, and she wasn't too pleased that I was basically wasting my life.

'You've got to get a trade,' she said, 'or you'll end up with nothing. You'll end up like your bum mates.'

She went around looking for apprenticeship vacancies and it wasn't long before she got me into Goldstein in St Peters, learning 'shoe clicking', basically cutting shoe patterns out of leather. She didn't know anyone there, just walked in and told them her son needed to be doing something with himself. I ended up in a five-year indentured apprenticeship, the first three years of which was schooling at TAFE. That's when my education really picked up. The teachers would write stuff

---

* Online dictionaries define 'emu-bobbing' as 'carrying out a detailed search of an area'. Presumably Ugly picked up this term in the army, but in this instance it may refer to the fact that they took the class out to the field and did a whole lot of nothing.

My Dad Was a Boxer

on the board, I would write it down, and then we'd all talk about it.

Finally, studying clicked with me.

I also learnt everything I could about knives and leather, which would come in handy later on.

2

The Fighter

There was this motorbike cop who used to patrol our street, flying up and down and tearing up the pavement. One day he clipped the back of a car, his bike went skidding off, and the cop followed, skinning his leg pretty badly. I ran up to him to try to help – you see someone hurt, you want to help – but he got up all right on his own. The car didn't even stop, probably didn't realise anything had happened.

The very same cop later put a bullet in my pet Pomeranian.

The little dog loved it when the ice cream truck came down our street. One day, he was sniffing about near the back wheels when the truck reversed right over him. He was lying there in a lot of pain. You know how it is; they're injured, but not dead yet. You can't save them.

I saw the motorbike cop and waved him down. He stopped and looked at the dog. Then he looked at me. 'You gotta turn away, son. He's gone.'

The cop shot him with his .38 right there in the gutter.

UGLY

I can still remember the ringing in my ears, the sound of that gun – *bam!*

You wouldn't see that sort of thing happen now, but I knew the cop was just putting the animal out of its misery. We became friends after that. I wanted to ride around on a motorbike like he did.

I felt a bit lost after that dog died, but I got very interested in guns.

I didn't get to ride my first motorbike until I was fifteen. That was the year everything really started for me. A mate's dad had a 650 Matchless ex-cop bike, which we'd take out to the park when his dad wasn't home. I loved the power that rumbled in that machine. We did big circles through the dirt and the grass and when we brought it back it was so filthy and covered in mud we always had to give it a good clean.

Afterwards, all I could think about was when I'd get my next ride.

When I turned sixteen, I got my learner's permit and bought an old Triumph Thunderbird. It was a beautiful thing. What's that saying? You never forget your first. This bike had a nameplate on the back and my mates were telling me that I had to put UGLY on it, or some variation on that. Half of them were Italians, and they always came to my fights, so they made up a plate that said 'Uno di Brutti', which means 'One of the Ugly'.

I'd just stepped into the role of a man named Ugly.

•

I started up my first gang, the River Rats, with some mates from the area after I left school. I knew some of them from the Police Boys' Club in Parramatta, where I'd been training for

The Fighter

about a year as a boxer. One mate could see that I was a good fighter, getting into scraps on the street, and thought I could use the training to focus myself a bit more.

We called ourselves the River Rats mainly because we used to hang out by the riverside. The gang was mostly a bunch of older blokes, eighteen, nineteen, twenty-year-olds, and most of them had cars. It might seem odd, a bunch of older blokes hanging out with a fifteen-year-old kid, but it was normal back then. And besides, they saw how aggro I was and appreciated that I knew how to fight.

Like I said, strength got you respect.

I wanted to be as tough as my dad and my brother. My peers looked down at me because I was short. But as I grew stronger, if they looked down on me, they'd also be scared. Being disrespected was something I never wanted. It made you feel weak. I didn't feel weak, physically, because I'd been training to punch since I was a kid, but I wanted to be so tough that no one would ever look down on me.

This was instilled in me from an early age.

I didn't go to pubs with the older blokes; mostly, we'd just hang out at Collins Milk Bar. We kept to ourselves, but if someone wanted a go, we'd give it to them. There were no drugs at that stage, or at least none that I saw.

I had a couple of fights at the Police Boys' Club in Parramatta. One was pretty ugly and that's where I got my nickname. It wasn't because I had an ugly mug no one could stand; believe it or not, I was actually a bit of a looker back then.

No, they called me Ugly because of my style of fighting.

'You look like an octopus,' one of my mates said. 'Your punches were coming from everywhere.'

And so the name stuck.

UGLY

One day some boys came up from Bankstown looking for trouble. They'd heard about the River Rats and wanted to size us up. When we found out, we flew over the bridge and gave it to them. There were about fifteen of us brawling on the street. It was the first feeling of fire I remember. It was great being in the ring where there are rules and skill and movement, but a wild biff in the middle of the road really heated up my belly and turned my fists to stone.

Street fighting was satisfying because of the way the victory felt. Unlike in the ring, every tactic was used on the street; the boys would try to trip you, scratch you, hit you with whatever they could. It was a hell of a thrill being in a fray like that – especially when you won. I don't think the River Rats ever lost a brawl.

Soon after that little punch-on, we decided to drive to Bankstown to give it to those boys on their home turf. We couldn't leave it with them coming over our way, we needed to show them that we weren't scared, that we didn't think highly of them at all. So we drove down – a few of us had our licences by that stage – and parked at the railway station.

Before we got into it, I gave my boys a quick boxing lesson. I wanted them to know the basics: footwork, weaving, the importance of keeping your hands up. That way we'd have a step up on the other gang. Knowing how to fight is the key to winning. You can be the strongest bloke in the world, but if someone else knows how to fight better than you, you're going down.

Well, wouldn't you know it, right in the middle of our boxing lesson, some Bankstown fucker came up behind me and slammed a wooden crate from the fruit shop over my head! It shocked me more than it hurt. I whirled around and clocked him.

The Fighter

It was on.

Even with that bloody crate on my head I was swinging and punching blokes. The crowd erupted, people shouting on our side and theirs. But I couldn't get the damn thing off my head. Turned out it was a solid defence.

There were about thirty people on either side in that dust-up and we came out of it pretty well. We didn't back down. It ended when a few of the River Rats, who were laughing their arses off, pulled the crate off my head.

By that stage, the Bankstown boys knew it was all over.

We were all huffing and puffing, sporting a few injuries, but we'd sent those Bankstown boys packing. And we'd done it on their own turf. Charlie Costa was there, thank Christ. He was a mean puncher. He knocked blokes left, right and centre. It was what made him a good trainer later on. Charlie was five years older than me and already a professional fighter, but he never stopped being a professional street punk as well. Best of the best.

The boys from Bankstown had wanted to fight, so we showed them what the Fairfield boys were made of. If they wanted it, they were going to get it, but they didn't like what they got.

That was the thing: if you were going to be out on the street, in a gang like we were, you had to be a good fighter. You couldn't just talk it, you had to be able to walk it – to hit and get hit. We had some solid fighters like Costa; the Green brothers, Tommy and Tax; and the Bradshaw brothers. Every one of them was a hard fighter. Everyone wanted to be top dog. As long as we kept on top of our fighting, we'd be all right.

Charlie, being the shithead that he was, loved corking people, especially me. Corking is when you punch someone hard on their thigh and it goes numb. Hurts like a bastard. Charlie first got me when I was about sixteen. He made out like he was teaching me punches and blocks. He went in for a punch, and I put up my hands but he just manoeuvred down and thumped me right on the top of my thigh. I screamed. I was holding my leg, jumping up and down, and he's dancing around me going 'na na na na na', slapping me about the ears. Holy shit, he could really hit. He had hands like bricks.

They were just like my dad's.

•

Sometimes my River Rats mates and I would head over to Manly Wharf to hang out at this great penny arcade. We'd take the train to Circular Quay from Fairfield, and then catch the ferry over to Manly. It'd be me, Billy Burton, Macca McKinnon, Sammy Luguide and Freddie Briggs. Billy and Freddie were Aboriginal, Sammy was our local wog and Macca was just Aussie like me. Sammy was a hell of a fighter; he had a mean right hook. He was shit at boxing, but he knocked out a fair few blokes in our time as River Rats. I always told him the only way I'd fight him was in a phone box so that he couldn't use his reach on me.

When we got to Manly, we'd hang around by the ferry wharf and wait for people to start getting off. We never had any money, but we devised a neat little trick to earn some coin that seemed to work every time. As the people got off the ferry, the boys (not me) would dive down between the ferry and the wharf into the water and swim back out. It wouldn't take long before someone would yell out at us.

'Hey, look at those boys,' they'd say. 'They'll dive for money, I bet!'

The Fighter

And then they'd start throwing pennies into the water! As soon as the penny hit the surface, Billy or Freddie would dive down to get it. Macca only did it every now and then, but the other two were experts. The water wasn't that deep. Once they found the coin, they'd swim back up and put it on the wharf and sit there, ready for more.

The ferry goers ate it up. They'd cheer every time one of the boys came back up out of the water holding a penny.

'Look what they're doing! Come on, folks, throw some more money!'

That'd give us a whole day's worth of pennies for the arcade. Not a bad way to make money from some bored people with spare change. I guess it seems weird — and it kind of is — but there was less to do back then, so people got their kicks wherever they could.

Billy's lost half a leg now to diabetes. Freddie ended up becoming an Elder, but he got dementia, the poor bugger. He was a top footballer.

I miss those boys.

•

Up until I went off to Vietnam, I was doing a couple of fights a week and ended up going up against a few of the well-thought-of amateurs. Tony Williams, an up-and-coming Aboriginal fighter, was a good boxer, lighter than me; a bantamweight. We used to spar down at Smithfield Hall. I liked it there, looking for sparring partners, taking on blokes I hadn't fought before. The only way to improve is to fight as many people as you can. Everyone has a slightly different style, a different way they duck or throw a punch. Fighting the same people over and over is a good way to stagnate.

Anyway, Tony and I were sparring and he cracked me a beauty on the nose. I had a bit of seepage, and thought it was just because I had a cold, so we carried on. I didn't know my nose was broken in two places. I kept sparring until eventually I realised that I was bleeding pretty badly.

'I think there's something wrong,' I said as we were winding down.

'Look at your nose,' Tony said to me. 'It's all over your face!'

He was right. The doc had a good look but there's not a lot you can do for a broken nose. He tried to straighten it, but it's never been the same since. It's flattened from one side of my face to the other, which changed the way I breathed.

Just before I got called up for Vietnam, Charlie Costa took me to train at Jimmy English's gym in Merrylands. This was 1967, when I was twenty-one. Charlie could see that I had raw talent and had taken me under his wing ever since I was a kid in the River Rats. Jimmy was a professional trainer. You had to pay to train there, not like at the Police Boys' Club in Parramatta. Jimmy had a lot of good fighters: the Thussel brothers; Crawford and Johnny Digby. Those names might not mean a lot now, but back then, if you were paying attention to the circuit, you knew who they were.

Without Charlie, I wouldn't have been as strong a fighter. He wasn't a member of the River Rats, but he was always hanging around when he wasn't training. Whenever we needed someone for a fight, he was there. He had a big pro bout in 1963 against Peter Batelle at the Sydney Stadium in Rushcutters Bay. He won. He usually fought under his own name, but sometimes under joke names like I. M. Gentle, I. M. Whackit, or Carlos Cruz. He was a real character and had a great sense of humour. It inspired me and sometimes I'd fight under the

The Fighter

name Art Mawson instead of Phil. I fought a ten-rounder at the Cronulla Leagues Club under that name.

My brother Neil would occasionally come to my fights. I wouldn't always spot him in the crowd, but I could always hear him bellowing and cheering. He came to one in south Sydney, and one at the Sydney Stadium. We weren't all that close, even as we got older, but he supported me in his own way.

My first proper professional fight under my own name was with a local Aboriginal bloke by the name of Orb Roberts. He was a really good fighter. We fought in the same weight class: light welterweight. I'm not that weight class anymore – I'm more like a super-heavyweight – but I can still slap hard!

Anyway, we were going at it, trading blows, and I went in for a swing at his head with my right hand. Orb ducked, the bastard, and my fist caught the top of his head, the really hard part of the skull, and *pop*, I broke my hand. It was like I'd punched a brick wall. He definitely heard it, too, and kept at me, swinging and swinging. I pushed on for another two rounds with the busted hand.

My first ever pro fight ended in a draw.

Afterwards, Orb came up to me and said, 'I heard your hand go. I thought I had you, but then you kept going, you bastard!'

I said, 'Mate, me too.'

We became good friends after that.

The next day I got a letter from Arthur Tunsel, a bigwig on the amateur fight scene. He wanted me to fight at the Sydney Stadium as part of a team up against the Russian Olympic team. But I was still recovering and my hand was hurting like hell.

'I just had a pro fight and busted my hand,' I said, laughing, when I got him on the phone. 'I need to recuperate.'

UGLY

I would have loved to have fought those Russians. That would have been a huge status thing. It was an honour to even be picked.

Sometimes, though, fights weren't fought with your fists.

There was this older bloke who hung around us, Johnny Smiley, who fancied himself a tough man on the streets. He was about twenty-two and I was about sixteen.

He was pushing a mate of mine around, just being a tough guy, a dickhead. Back then we all carried fisherman knives. They were fold-up knives with two blades; one straight, and the other serrated with a two-pronged fork at the end. We didn't use them all that much; they were mostly just for scaring people. Someone sees a knife and they usually run right off.

Well, Johnny Smiley was pushing my mate around and I was having none of it. I went, 'Hey, back off!'

He looked at me, fixing me with this leer.

'We're not here to fight,' I said. And I meant it, I didn't really have any intention of fighting him. But I wasn't going to let him push my mate around, either.

I don't remember exactly what he said next, but he said something, probably something smart, and so I pulled out my knife and flicked it open. I was hoping he'd get the hint and back off and then we could all go on our merry ways.

But no.

'Ah, you've got a knife,' he said.

He rushed me and grabbed my wrist, trying to wrench the knife away.

But he ended up pulling me into him and I stuck him.

The blade slid right in.

He cried like a wounded pig and just ran off. It was over so fast. One minute he's in front of me, the next there's blood on my knife and he's gone.

The Fighter

That night I went to a party and people were talking about how Johnny Smiley was one of the best street fighters around.

'That bastard?' I said.

'Yeah. But today someone *stabbed* him.'

'Yeah, it was fucking me!'

I never finished the job. Johnny Smiley stabbed himself by grabbing me and pulling me in. I know it sounds like bullshit, but it's one of those dumb, quick things that can happen in a street fight. He never reported it. He was a hard nut who never would, so that was good. I thought I was going to get charged, but I didn't. To this day I'm glad Johnny Smiley* had the balls to keep it between the two of us.

•

Besides training and fighting, we were always chasing girls. We'd go out, cruise around the neighbourhood, and chat them up. It's different now, but back then we'd just walk up to a group of girls and start talking. I remember once there was a bunch hanging out at our favourite joint, Collins Milk Bar. They were laughing and carrying on, drinking milkshakes. We walked past and one of them said something smart to one of my mates. I jumped down and gave them all smacks on the bums. I said something like 'smart-arses get smacks on the arses'.

Well, just my luck. The cops happened by at that exact minute and arrested me for accosting women.

It was the first charge on my sheet. I was nineteen years old.

The funniest part is, in among that group of girls was Patty

---

* *Author's note:* Ugly called me one afternoon in June 2021 to tell me that he had just found out that Johnny Smiley had died a couple of years earlier. He laughed and said, 'I guess I finally got him. It all came back around to him in the end, eh?'

Baines. I ended up marrying Patty. I smacked my wife's arse before I even knew she was going to become my wife! I was also sweet on another girl from that group, Ruth Tuff, and we were together for a little while when I went away to Vietnam, but it didn't last.

So Patty and I got back in touch when I got home. She was a real sweetheart, but things didn't work out. We were only together a couple of years, and my temper did us in. These days they'd say I had PTSD after Vietnam, and they'd probably be right. But what it really came down to is I didn't treat Patty right because I was an angry bastard. Let's leave it at that.

•

There were motorcycle clubs around in the late 1950s and early 1960s, but they were mostly social clubs and race clubs, places for motorbike enthusiasts who wanted somewhere to hang out and talk shop. When I was about eighteen, I joined St Mary's Motorcycle Social Club, which was also a racing club. I'd signed up for Vietnam by that stage, but hadn't had my marbles drawn yet. My bike at the time was a 1959 Triumph Bonneville with an orange and white fuel tank.

I wanted to race. I always thought I'd be able to do it. Problem was, I was never that good. My mates were better, especially my childhood mate, Damon Tippen. Sometimes in life your abilities don't match up to your passions.

The St Mary's boys would meet up on Thursdays at the Namatjira Hotel, a pub in Rooty Hill. It was a bit like the River Rats, just a bunch of blokes hanging out and chatting about what had been going on, except we all had bikes and were now drinking beers instead of milkshakes.

The Fighter

One of the presidents of the club at the time, Guitar Zaan, was this would-be, could-be sort of bloke. Always bigging himself up, always trying to get his nose and name into things, the kind of dickhead who tries hard to build up a legend around himself. In the end, he joined the Hells Angels and flew over to the United States to hang out with them. This was before the Angels here were affiliated, so going over to them from Australia was a part of that.

Turned out Guitar got on their bad side.

He had this trick where he'd go to discos and when the girls would get up to dance, he'd rifle through their bags and steal their money. Well, one night he got caught, and naturally enough his new mates weren't all that keen on this sort of behaviour. He was stealing from the Angels' girls!

Which is basically stealing from the club.

And that's against the rules.

Apparently the Angels boys took Guitar out into the desert and no one's ever seen or heard from him since.

It was a really stupid thing to do. The bastard's probably buried out in the sticks somewhere. If he was still in Australian biking, he'd be around, I'd have seen him, but he isn't, so I reckon he's gone.

I met Browny and Wally at St Mary's. We used to go out on the Bathurst Road and ride to Tarana, and then beyond to Lithgow. We'd take our sleeping bags and just set up camp wherever we liked, sleeping under the stars, curled up around a fire. That'd keep us warm all night; as well as the longnecks. It was good fun. Drinking on the road wasn't as much of a big deal back then because there weren't really any breathalysers. We could have a longneck or three and then ride on without worrying about the cops.

UGLY

I don't know why we always went down that way, because it was always freezing cold. I met a bunch of fellas on those rides who hung out together, but who didn't give their club a name. They eventually became the Fourth Reich 1% Club. The '1%' means 'outlaw', as in '99% of motorcycle riders are law-abiding citizens', and outlaw club members make up the other 1%.

Being a member of a regular motorbike club is like going to the RSL; you just socialise, have a feed and a drink, maybe play the pokies. With a 1% club, you do all that, but you also keep to yourself. You don't mix with others. You keep everything closed off from the outside world. You're a tight unit.

Another way we liked to see it was social motorbike clubs were the regular army, while one percenters were the special forces; those elite soldiers who didn't mix with the other troops.

When I eventually set up the Jokers I decided we would be one percenters, too.

We didn't mix well with others and that suited us just fine.

•

At first, they said I wasn't allowed to go to Vietnam because my five-year apprenticeship at Goldstein wasn't finished. I'd signed up as a volunteer, but they didn't want me to stop working. Vietnam was on and I was ready to do my bit, but I was stuck doing shoe clicking.

A lot of my mates were bricklayers or builders or labourers and earning decent money. I wanted to get out of my trade so I could make some money too, but I couldn't. Not that I was ungrateful, mind you. I was thankful to Mum and Dad for getting me into Goldstein, bless their hearts. The trouble was, I'd be stuck doing shoe clicking until I was twenty-one. Most

The Fighter

blokes would have done their Vietnam tours by then. I'd be twenty-two by the time I got over there – just when everyone else would be coming home.

I thought enlisting in the army would be a good way to get over there sooner, as well as making a few dollars at the same time. So I signed up for the infantry. I didn't know you had to take a test. I failed because I wasn't very good at maths.

And that meant more bloody shoe clicking.

When my marbles finally came up again, about a year later, I was over it and didn't want to go. I was breaking into the fighting game, doing some tent fights, and I was faring pretty well. I had a few wins under my belt and I had nowhere to go but up.

Still, when the army called, I did the right thing and went down to the recruitment office. They had a look at my broken nose – which actually caused another deferment on its own – and sent me to see a nose and throat specialist called Dr Arnett in Macquarie Street in the city.

He took a look at me and how my nose had set.

'There's nothing wrong with you,' he said. 'You can breathe in the jungle.'

I tried some cheek, looking for a way out. 'No, I won't be able to,' I said, although it came out more like, 'Nah, won' be ab'e to.'

'Nah, you're breathing just fine,' Dr Arnett said. 'You'll be right.'

Bang. That was it. He gave me my pass and I went in as a volunteer reinforcement.

That doctor's son ended up in the army, too. I found out much later on when a young bloke named Paul Arnett stopped by my tent one day and introduced himself.

UGLY

'Is your dad a nose and throat surgeon in Sydney?' I asked him.

'Yeah,' he said.

'Small world. He was the doctor who checked me out 'coz of my nose.'

He thought that was pretty funny.

I wrote Dr Arnett a letter, telling him his son and I were good mates. It was funny to me, but I'm not sure how funny he found it. His son and I were in different battalions and I don't know what happened to him.

But I'm getting ahead of myself again.

Even though I'd finally been accepted by the army, they still wanted me to finish my trade before I shipped out, so I had to wait *another* year. In my eyes, this meant I was definitely going to war as an old man.

I was doing well in the ring, too, so I thought to myself, *bugger this*. I decided to take a ride up to Southport in Queensland, about an eight-and-a-half-hour trip from Fairfield. It's rough on your shoulders, arms, legs and arse but I ended up doing it in two days, sleeping by the side of the road, drinking beers next to a camp fire. It was pretty bloody good. I'd sleep in carports, next to my bike, so that when the trucks pulled over to park overnight they wouldn't run me over. Looking back, some of those longer rides might have contributed to the kind of pain I've got now, but it was worth it.

A motorcycle club up there, the Southport Cycles, had a logo with a triangle with an S and a C through it. I'd never seen that before, so I asked the head honcho, Dave Lane, what it meant.

'Well,' he said, 'you start life at the bottom, then you go up, you level out, and then you come down. And then it's all about whether you come up again.'

The Fighter

'Yeah,' I said. 'I like that.'

That stuck with me, that idea of the flow of life.

'Where are you staying?' he asked me.

'Out by the weir. Camping.'

'I've got a farm a little further up.' He pointed off into the distance. 'I've got an empty place. You come up and stay there. I don't want a bike bloke sleeping by the river.'

I told him it didn't bother me, but he was insistent and took me up to his big property. There were two houses, and one was empty. He said I could pay my way by doing some picking on his farm. I thought that sounded fine.

He didn't tell me that every Friday night he and the Southport Cycles fellas would have parties in the house I was staying in. They'd go all night, all the bike club blokes and hangarounds and girls. Hangarounds were blokes like I was at the time, people who were friends of the club but weren't a part of it. I had a pretty good time, drinking beers and sitting by the fire and talking shit. Just being a young fella with no worries in the world.

I ended up staying at Dave's place for three months. We'd sometimes go into town to see a movie. The club members weren't really into pubs, preferring a few longnecks around a fire. I got a bit of a taste for it up there. The Southport Cycles boys treated me really well. It was a good connection to have.

But even in faraway Queensland, I wasn't unfindable.

Sure enough, I got the call.

I'd told Mum and Dad where I was going because I didn't want them to worry. They'd done everything for me and it would have caused them a lot of unnecessary pain if I'd just disappeared off the face of the earth one day. They tracked me down at Dave's place and told me the army and the police were

UGLY

looking for me. They thought I was some sort of 'conscientious objector' to the war because I hadn't appeared for the call-up.

They wanted to bloody arrest me!

'But I'm not objecting,' I said. It was the truth.

'Yeah,' Mum said. 'But you also don't want to go in for your service.'

'They didn't want me in the first place!'

It never occurred to me that it must have looked like I was a conscientious objector. I was in shock. I didn't want people thinking I was a gutless wonder.

So the next day, I rode back down to Sydney.

I went straight to the recruitment office and said, 'I'm Mawson, I'm the one you were looking for.'

'Righto,' the woman behind the desk said. 'Go down to Marrickville and then you'll be off.'

When I walked out of there, it hit me. *Fuck this, I didn't want to go and now I'm actually going.* A part of me cursed myself for signing up in the first place.

The six weeks of basic training went by in a blur. It didn't feel all that different from gym training to be honest. There wasn't time to be scared. All the exercise and the adrenaline kept us gung-ho. They taught you how to march, how to sleep rough, and drummed you full of discipline. That's where the movies get it right – those angry sergeants yelling at you – because if you can't take the discipline, you'll be no good in the field.

I was fit as a fiddle because I'd been doing all that fighting, so the discipline didn't bother me. That probably comes as a surprise to some people, considering the River Rats and the Gypsy Jokers, but discipline was never the issue. I actually enjoyed it. There were a lot of drills, which felt familiar given my training. It's all about getting you into a proper routine.

The Fighter

A proper mindset. I used to be able to climb up a rope, hand over hand, with my legs out straight like the circus blokes do. In another life, I might have been in *Cirque du Soleil*!

On one of our leave days, a bloke in Third Battalion, Peter Christie, and I decided to go back over the obstacle course we had to do during basic training. Exercise was a great way of blowing off steam, so running that course over and again was good for my mind. Peter was a fitness fanatic like me, and neither of us wanted to go home.

'Obviously, we've been through the course once,' he said. 'When we go through it again we'll just get better and better.'

So we were doing the obstacle course by ourselves, just the two of us, when out of nowhere this officer showed up. He had some families with him, either for a tour or visitation, and saw us come bolting through on the ropes. It must have been quite a sight.

'What the hell are you soldiers doing?' he yelled.

Pete and I just looked at each other. We were about to stop but the officer shook his head and said, 'Keep going!'

When we finished, he was still there with the families. They were watching over his shoulder. We knew we were in trouble now.

'Mind telling me just what it is you were up to?' he said.

'Practising the obstacle course,' I said. What else could I say?

'What are your names?' he said, and we told him. 'Get back to your lines, I'll talk to you later.'

When he'd got rid of the families, he came and found us. We thought we were in for a whipping: extra push-ups, sprints, you name it.

'Jeez, I'm proud of you boys,' he said.

UGLY

He just needed to make a show of authority in front of the civvies, to keep us on our toes. Lucky us. We'd been caught by the right officer!

•

At the end of basic training we had to put down our three preferences for the corps we wanted to join. I had the sheet in front of me and was holding the pen and I was just staring at those three boxes. I wrote *Infantry, Infantry, Infantry*, then handed it back.

'You can't do that,' they said, and gave me another piece of paper.

'Right.'

On the second bit of paper I wrote *Infantry, Artillery, Armour*.

They looked at that and laughed.

'You're a volunteer, are you?' they said.

'Fucken oath I am,' I said. 'I'm in. If Sarge says to jump out of a plane, then that's what I'm gonna do.'

'They're gonna like you over there,' they said and stamped my sheet.

They assigned me to the infantry as a reinforcement. They probably read my report and saw 'fitness fanatic and loves the infantry' and the two pieces of paper with the two versions of my three options for the corps, and realised how easy it was. I can only imagine that they laughed at what I'd written. I would have.

But it felt like I was in the right place. That's probably because I'd volunteered. Other blokes had been called up. Even though it'd taken a while to get organised – and even though I was an old man – I wanted to be there. I doubt anyone else wrote

The Fighter

down infantry on their preference sheet. They all wanted to be drivers, or non-combatants like cooks, or even MPs.

Training was at Singleton in the Hunter Valley and it just so happened that two of the corporals there were instructors at the Merrylands gym where I boxed. They hadn't taken much notice of me at the gym, but they gave me an extra hard time now. Friendly, but still. They were good blokes; they looked after me and pushed me. Made sure I did what I needed to do and that I was all right.

Infantry training was more detailed than basic training. It went for about six months. We learnt map reading, compass work, stealth, and wilderness survival techniques. We were going to be in thick jungle over in Vietnam, so we needed to know how to survive and how to hide. And of course, we practised shooting nearly every day. By the end of training, I was a pretty good shot, but I was an even better night shooter. I don't know why, but I could always pick things out better in the dark.

I kept up shooting when I got back from the war and was a member of the Port Jackson Rifle Club for years. I'd shoot every Saturday morning. I even took out the C Grade Championship one year. Shooting stuck with me. I remember my first day on the range, I got a bolt-action rifle off of a mate, Leon Moon, and was only supposed to shoot the target once. I was so quick with the bolt that I unloaded all my ammo into it. It was just muscle memory.

'No, no,' Leon said, running over to me. 'It's not Viet Cong!'

'Well, I got the bastard.'

At the end of infantry training, I was assigned to Seventh Battalion as a reinforcement. I was now Private Rifleman Mawson. I ended up moving around a couple of different units, especially after I found out that Seventh Battalion was going home early. I wanted to do my whole ten months, which was the minimum requirement. If I didn't, the government wouldn't give me my second medal and my war service loan. I wanted to get everything I could get.

In early November 1967 I flew out to Saigon via Malaya.

I wouldn't be home for over a year.

3

The Soldier

As you'd expect, we didn't fly first class to Vietnam. Flying is a shitshow at the best of times, and we were going somewhere we didn't know, with people who spoke a language we didn't know, to walk around the jungle and get shot at.

When we arrived at Tan Son Nhat Airport, I got what was probably the most intense welcome anyone's ever received. As we disembarked, we saw all these trolleys being wheeled towards the plane. Getting closer, we realised what they were: coffins full of dead Americans about to be shipped back to the United States. It was one thing to hear about how many boys were dying. Seeing it like that, the evidence of it in broad daylight, was something else. That stayed with me as we arrived at base.

That first night, we were issued our rifles. We were told to remember the serial number; if you picked up the wrong rifle and it was dirty, you got in trouble. Keeping your weapon clean was a high priority.

UGLY

Each and every night, you could hear the planes and jets roaring overhead. We couldn't help feeling on edge. There was just this constant tension. We were told that when we were out in the jungle, anyone in black pyjamas was Viet Cong. *Anyone.* We had to be locked and loaded whenever we left the gates because we might have to engage the enemy, who could be anywhere.

There was a bit of friction between us reinforcements and the guys who were already stationed in Vietnam. They thought we didn't know anything because we'd just arrived in-country. They'd test us to see if we had the balls to hack being in a warzone. They'd push us around, pull tricks on us while we were in the camp.

Only about two weeks into my tour, I was out on patrol with a few other blokes. Part of me was hoping for an easy, quiet patrol; another part of me was keen for *something* to happen. You know how young blokes can be – that adrenaline just gets into your brain and fires you right up. Anyway, we were out walking past this banana plantation. It smelt good.

I looked over and I saw a couple of Vietnamese soldiers hiding in the bushes.

'Nogs! Nogs!' I shouted. That was what we called the Viet Cong.

Then I saw one of them putting what looked like a rocket launcher onto their shoulder. They looked at me and the next thing I remember my gun's going *boom, boom, boom.*

Turned out it was just a farm girl.

She had a hoe and she and another villager were just working in the plantation, cutting bananas.

She hit the ground. I nearly cut her right in half. The other farmer had dropped to the ground to avoid my spray of bullets.

The Soldier

'You fucking idiot!' one of my blokes yelled at me. 'You killed a villager! They're fucking farmers!'

'Well, I didn't know! She had a hoe and she was in black pyjamas so I thought, you know, Viet Cong!'

The boys put the body into the Jeep and drove her and the other farmer back to the village.

They kept a close eye on me after that.

I felt really bad that my first kill had been an innocent civilian. It didn't seem fair. It didn't seem right. And not only was I upset about it, they made me feel upset. I was a young bastard, it was my first two weeks in the battalion, and I'd killed an innocent woman. There was no support like there is now. It started to eat at me.

I was jumpy and nervy after that. I thought I might get charged, but I didn't. When my superiors confronted me, I told them that I only did what I was taught to do, and that the hoe the woman was carrying looked like a grenade launcher.

A fellow soldier who was there – still a good mate of mine – Mick Evans, looked after me. What I'd done really played on my mind. It must have been obvious and made me stand out.

Around this time, the officers needed volunteers for some RIC – Rest in Country – down at the holiday resort of Vũng Tàu, south-east of Saigon.

'We want some defence and employment infantry down there,' they said. 'To guard the place and look after it.'

Lucky me, I got sent there. It was an easy assignment for a young bloke who was having a hard time so early in his tour.

Vũng Tàu was officially listed as the Headquarters First Australian Logistics Support Group. We were guards on the gate and had to search any Vietnamese coming in to work in the compound. We also had to patrol the beach part of the resort. It was basically a holiday camp, and you bet I made the most of it.

There was a piece of wire on the front gate which we used to let in any of the boys who came back late after a big night. We were supposed to tell the MPs and lock them up, but we didn't. I wasn't going to call the army coppers on some blokes for being out having a good time.

There was a lot of surfing at the beach in Vũng Tàu and my mate David Cripps was a lifeguard back in Cronulla and organised for a Cronulla lifesaving boat to be flown out. A book called *Charlie Don't Surf but Aussies Do* by Stuart Scott has a photo of me lying on the beach, skinny as, next to some surfboards. The bastard captioned it, 'A lifeguard, Phil Mawson, having a rest'.

Well, it was a damn fine place to serve some rest-in-country.

But then, in January 1968, things took a turn for the worse.

The big military push by the North Vietnamese and the Viet Cong known as the Tet Offensive began.

The Vietnamese celebrate dates on the lunar calendar. We did too. For the big celebrations, the army got some leave, and everyone got to go home to their families.

In other words, everyone's guard was down.

Our officers figured that both sides – the South Vietnamese and us, and the North Vietnamese and the Viet Cong – would have an unspoken truce during this time. A bit like the soldiers in the trenches during World War I putting down their weapons and having a ceasefire and a soccer game over Christmas.

But the Viet Cong had other ideas.

In January 1968 – right in the middle of the New Year festival – they hit. And hit hard.

The Soldier

They infiltrated cities, caused massive disruption, attacked wherever they could. They even got into the embassy in Saigon.

Mick and I were put on a machine gun on the beach. This would be our first enemy contact together. It was dark. Our blood was pumping. My heart was beating so loud I couldn't hear anything else. When your heart's making that much bloody noise, you think the enemies hiding in the trees are going to hear it. You're sure they're going to find you and kill you. We were holed up with an M60, ready for anything the night had to throw at us.

I saw something in the water. It looked like a little sampan or a canoe winding up to the beach.

'Let's give it to 'em!' Mick said.

I pressed the trigger and unloaded. Shot the shit out of it. I put at least a hundred rounds into it. There was almost nothing left.

I ran down to the water to have a look. I thought I saw a body.

'Someone's out there!' Mike shouted beside me. His voice was reedy from screaming.

That alarmed the hell out of me, so I went back to the gun, reloaded and unleashed another hundred rounds into the water. Whatever was there sure as hell wasn't there anymore. We waited for a bit, to see if there were any other boats coming our way.

Then the whole place lit up.

Captain Maisenguard showed up and shouted at us, 'You infantry blokes, you come from a battalion, and when you show up you're nothing but trouble!'

'It's war!' I said. 'It's an offensive! It could be Charlie coming in.'

Maisenguard sent a chopper up with spotlights. When they got there, they radioed down. 'Bit of debris,' they said, the radio crackling. 'But we can't see nothin'.'

I didn't know what they were talking about – I'd shot an enemy boat and a body – or bodies – in the water. It wasn't a log, it wasn't just debris. They just couldn't see it from the chopper because I'd ripped it apart with the M60. The canoe had sunk for sure. Mick backed me up because he'd seen it, too.

We started making our way back up to the garrison, and the next thing we heard was planes overhead. There was an airport nearby. We looked up and there were more helicopters with blazing searchlights.

Which was great for them, but it blinded us down on the ground.

We heard noises from the bushes all around us and so we shot at that. The noises stopped. Whatever it was, we'd got them, too. What else were we supposed to do?

But Maisenguard wasn't having any of it. He was hellbent on giving us shit.

'Fuck this,' I said. 'We're out of here.'

'Good,' Maisenguard barked. 'I'm happy to be rid of you. Go back to your battalion as reinforcements.'

'Well, you know,' I said to him, 'those blokes have gone home. If I'd have stayed with them, I'd have gone home already, but I don't want to. I want to do my full ten months.'

He stared at me. I couldn't tell you if he smiled, but he might have. He sent me and Mick back to the reinforcement wing.

When we got back to the battalion, part of me started to wonder if I might be cursed.

One night, we were doing a training ambush. Mick was at the rear with the New Zealand blokes, because in reinforcement

The Soldier

it was half Kiwis and half Aussies. It was humid and hot, like most nights in the Vietnamese jungle. We were walking down this path, when I saw a bullock right in front of us.

It stopped me dead in my tracks.

This was a trick I'd seen before. The Viet Cong would send a bullock down ahead of them and wait. If they heard us shooting at the animal, then they'd know we were there and ambush us. If nothing happened, odds were good there was no one there.

I said to the guys, 'Hold on, they're coming.'

'What do you mean?' one of the blokes said.

'The Nogs, they're coming. Just wait until the bullock goes past.'

Those seconds while the beast wandered past went on forever. I could tell the soldier who'd spoken before was getting restless, so I whispered, 'Behind the bullock, you watch.'

Sure enough, a group of Viet Cong came creeping down the path.

Unbeknown to us, they'd also sent some guys round the *back* of us.

Next minute, we're in the middle of a full-on shootout.

Bullets were flying in front of us, behind us, all around us.

It's impossible to describe the adrenaline rush you feel in a firefight. Your heartbeat's going a million miles an hour. Your hearing is muffled by a numb roar. To this day, I still get that sound sometimes in my head. It just comes rushing back. I have earplugs that I'm supposed to wear, but they give me the shits. So I don't wear them. Point is, it's noisy as hell in the middle of a firefight. The smell of gunpowder hangs heavy in the air, even when it's humid. It's a bit like when you get caught in a cloud of haze after fireworks are set off.

UGLY

By the time it was all over – and it couldn't have been more than a couple of minutes – the soldiers in front of me were dead. A firefight is like boxing; a few minutes doesn't seem like much until you're actually in the ring. It was scary as hell. Mick had taken cover behind an old well. When he checked it afterwards, there were bullet holes all around where he'd been hiding. They'd missed him by centimetres.

We lost five men that day.

We collected them and marched back to camp.

Mick and I were then assigned to Third Battalion at Balmoral, north-east of Saigon. Sure enough, we got caught up in the Battle of Coral–Balmoral which kicked off in May 1968.* By now I was sure I was cursed. The Viet Cong attacked the lines over and over again. In a big gunfight like that, your nerves go haywire with the excitement. You're jumpy and your adrenaline is spiking. It's not like being in a fistfight, but you remember everything you've learnt about dealing with that sort of situation.

That's the good thing about the army, they teach you properly.

I ended up getting a citation for bravery for that battle.

•

I spent my twenty-second birthday covered in mud and avoiding bullets and landmines. As a birthday gift, I got a Dear John letter from Ruth Tuff, the girl I was going with at the time. It said something like, 'I met someone else and you're no more'.

Terrific, now I'm single and getting shot at in the fucking jungle.

Life was looking *really* good.

---

* Although it is not as well known as the Battle of Long Tan, more Anzacs were killed during the Battle of Coral–Balmoral than in any other engagement during the Vietnam War. It began on 12 May 1968 and went for 26 days.

The Soldier

I needed a way to let out what I was feeling so I did the only thing I could think of. I got my mates from camp – Dave Cripps and Mick Evans – and we went out into the jungle. I took the knife I always carried with me and pinned that Dear John letter to a nearby tree. I walked back to the others and told them to take aim.

'What's in the letter?' Mick asked me.

'Never mind. Just fire.'

We made our guns ready and then all three of us let loose.

The bullets tore it to pieces.

It took some of the anger away, but I still felt pretty shit.

Ruth's married now and I hope she's well. No hard feelings, eh.

•

The fact that I'm still alive proves I was one of the lucky ones in Vietnam. But I did find myself in certain situations that even to this day I'm amazed I survived.

While in Third Battalion, my corporal, Robert Gould, sent me, Mick Evans, Dave Cripps and a few others down to the Firestone Trail on claymore landmine duty. Claymores are those small green boxes with little legs that have FRONT TOWARD ENEMY written across them. They're easy to disguise on the jungle floor. When someone steps on them, a deadly explosion shoots out hundreds of ball bearings. They tear people apart. You want to make sure you're nowhere near a claymore when it goes off because there won't be much left of you otherwise.

We were on the trail, planting landmines, and a bloke named Samuel pricked his ears up. When I saw that, I smiled.

'They're comin',' he said.

UGLY

'Oh, yeah.'

He had a look over the bushes where we were hiding. A moment later, he came back down and told me there was a group of Viet Cong approaching. 'Wait for the second one to pass,' he said. 'We'll get the ones in the back and the next ones in the front.'

He wanted to catch them in a claymore landmine crossfire. We'd set three claymores on the track. That meant that there'd be something like 900 ball bearings from each one, which means over 2700 ball bearings were going to come ripping through the jungle and tear the enemy to bits.

After setting the claymores off, the plan was to run back towards the machine guns so that we could mow any survivors down without any worry of hitting any of us.

We waited.

We waited some more.

Samuel put his hand up.

Finally, the first couple of Viet Cong crossed the claymore line, with the others close behind.

I set the landmines off.

Voompt.

It's like no other sound, just this weird, dull explosive roar. There was dust and shit everywhere and the Viet Cong started yelling and screaming. We ran back to the machine guns, but I couldn't tell which way was which.

I ran into someone and yelled, 'Sorry, Nobby!'

I thought it was our machine gunner, but all I got in response was loud, angry shouting. *In Vietnamese.*

I'd run the bloody wrong way.

I'd run right into the Viet Cong!

'Oh, fuck you!' I yelled.

The Soldier

I always carried my KA-BAR knife on my belt. I had an M79 grenade launcher with a couple of cannister shots as well, but the knife came in handy in close combat situations. KA-BARs are small, curved knives, about three inches long. Mine was sharpened on both sides so I could use it as a slasher as well as a stabber.

I pulled it out quick as you like and slashed the Viet Cong in front of me. Everyone was screaming. I was too, just swearing my head off. There's nothing else your brain can do. You just move and swear and scream. And fight.

The Viet Cong screamed and buckled underneath me.

I went to the ground and started firing. There was nothing to aim at, so much dust was getting kicked up. All around me I could hear enemy soldiers screaming and dying. I knew I needed to get back to my unit. If I stayed here too long, I'd die. They'd be calling in an artillery strike and I'd be right underneath it.

I got up and tried to get away but I ran into another Viet Cong. I slashed him and ran in the opposite direction. That's when I found the trail back to our machine gunners. I was covered in blood. Most of it wasn't mine. I bolted towards them, screaming, 'Don't shoot! Don't shoot! It's me, Mawson!'

I was ready for them to shoot me because they'd think, with me running and screaming out of the dust cloud, that I was the enemy. But they didn't. I got lucky again. Maybe I wasn't cursed after all. I scrambled back behind their position and the corporal said, 'We were gonna charge you with desertion!'

It was such a relief to be safe with the unit again. I couldn't have been more than a hundred metres away when I was attacking those Viet Cong, but it felt like forever making it back.

UGLY

Our lieutenant, David Barclay, then called in an artillery strike. We weren't far away and could hear the Viet Cong still screaming. It was a horrible sound. But the Kiwi on the radio had other ideas. He said, 'I've got to talk to a commanding officer if I'm bringing artillery in that close to where you boys are.'

'I'm the fucking commanding officer!' Barclay yelled, stomping up and down. 'Bring it in now!'

He got his way. Minutes later, the artillery started raining down. We took out our shovels and unscrewed the blades and held them over our heads like helmets. We only had bush hats, so there wasn't much protection from shrapnel and debris.

You've never heard anything so loud until you've been a few metres away from exploding artillery. It was like the end of the world. Like the earth was splitting apart. A few blokes had shrapnel pieces bounce off their shovel-helmets, but otherwise we were fine. Those artillery boys were bloody accurate.

The whole event scared the shit out of me. We all almost bit it right there, but none of us did. The artillery saved us. And my trusty KA-BAR knife.

I got another nickname that day: 'Wrong Way' Mawson.

My army mates, including my Third Battalion major and sergeant, kept calling me that long after we got back to Australia. Barclay still jokes that I was trying to run all the way home. After that day was when I started drinking. Before that I'd drink like any normal person, but after being stuck back there, almost dying, the drink quenched a thirst I didn't know I had.

Out on another patrol one day, one of our blokes found a skull on a spike. It had been there long enough for the bugs to have eaten all the skin and eyes and brains. Our boys took the skull back to camp, put ping-pong balls in its eye sockets and

The Soldier

a little battery and a light switch in its mouth. When we got on the booze, we'd switch the thing on. Its eyes would light up in the bush and that way we could find our way back to the tents.

It sort of became our mascot.

•

Not every day in Vietnam was hard. We weren't always on patrol. Some days you got kitchen duty. Other days, if you were lucky, you got bar duty. That was the best job. I didn't get to do bar duty very often because I usually drank more than I poured.

Our major in Third Battalion was an intimidating bloke who we called 'Birdy'. He was big and tough, about six-foot-four, and could be a loud, bombastic bugger. He'd been in the SAS before he signed up for the army. Covered in muscles, he didn't waste words. We all called him 'Big Bad Birdy'. When we arrived, he lined us new recruits up, climbed onto a platform and said his piece.

'My name's Birdy. I'm thirty-two years old, I'm a major, and I take no shit. You give me shit and I'll take you behind a tent.'

In other words, if we gave him any trouble, he'd bash us black and blue.

It didn't scare me and, like I've said, I can be a bit of a smart-arse at times. While he was still banging on, I muttered, 'Suits me.'

It was only meant to be a joke, but I must have said it a little too loudly because he turned his head, quick as a whip. 'I heard that,' he growled. He jumped down off that platform and got right up into my face, just centimetres away. 'I've read your record, Mawson. You're *mine*.'

UGLY

I knew he wasn't lying. He would have known I was a full-time fighter back home and that I wasn't there to fuck around.

'Oh,' I said, 'any time, sir!'

'Yeah,' he said. I definitely didn't miss the little smile on his face. 'Remember that. You're *mine*.'

From then on, every time he wanted something done, he'd come to me. I was his enforcer, what he called his 'batsman'. If blokes were playing up, being smart-arses, or up partying late, he'd send me and another bloke named Jock Smith, who was a wild fighter, around to sort things out.

We were the battalion fixers.

Most of the time, all we had to do was show up and have a quick word with the boys and they'd soon settle down. If that didn't work, if someone decided to be a big dog and say something cheeky, we'd give them a whack.

About half of them said, 'Fuck Big Bad Birdy.'

That sort of thing got the toughness knocked out of them real quick.

Jock was a hell of a batsman and I'd been working on my rock-hard fists for years by then. Most people like to talk big but when it comes down to it, they never really expect a proper fight.

I got on well with the battalion sergeant, too, an ex-SAS bloke by the name of Sergeant Young. Youngy was a killer and a half. I saw what he could do. He'd won a military medal in Malaya. I also heard that back home he'd had some trouble with the law and with his family. Apparently he caught his wife in bed with some other bloke. He bashed them both. The law said he could either go to jail, or go into the army. It was an easy decision, but he wasn't allowed back in the SAS – at least, not for the time being. If he wanted to get back in, he'd have to reapply and do the cadre again.

The Soldier

So he joined the battalion.

Youngy was like a walking lead balloon; nothing could touch him.

After that, I was pretty gung-ho about going for the SAS, too. I fancied I was suited to it, given that Youngy and me seemed to be the same kind of build. I got talking to Birdy one day.

'You know, me and Jock are going to go for the SAS,' he said.

'Good,' I said. 'So will I.'

'You're a natural. You should sign on and go for it. When we finish up here, we'll go and try out and, you know, we'll put shit on Youngy.'

I laughed and said, 'That sounds great.'

After a minute, Birdy said, 'Actually, let's get Youngy to come with us, too. He can show us the ropes.'

We got really chummy after that. Like I said, I was already Birdy's fixer. No matter what it was, I was up for it. He knew that and so when he had something that no one else would do, he would come to me.

We were told that Viet Cong soldiers were not to be left alive. No survivors, no prisoners. And we should always try to shoot them in the head, even after they were dead. We had a shot pattern called 'the cross', which was one bullet on either side of the chest and one in the forehead.

The reason we shot them in the head was because the Vietnamese people had a superstition about anyone who had their head blown off. They believed that the spirits of these people would be set loose in the jungle and be lost forever. Each and every Viet Cong soldier was afraid of this happening to them, because it meant they'd be stuck on earth as a wandering spirit and not move on.

UGLY

'Whether they're injured or dead,' the saying went, 'they get a bullet in the head.'

It made me feel as if I was part of an execution squad.

We were also encouraged to take as many of these bodies as we could and leave them out in the open, where they would be easily found by the Viet Cong, so they could see the bullet holes in their foreheads. The point was to scare the enemy soldiers, to make them afraid of us so that they'd know fighting us had spiritual consequences.

I followed my orders.

I didn't keep count of how many bodies I saw. It would have been impossible to do that and carry on with my duties. There was no time to feel bad for anyone. When you came up against the other side, it was them or us.

They'd come out of the jungle and it would be chaos. Sometimes we'd be ready for them, and sometimes they'd take us by surprise. They knew the area better than us, that's for sure, but I felt that we were better trained.

Sometimes, after a fight had died down, there would be enemy combatants who were critically injured but still alive. They'd be lying there, moaning and crying. No one really knew what to do with them, because it was unlikely that they would survive being transported to any kind of medical care. They'd just end up dying in the mud, crying out in pain. A lot of them did, crushed under the bodies of their fellow soldiers.

At times like this I felt it would be kinder just to shoot them, or drop a grenade on them. I knew if they ordered me to do it, I would. That might make me sound like a cold-hearted bastard but it's how I was trained. You followed orders. You locked yourself into a killer's headspace so you could do what

The Soldier

had to be done. Disobeying orders could mean you died, or your mates died.

I think back on it now and it makes me sick. Being at war isn't fun. Dodging bullets isn't fun. Anyone who says any different is a fuckhead.

Seeing wounded men lying in pools of their own blood – that look in their eyes – you don't forget that. I can still hear it, smell it, feel it, when I think about it today. It stays with you forever. You dream about it.

It probably explains why we were all so quick to get on the piss when we got back to camp. Drinking to forget doesn't always work, but it beats the shit out of anything else. After a day of not knowing if you were going to die or not, a bottle of beer took the edge off.

We had to be careful not to get too pissed, though, because there were still patrol duties around the camp. We took it in turns as to who got to have a booze night and who had to stay at the ready.

Youngy would go out on patrol, sometimes by himself, sometimes with two or three others, on the lookout for any stray Viet Cong that might be in the area. I was always a part of his team. Even if I was in the middle of a booze night, he'd find me and pull me out of the tent. 'You're coming out tonight.'

We were supposed to harbour up, spread out in a semicircle where you reckoned the enemy were going to come through, and just observe and report. We weren't supposed to make contact unless it was absolutely necessary. But Youngy was a contactor. He liked to wait until they were close and then shoot them. He figured it was better than waiting until there was a threat to the rest of the unit.

UGLY

He was an angry man. A good soldier, but an angry man. Those two often go hand in hand. A lot of people would say that about me, and they wouldn't be wrong, but Youngy showed his anger more. He seemed to hate everybody. He got on with me, but that was because I had contacts in Seventh Battalion and Defence and Employment. I don't know what he would have been like if I hadn't, though it helped that I just followed whatever orders he gave me. I think he was always like that, but the army trained him well. When you take someone like that and give them focus, they become sharp and hard, like a dagger.

Birdy liked him, and he wasn't an easy man to please, but Youngy could definitely get in people's faces. When Jock and I were going for the SAS, Youngy attacked my lieutenant, Barclay. Barclay was a good bloke, and I didn't like that Youngy was having a go.

'What'd you fucking go and hit Barclay for?' I shouted at him.

'Ah,' Youngy said, waving me off. 'He's fucking slack.'

'No, he's not. He's a fucking good soldier.'

'I should attack *you*, then.'

I looked right into his eyes and said, 'Well, I'm ready.'

He cracked a smile, a mean one. 'Yeah, you would be, you bastard, wouldn't you?'

When someone's willing to have a go, that's when you really know them.

Only fighters understand that.

Youngy never really left the SAS. He just couldn't keep away from it and ended up re-joining after his stint in Vietnam. He's gone now, bless his heart. He died in the most hard-arse way possible: he fell off Mount Everest doing an SAS mountaineering climb.

The Soldier

Unlucky?
Maybe it was the world taking back what it was owed.

•

While I was in Vietnam I met a bloke who would completely change the direction of my life. I was reading a bike magazine, *Easyriders*, one day when this Yank came up to me. 'You're into bikes?' he asked.

'Yeah, love 'em.'

'Oh, yeah? I ride with the Gypsy Jokers.'

'Who?'

'The Gypsy Jokers,' he repeated. I think he was taken aback that I didn't know who or what they were.

'Who are they?' I said again.

'They're the number two in America. Number one are the Hells Angels.'

'I know them from Sydney,' I said. 'I don't think they're much chop.'

'Yeah, well, the Gypsy Jokers are the number two.'

I wouldn't mind getting back into that, I thought to myself.

The name stuck in my mind.

We chatted a bit more and the Yank, who was called 'Fingers', wrote me a letter that basically said if I wanted to start a chapter of the Jokers in Australia, I had his permission. He signed it, 'Gypsy Jokers America, with all the best'.

That piece of paper ended up causing me quite a bit of trouble down the track.

•

Even at war, being shot at, when you're with your company, your mates, you find ways to make life bearable. One time, we stole the grog from the officer's mess from D Company and hid it beneath the floorboards of our quarters. Each night, we'd end up on the piss if we weren't on patrol, chatting away and having a good laugh.

Then Youngy found out about it.

He stormed into our tent. 'Right, boys,' he said. 'I won't turn you in if you give me one bottle of booze a night.'

'That's blackmail!' I said.

'It is indeed. But it's a reasonable price to pay.'

We had no choice. We liked Youngy and he was good to us so why shouldn't he get a share?

Another night, we were all in the tent talking and getting on the grog. I wanted to say something, but Dave Cripps wouldn't let me get a word in. He was telling a long and boring story and I wasn't having it.

'Ah, you fucker,' I said, and threw out a solid punch with my right hand.

I wasn't in top form and Crippsy saw it coming a mile off. He ducked his head out of the way. Our tents were only lit with hurricane lanterns and my hand sailed by Crippsy and went right through one of them, smashing it completely. The tent went dark.

'That fuckin' hurt!' I said and staggered outside. I sat down on the ground. My head was spinning from all the drink. I needed to breathe some fresh air.

A few seconds later Crippsy came out.

'You silly old cunt,' he said. 'There's blood everywhere.'

I looked down at myself and I was covered in it. 'Oh, look at that,' I said, mumbling. 'It's all over me.'

The Soldier

Crippsy went to look for Youngy. A few minutes later they came back with Youngy bellowing, 'What's the bastard done now?'

'He's cut his hand open,' said Crippsy. 'Look at him.'

'Ah, shit,' Youngy said. 'Hold on. We've got to get you to the medic.'

He radioed for a Jeep to pick us up and take us over to the medics up near the R.P.* It didn't take long for the Jeep to arrive. I hopped in and Youngy said, 'I'm getting in the front 'coz you're bleeding everywhere.'

The Jeep started off down the trail. I wasn't feeling too good because of my hand and the grog and the bouncing Jeep. 'I don't wanna go to the medic,' I mumbled, squirming around. 'I want another beer.'

'Sit down and shut up, you fuckin' idiot,' Youngy said.

'Fuck you!'

I got up, opened the door, and jumped out of the Jeep.

We were still going about sixty kilometres an hour.

Boom.

I hit the ground on my shoulder, spun around, bounced off the road and went flying into the bushes. I landed in the dirt, in a pile of wet leaves, in the dark. Next thing I remember, I heard shouting.

'Where are you, Mawson?' It was Youngy. 'Where are you?'

'Fuck off!' I shouted.

That led him right to me. After a pretty pitiful struggle, he grabbed me in a headlock and dragged me back to the Jeep. I was in that headlock until we reached the RP. It was pointless to struggle. He was such a big bastard, strong as hell, and I was drunk and injured.

---

* Regimental Police.

When we got to the RP, Youngy explained what had happened. I was still in the headlock at this point. A doctor – a major – and a university medical student were on duty.

'Look at his hand,' Youngy told them, 'and tell us what you think.'

He finally let me go and the doctor examined my hand. The finger was cut bad, into the flesh of the palm and around the back of my hand, and looked like it was hanging on by a thread.

'Oh,' the doctor said. 'I reckon that'll have to come off.'

I didn't like that one bit. 'You're not taking my finger!'

Whack.

I king-hit him with a hard left right to his face. He flew backwards and crashed into his instruments. Everything spilt onto the floor. The doctor was out cold. Youngy jumped on me and held me down, shouting the whole time. When things had calmed down a bit, the medical student came over and had a look.

'No, no,' he said. 'We can sew that up. And with a bit of exercise, we'll get that finger working again. It's only cut through the sinew, not through the bone.'

'He's going on R&R in a couple of days, anyway,' Youngy said. 'So that'll be fine. He can heal up then.'

He was right. I'd put in to go to Hong Kong or Bangkok for my R&R, and they'd given me my second choice: Bangkok. In a couple of days I'd be heading out.

'Good,' the medical student said. 'Let's stitch it up, then.'

It took eight stitches to keep that finger. I've still got a big scar.

When the medical student was done, Youngy got me in a headlock again and marched me all the way back to camp. Well, he jogged, so I was forced to jog alongside him with my head in the crook of his arm.

My shoulder's still fucked from jumping out of that Jeep.

The Soldier

But I was never charged for punching that major.

The next day, I was shipped off to our task force headquarters at Nui Dat. The name just means 'dirt hill', which is all it was. From there, we went to Saigon, where I had to wait for the following day's flight to Bangkok to start my R&R. Mick Evans had put in to go to the same places as me so we could take some time off together. My hand was all bandaged up – all reddish and tender – so I wasn't in the best mood. I just wanted a drink.

The Americans had a big PX* down in Saigon. Biggest bloody PX we'd ever seen. They're like markets, where they buy and sell things like radios. The grog is cheap and there's often a bar attached. All the Yanks were drinking, and there were all these Vietnamese girls walking around with trays serving drinks. I ordered a couple from the first one I saw. But I didn't know you had to tip them. I had no idea they were working off an American model. So when the drinks came around, I took them, paid and then reached for my change which was on the tray.

The waitress started yelling at me in Vietnamese.

'Shut up, ya fuckin' Nog,' I said, 'or I'll fuckin' shoot ya!'

There were bouncers at the bar, but because of the set-up they were dressed like civilians. One of them came over and said to me, 'Right, you can get out. You've had enough.'

I looked at him and thought he was just some punter stepping in, getting in the way. 'Who the fuck are you?'

'I work here,' he said.

'You don't look like you work here.'

He didn't like my smart mouth. He threw a big punch, but I was lucky and ducked it. I knocked him in the face with two

---

* Post Exchange.

straight jabs with my left. I couldn't hit with my right because I was all bandaged up, so all I had was my left.

He swayed for a bit then came back at me, throwing punches, but every time I took a couple of quick steps back, just like I was taught. Each time I'd dodge one of his hits, I knocked him with a couple of sharp lefts of my own – *whack, whack*. He kept at me all the way to the back, up against the officers' room, where he threw out one really big punch. I side-stepped it and he crashed right through the door. I went after him and got on top of him and was just letting him have it.

Bang. Bang. Bang. Bang.

Next thing, I felt hands on me. The officers were on us, pulling us apart.

'What the hell's going on here?' one of them yelled.

'This mug picked a fight with me and I don't know who he is!' I said. 'And I've just got blown up!'

It was a little white lie but I waved my bandaged hand around anyway.

They marched me out of the PX and over to a barracks, where they told me to quieten down and sleep it off. I was stuck there until the next morning, when I was due to fly to Bangkok.

After all the drama, R&R was good. Mick and I went and watched some Queensberry rules and Thai boxing. At one of the matches, a big fight broke out in the crowd. The guards waded in and just started whacking people on the heads with the butts of their rifles. It was horrific.

Mick and I didn't get involved. We had a little bit of money so were sitting in the luxury seats with a couple of girls either side of us. We were pissed as and laughing our heads off.

●

The Soldier

When I got back to the battalion after my R&R, I couldn't shake the bad feeling that my first kill had been a civilian. It just wasn't right. That banana farmer didn't deserve to die. But as a young fighter, you're thrown into these sorts of situations and you just react.

On the other hand, I didn't feel at all bad about the enemy combatants I killed down by the water.

I was in the middle of a warzone. We both were. If I didn't kill them, they would have killed me. I got lucky that it worked out in my favour, because I could just as easily have eaten one of their bullets. I had no idea if they were about to rush me with a gun or a knife. So I just let fly and they disappeared into that inky black water.

The enemy was gone and I was still standing.

Sometimes, though, something like remorse – I call it a dark cloud – comes over me. Even to this day. It's heavy, like a weight. I got it back then, when I was in the thick of it. The gravity of what you're doing, of what's happening and what *can* happen just all comes together in your head. But you can't stop, because you're already doing it.

If you stop, you die.

We shot the enemy in the head because then their spirits are set loose in the jungle. A few times I actually saw it happening, dark shadows escaping into the night.

When I got back home, I witnessed it again, but not until much later on.

That's another story.

For now, I was still in Vietnam. The officers suddenly realised that I'd done twelve months in-country, when you were supposed to only do ten. Somehow, I'd fallen through the cracks. I'd always managed to dodge the question whenever anyone asked, which was easy given that I kept moving around battalions.

When they tallied up the dates, it turned out I'd been in-country for 359 days by the end of my run.

It was all over. I was told I was to be sent to Nui Dat to ship out. It was November 1968 and I was in the advance party. We moved out from our lines towards the airport. In the jungle we could hear what we always heard: gunfire. It was what we called 'Battalion Patrol Charlie'. They were never far away.

A bastard in another squad decided it was a good time to light a cigarette. Having a smoke at night while you're in the middle of a warzone is the perfect way to get yourself or one of your squaddies killed. It's like putting a big fucking neon sign above you that says, 'SHOOT HERE!'

And of course that's exactly what happened.

Charlie came down the road, saw the cigarette and just lit it up.

Sergeant Quigley and another bloke – the new recruit who'd lit the cigarette – were killed instantly. But given the commotion of the firefight, I didn't find this out until later.

Gary Martin, the Regimental Sergeant Major (RSM), was the one making sure we all got on the plane. He had this big moustache. After the firefight, I was laughing and joking around. I was young, I was alive, and I was going home. 'I'm gonna sign up for the SAS,' I said, because I was still thinking about it then.

Martin turned to me. 'Shut the fuck up, you fucking snotty-nosed nasho. You wouldn't make a soldier's fucking arsehole.'

He had this dark look on his face, real deep fury inside. He knew that Quigley and the new recruit had been killed but I didn't. He was fuming and instead of shutting up, I got right in his face.

The Soldier

'I'll shove your fucking moustache up your arse!' I shouted at him.

We were about to get started when the other soldiers pulled us apart. I didn't give a fuck about squaring off against a major, I was going home.

'You fucking thinking that way, I'll stick your arms up your arse!' I went on. I didn't really even know what I was saying, I was just seeing red. 'I'll start my *own* army when I get home!'

And that's exactly what I did.

•

It wasn't until after my run-in with Major Martin that I found out that Quigley and the new recruit had died. I realised that my laughing and carrying on was a shit way to behave. And I understood why Martin was so worked up. Not that I could have known, but I can see now why he acted the way he did and I don't hold it against him. You get torn up when your squadmates – your brothers – are killed.

I ended up making peace with Gary Martin many years later. One day, he called me, Mick Evans and Dave Cripps and said he wanted to have lunch. He knew we three were tight and had kept in touch. I don't know how he knew, but that sort of thing always has a way of getting around. So we took our wives with us and we all had lunch with him.

Gary talked about how he would have beaten me in the fight when we were in Vietnam. I gave it right back, saying I would have floored him. In hindsight, it's hard to say who would have won, but I'd have put pretty good odds on me.

A little while after that, Glassonby, another mate from the battalion, called and told me that Gary was dying. He was at St Vincent's Hospital in Darlinghurst. He'd always been an

UGLY

advocate for others and it didn't seem right to just leave him there alone. This would have been fifteen years after we were in Vietnam – in the early 1980s – and I wanted to bury the hatchet once and for all. There's just no point taking a grudge to the grave. So I went to see him.

At the hospital, there was a Vietnamese woman in the waiting room. 'You're army, aren't you?' she said to me.

'Yeah.'

'I'm Gary's wife.'

I went over and shook her hand. She hadn't been at the lunch and although Gary and I had seen each other a couple of times afterwards, I'd never met her.

'We'll go in together,' she said with a nod and a smile. She got it, how we army blokes are.

Gary was connected to lots of tubes and machines and was clearly in a bad way.

I couldn't help thinking that I'd been a real smart-arse back in Vietnam.

'Oi,' I said. 'It's Private Mawson here, you arsehole.'

He squeezed my hand. As a young brat all I wanted to do was bury him, but he ended up with cancer and all that petty shit just evaporated. He'd been this big imposing figure in my mind for all these years and here he was, lying in a bed, dying. I felt sorry for him. He was a hard man, but fair.

But in 1968, I was young, hot-headed and steaming mad. I knew my time in the army was almost over. And I knew I wanted my own group of blokes, somewhere where I belonged.

Birdy and Jock ended up getting into the SAS. They told me I would have been a shoo-in with my level of fitness. But that wasn't for me. Not anymore.

When I got home in November 1968, I had other plans.

4

The Bikie

We flew back into Australia on a Qantas flight in the middle of the night. My parents had one of their neighbours drive them and they met me at the airport. Before the officers let us go, they strip-searched us to make sure we weren't trying to sneak any guns back into the civilian population.

I had a bunch of knives on me, but no guns.

They let me keep those.

After that, we had to spend a month at the naval base at Watsons Bay, in Sydney's eastern suburbs. I was bored out of my mind, counting the days until I could get on my bike and ride out of there. One day, during rollcall, I got in line as close to the rocks as I could. When they called my name out and told me it was time to go, I shot out of there like a bullet.

They told us never to wear our uniforms and ribbons out on the street, except for on parade days. After we came home, people looked at you funny when they saw that you'd been to Vietnam. There were protests and the public was basically against the war. If you went out in your uniform, you were likely to be attacked, if not physically, at least verbally. People would have a go and shout stuff like 'baby killers'. I remember a young bloke came up to me, right in my face, and yelled, 'Are you a baby killer?'

I said back to him, real quick, 'The youngest I got was fourteen, but he had an AK-47.'

That shut him right up.

Shit like that made you feel dejected. And disrespected. Like I said before, I was already feeling dark from all the action while I was over there, but it was bloody awful coming home and being made to feel even worse. On top of that, I was still pissed at Gary Martin for having a go at me. I felt let down by the army, and let down by the public for their reaction to me doing my job. It's not like the war was my fault. Our parents and grandparents served in World War I and II and they came home to tickertape parades. They might have been fucked up – with PTSD or shellshock or whatever they called it then – but the public was behind them.

Vietnam vets were abandoned. By the public *and* by the government.

My time over there had had a big effect on me, but it was a long while before I ever really figured it all out. As soon as I got back, like so many others, I got straight on the grog. I didn't really sort myself out until I got the Jokers up and running.

Before I left for Vietnam, I'd had a good relationship with my folks, but after I came home, we grew apart. I was more distant from them. I was bottling everything up inside, keeping everything to myself. And of course, the PTSD started its work on my system.

That wasn't good.

The Bikie

Mum and Dad understood that I needed the space, so they let me be and let me do my own thing. Dad recommended I get back into training, in order to clear my head. I thought that was probably a good idea.

Neither asked me what I'd done over there in Vietnam. Or what I'd seen. Back then, you just didn't ask that sort of thing. Asking what someone had done in war was, if not rude, then just not done. It was digging into a hole and not knowing how deep it was.

I didn't want to tell anyone about what had happened. I was so embarrassed. I had killed so many people. It weighed on me like a boulder on my back. Unless you've been there in the thick of it, it's impossible to understand that kind of weight.

Especially since my very first kill was an innocent civilian.

Of course I knew I'd signed up to join the army and go to war – I thought I understood what that would entail – but killing that farmer really broke me. It shook me up. And maybe other people saw it more than I did, how much it troubled me. I thought I could tough it out, I thought I'd be fine, but there was a reason they sent me down to Vũng Tàu.

Obviously, I wasn't fine.

Back home, I soon caught up with all my old mates. It was easy being with them. Just like old times. We fell straight back into socialising how we used to. We'd go for a big ride on Saturday nights – me and Browny and Wally – and light a fire and sit around it with a few longnecks and have a good chat. That made the transition from army life to civilian life much easier.

To set myself up, I bought a two-and-a-half-bedroom war service home in Hurstville in Sydney's south. Then I got right back into training and fighting. Fighting was what I knew best.

UGLY

And it was all right money. I worked at my trade, shoe clicking, and did some gyprocking as well, but I had all this anger, and not just my normal anger, but the anger at Gary Martin and the army and the public and all the shit I'd seen and done in Vietnam.

Of course it all boiled over.

How was I supposed to deal with it? It's not like they gave us any resources, any support. It seemed like the public and the government just didn't care.

For me, the easiest way to get all that shit out of my system was to drink and to fight.

Starting my own motorcycle club was the only thing on my mind. That was goal number one. Clubs were where I felt at home, and I knew I could round up a few like-minded blokes who liked to fight and who loved bikes. None of my River Rats mates were keen on joining, not because we weren't close anymore, but because they just weren't into bikes. The love of bikes was key to the whole thing. I was a River Rat for six or seven years before I went away to Vietnam. Now I was starting all over again.

But where to start?

One of the first things I did was buy a new bike. I had the 1959 Bonneville, so I bought myself a 1969 Bonneville Triumph. That was a good bike. I had her for about five years before I needed to take a proper spanner to her. Shame. I ended up blowing her up on the Hay Plains out in the New South Wales Riverina doing 140 km/h trying to keep up with some Harleys. That didn't work out too well. I was in the middle of a ride and they had to put me in the backup truck when we got to Adelaide. I rode in a sidecar with a guy named Pappy. I had big whopping sunglasses on and everything. Pappy died not long ago, but that memory still makes me smile.

The Bikie

Anyway, I was back home from the army and back at my old haunt, the St Mary's Motorcycle Club. I went and saw my mates Wally and Browny and told them I wanted to start up my own club. I had a book on clubs in America and said I was going to found a chapter of the Gypsy Jokers. I told them all about the American bloke, Fingers, and the permission letter he'd given me. They had the same reaction as I did.

'Who the hell are the Gypsy Jokers?'

'They're number two in America,' I said. 'And I want to be number one in Australia because the Hells Angels are shit.'

I was a young arsehole with a smart mouth, but I knew what I was about. Guitar Zaan had told me that if I wanted to start up a club, I'd need to talk to the Angels first, to basically get their permission. But I didn't see why I couldn't just take my mates Browny and Wally and start up what I wanted to. Patience wasn't one of my virtues, especially back then.

'Well, the thing is,' Browny said, 'I'm already a nominee for the Angels.'

'Oh shit,' I said. 'How are we gonna get you out of that?'

He kind of just sighed and said, 'We'll have to go in front of Jan.'

'Same for me,' Wally said. 'I'm a debt collector for them. We're gonna have to have a big chat with Jan.'

Jan was the leader of the Hells Angels at the time. We'd need to ask his permission for the boys to come over to the Jokers. Bow to the king, that kind of thing. Browny was a nominee and Wally was collecting money for the Angels, so getting in to see Jan wasn't going to be an issue. Getting him to agree to let Browny and Wally go would be another thing entirely. It turned out Jan knew me from my street fights, the ones I'd been in before I went away to Vietnam, as well as a few of the ones I'd been in since I'd got back. I'd made a bit of a name for myself, so it wasn't as if I was going in half-cocked like some nobody.

Jan was an all right bloke. The biggest issue the Sydney Hells Angels had was that they hadn't gotten permission from the States to start up as a club at all, but the Melbourne chapter – who came along a bit later – had. I learnt all this afterwards, so at the time I thought Jan had permission, like me with my letter from Fingers.

'I want to start the Gypsy Jokers and a 1% club,' I told him. 'The Finks are running around as one percenters and I want that, too. If you've got any objections, let's have it out.'

He sort of just looked at me, like he expected me to go on. I cleared my throat and asked what I really went there to ask. 'I want Browny to come with me.'

That's when he smiled. It must have been what he was waiting for. He was a smarty.

'You can have Browny,' he said. 'And, on top of that, you can have our set of rules, and our red and white 1%.'

Back then, the Sydney Hells Angels weren't technically a proper 1% club. But Jan was planning something, so here he was 'giving me' their 1% patch.

'And,' he went on, 'you have to make Browny the leader.'

Ah. There it was. Jan's plan was to start a new branch of *his* club, with one of *his* nominees heading it up. It was like installing a branch manager of a franchise restaurant or a bank.

I didn't want to make that kind of decision then and there.

'Right,' I said. 'I'll need some time to think on everything. Then we'll come back to you.'

We had a month to decide. I didn't want to give in because I thought he was being right smart about it. My vision wasn't to be under the Hells Angels' wing – I wanted my own club. And

The Bikie

although Browny was a good mate, if anyone was going to be leader, it was going to be me. Browny could be vice-president.

At the time, the Hells Angels had a fair few hoons in their ranks. A month after our meeting with Jan, they came down to St Mary's because a few of them used to hang out there as well. It was a regular social club, so there was no stopping them. Jan came over and gave us the word. And so we all went out the back of the Namatjira Hotel to have a little chat because there was a bit of a paddock out there.

About fifteen Angels were there, all on their bikes. All Harley-Davidsons. There were about thirty or so of us in Jokers patches with our bikes. We outnumbered them, but the Angels were pretty hardcore.

But I had my own way of doing things. What was important to me was that I only took in blokes who knew how to fight. One of our blokes played jersey flag for Parramatta. He was actually a hooker, back when they had proper hookers, when the ball landed in the middle and you had to fight for it. Boofheads and fighters and footballers made up the ranks because that's what I knew. From the streets, to boxing, to the army, it was always fighting, so why would my Jokers be any different?

Jan had obviously been watching all that. His plan was pretty clear: he wanted to use us as a nurture club and then get us to fold into the Hells Angels. He knew I'd get fighters on board, and he wanted those fighters. Then he'd have a stronger club, which is what he needed, because another club, the Gladiators, were getting bigger all the time, and the Finks had turned 1%.

So, there we were, facing off against each other in this paddock out the back of the Namatjira Hotel.

'Righto,' Jan said. 'You're doing pretty well now; we want you to change from Gypsy Jokers to the West Sydney Hells Angels.'

Just like that, he said that to me. Just change over.

'Who's gonna pay for the patches?' I said, with my smart mouth. 'You'd better, because I ain't changing. And Wally ain't changing, either.'

Wally nodded.

'Well,' Jan said. 'You've got our nominee over there.'

I turned around and there was Browny, chucking down a beer. He just stared at us.

'What's he got to say?' said Jan. He had his arms folded like, *See? I win.*

'Browny,' I said. 'Come over here.' Browny came over and stood next to me. 'Jan reckons you're still a nominee for him.' I must have had a shit-eating grin on my face. I don't know for sure, but it's easy to imagine. 'Are you going to stay with him or come with me?'

Quick as a flash, Browny said, 'I'm coming with you. Fuck off, Jan.'

You could tell that no one ever spoke to Jan like that. He just stuttered, '*What?*'

He was fuming. It got all quiet and tense. There was definitely a fight coming, I could feel it. I squeezed my fists, ready to throw the first punch. But then, the damnedest thing happened: Jan got all his blokes back on their bikes and they rode off in a huff.

And that was how we got out from under the Angels once and for all.

It took almost a year to get properly up and running, but by November 1969 the Gypsy Jokers were a fair dinkum club.

The Bikie

I made Wally my sergeant. We didn't have to affiliate in any official way with the Angels, we just did our thing. We did model ourselves after the Angels' rules, as a way of kind of keeping the peace, and our 1% patch was red and white, in a nod to them. That was something else that ended up being a problem a bit of a ways down the line.

For our Gypsy Jokers patches, I took the triangle from that bloke from the Southport Cycles, because that really resonated with me, and then we put a skull in front. That came from my time in Vietnam. The boys who found the skull that we used as a light in the bush somehow got it back into Australia. Don't know how, but they let us bring all kinds of stuff in those days.

I thought it was right to put that skull on the patch because it had brought me out of the darkness and back to safety more than enough times. We had a lady named Rhonda who hand-sewed those first patches. She's dead now, unfortunately, but she was integral to the starting of the club. She was never a patch-wearing member, she didn't have a man in the club, but she was a good friend.

•

Other than the fact that we were now 1%, we basically behaved like we always had. We wanted to do whatever we wanted, whenever we wanted, and we wanted people to know that that's how we were.

Being a 1% club doesn't mean that you plan on being criminals, it just means that you're not going to listen to some bloke just because he's wearing a uniform. Most people think of the 1% and go, 'Oh, they're a criminal organisation', but that's not how it was, not back then, anyway.

The point of being in a 1% club was to live outside of the rules, to live outside the law. To be able to bash some dickhead for starting shit, to not have to look over your shoulder. Ever. It was a form of protection, as well as a form of freedom. I suppose to a lot of people there's no difference between that and just acting like a criminal, but back then there was a difference. Being in a 1% club meant acting out against the bullshit we saw going on around us; the crooked coppers, the laws, the way we were treated. Being 1% means you look after yourself, your club, and you tell everything – and everyone else – to get fucked.

Being 1% meant rebellion. Like telling Gary Martin to stick it up his arse, being 1% was like telling society to stick it up theirs. We didn't want to be part of the 99 per cent of the population who wore a tie and had a desk job. If someone tried to tell us we had to wear a tie, we'd tell them to fuck off and throw the tie away. We just wanted to do our own thing; to hop on our bikes, go for a ride out to the bush, light a big fire and just hang out.

The club met once a week at first – usually on a Tuesday or a Wednesday – and then we started meeting every weekend as well. Weekends were good because we'd organise a keg. Everyone would chip in, a couple of bucks each, with a bit more on top which would go to the club. Some weeks we'd only pull in about five bucks in profit, but sometimes we pulled in more. Members were expected to pay dues, but they were pretty low. I think it started off at fifty cents.

The club rules were simple and there wasn't a massive book of them. You had to follow them, and if you didn't, you'd end up bashed bad. It was simple stuff: don't steal, stick by your brothers, that kind of thing. On top of that, we had regulations

The Bikie

for the kind of bikes that you could ride. You didn't have to ride a particular make or model – most of us ended up riding Triumphs, but that might have been because we all knew how to maintain them – and it wasn't like with the Angels where you had to ride a Harley-Davidson. It was more about the power.

Your bike had to be 500cc or upwards, and either British or American. We had that rule because otherwise you'd have blokes swooping in on those fast 250cc Suzuki Hustlers and blowing the rest of us into the weeds. Those bikes were fast as hell. Also, we liked having that *pump pump pump* sound, that big noise. It gave a sense of strength and announced our presence. The other reason we didn't want Japanese bikes was because a lot of our parents had fought in World War II and something about riding Japanese bikes felt disrespectful.

A lot of people don't think of clubs and bikies as being organised, but when I got back to Australia from Vietnam, I still had plenty of army ideas in my head. So, to me, the only option for my club was to have a committee. That meant we needed a president, a vice-president, a treasurer, and a sergeant-at-arms.

The United States' clubs gave us the idea for it initially, because they have all the same roles, and a lot of those blokes, when they originally formed the clubs, were veterans as well. Other clubs around us saw the value in that, so it became kind of the standard. The point is, clubs aren't autocracies. What a president wants might go counter to what's good for the club. It's not useful to have someone in charge who would just pursue personal missions or vendettas. The whole club could get dragged into the shit, so the committee is there to tell the president to back off if necessary. It's a community.

We'd go between different pubs and drink – the Carlton, the Windsor – but there was no fighting. We didn't fight really with each other, and we didn't get into fights with people outside the club if we could avoid it. If someone tried to start something with one of us, we'd all just stand up. That usually put an end to things pretty quick. As a result, we had no enemies.

We'd often travel down to Wollongong and meet up with the Fourth Reich boys. They'd started up at a similar time to us, and we had the same colours: green, gold and black. We've been friends ever since.

The first ever Jokers patch actually had a swastika on it, but I wasn't keen on that. Didn't like it at all. I pushed and pushed and finally we got rid of it. Wearing a swastika felt disrespectful to the soldiers who'd fought in World War II. And I felt sorry for the Jews. It was persecution, it was wrong, and I didn't like it one bit.

Wally didn't mind the swastika, but I overruled that. Some of the blokes in the Jokers used to say that there'd never be Aboriginal blokes in the club, but that was dead wrong, especially once we joined up with the boys from the Outback chapter.

The Jokers and the Fourth Reich were always niggling at each other that we'd make them join our club, or they'd make us join theirs. It was friendly digging, because we were all mates. There'd be small blues between some of us, but not full-club fights. Just friendly biffs; we'd break it up and then everyone had a drink and forgot about it.

The Fourth Reich's main bloke, Ziggy, always said that they weren't going to change, they were staying as they were, and that was that.

'Okay,' I said. 'How about a brother club, then?'

'Yeah,' he said. 'That sounds good.'

On top of that, we were all working. I carried on with my trade in the 1970s and got a job as a shoe clicker at Dunlops

The Bikie

in Bankstown. I showed them my certifications and they just walked me right onto the factory floor, put me in front of a machine, and I was off. I didn't have to do all of it by hand because by then there were machines that stamped out the bits of leather for you. It was a pretty good job. I also worked for a construction company called LW Giles, doing some bricklaying and gyprocking.

We had a strict no drugs rule in the club. None of that shit. Anyone caught wheeling and dealing was kicked out. At one point, I heard rumours that a couple of fellas were pushing drugs while wearing our patches and making some money. I never found out if it was true, but I had a bit of a chat with them and made them pay some money into the club coffers. They didn't fight me on it. I made it a rule that if anyone was dealing drugs, they would have to give a cut to the club. I hoped that this would dissuade anyone from doing it. I didn't want their drug money, and I was sure they wouldn't want to give their profits to the club.

But you can't stop that shit forever. Drugs became a fact of life in the club, at least in our chapter, so we had to make some other rules as indulging became a bit more commonplace. I didn't want anybody selling drugs at all, especially not with the club patch on their backs. Whatever they did outside of the club, not wearing a patch and away from me, was none of my business. I never found out for sure if anyone was dealing, but that's probably because they were good at hiding it from me. However, I was very clear on one thing: if you stick a needle in your arm, you're out of the club. That's still enforced by our club, if not by all the others. Although a lot of the blokes who do drugs end up putting it up their nose instead.

UGLY

I tried my best to put a stop to it, but there's only so much you can do.

•

The club rules were in place largely because of my first wife Patty. She was adamant that without rules, everything would fall apart pretty quick. We were a bunch of unruly dickheads, and the structure — not unlike the army — of a committee and basic rules would keep us together, united against outsiders.

When I got back from Vietnam, Patty and I got married. I was back into fighting, the club was up and running, and Patty was a top sheila who I'd been hanging out with a lot at parties. She was good to me. I can't say the same about me to her.

Coming out of the army, like most other blokes, I was, in a word, fucked up. PTSD had a stranglehold on me — nightmares, flashbacks, always on edge — and all I knew how to do was fight. I'd wake up at three o'clock almost every morning in a cold sweat. To calm down I'd go have a drink of water, have a piss, and lie back down and try for more sleep.

But the dreams wouldn't let me go. I still get them, same as back then, as if it just happened yesterday. Three o'clock in the morning was the time of that ambush, the one where I got caught behind enemy lines and had to stab my way out from those Viet Cong.

I dealt with it all by lashing out at Patty. My temper was out of control. We'd get in fights all the time and I'd throw things, break stuff, punch walls. You name it, I did it, but I never hit her. Never. I'd raise my voice and storm out of the house and slam doors, but I never hit her. That wasn't acceptable. There

The Bikie

was once a bloke at a Jokers party who was manhandling his missus and so we booted him outside and manhandled him. It's just not the done thing.

Still, I'm not proud of how I behaved. Patty's a good person. We're still on good terms now, but I terrorised her back then. She helped me get away from self-medicating with booze. I was doing a lot of that then. She also helped me with my anger, which must have taken a lot out of her. It couldn't have been an easy job.

She was the first woman to ever get a Gypsy Jokers patch.

And she bloody earnt it.

Patty was always by my side when shit went down.

I always had a nasty sort of look on my face, like I was ready for a fight, always looking for someone to smack. Plus I was still boxing, so I had hard fists and must have come across as a real bruiser. One night, Patty and I were with some of the Jokers at a pub in Glebe, when this cop walked in. He was giving everyone filthy looks. He had that real kind of power strut, like he was king shit. Coppers in Sydney in the 1970s were a different breed. It was a bit more biff-baff than what you see now. Now they just fuck you over using paperwork.

But back then, this cop was strutting through the pub eyeing people off. When he clocked me he gave me this filthy look. What did I do? I gave him one right back. Now, we were both just glaring at each other. Everything else faded into the background because my nerves were focused on this cop. Then, just as quick as he came in, he walked out. I didn't notice that he'd come in with a couple of plainclothes police, but they turned around and left with him.

Next thing I know, the door burst open, and there were coppers everywhere. They started running at people, yelling at us. It all happened so fast I barely had time to move when three of them grabbed me and dragged me outside. The bastards threw me in the back of a paddy wagon. And then they started laying into me. The ringleader was the one I gave the filthy look to; who else would it have been?

I just covered up. It's not a fight you can really win. This copper was really going for it, but then the other two jumped in the wagon and joined in, kicking the shit out of me.

When they got tired or bored or maybe they'd just had enough, they took me down to the police station at the Rocks. The ringleader copper threw me in the lock-up and gave me another smack.

'You have a go, will ya?' I yelled.

I was ready to fight. I didn't know why, but he wanted to fight me specifically, and I was more than happy to oblige. But he didn't want a fair fight. The other two coppers came in and grabbed me and the king shit copper smacked me again, twice.

'Let me go,' I growled at him. I could taste blood in my mouth. 'I'll have a fucking go!'

He told the boys to take me to the back room.

That's where I got a few more smacks.

When all of that was said and done, they ended up charging me with assault. *They* charged *me* with assault. All I'd done was return this bastard's dirty look. Before I knew it, he'd jumped me with two other blokes and was giving me a good old hiding. I didn't even get to fight.

I went to court at the Downing Centre, near George Street in downtown Sydney. The official charge was assault on a police officer. They ended up fining me, which was lucky. I think the judge could sniff out what had really happened. I was scared because that kind of charge can land you in jail.

The Bikie

The more I thought about it, I realised that's *exactly* what those coppers were angling for – they wanted me back in jail. Because I'd been there before.

For assaulting a police officer.

•

Not long after I returned from Vietnam, Patty and I were at a party at a mate's place. He lived on a corner block, so we were all out on his front lawn. You know, out in the sunshine, having a few beers, enjoying a bit of banter, some music. Just having a good time.

Someone, of course, called the cops. They came around to tell us to keep the noise down. I was a few beers in by that stage so I didn't respond as diplomatically as I could have.

'Fuckin' grow up,' I growled. 'It's not even six o'clock. It's still light out.'

Well, this cop walked straight over to me and cracked me on the head with his baton.

So I just cut loose on him. I went straight into boxing mode, *whack, whack, whack*. I even took his baton from him and hit him with that! The other coppers got tangled up with the rest of the boys. In the end we all scampered, running down streets and over hedges. They ended up raiding my place, but I wasn't there.

A bit later on, I decided it was probably best to hand myself in. So with a solicitor, I went down to the station and gave myself up.

'I've got no internal or external bruising,' I told them, which was true. The copper didn't get any good hits in. In my mind, that should have taken the air out of the charges they had on me. It only occurred to me later that that might actually work *against* me, make it look like I'd just attacked that copper on my own without provocation.

'I'll take him down to the cell, Sarge,' said this young constable, grabbing me by the arm. 'I don't need anyone to look after this bastard.'

I turned to look at him and realised it was a bloke I knew from rugby named Franky Toggs. Another one of my weird backwards strokes of luck. As he was walking me down to the cells, he shushed me. I nodded and then he just started smacking his hands together, making like he was beating me up. He knew they'd want to tenderise me a bit, so he put on a little act for them. I'm forever grateful to him for that.

It seemed to appease them.

The next morning, Dad came and bailed me out. I ended up getting three months for that assault charge. These days it would be three years.

Patty's parents looked after her while I did my stint in Parramatta jail. My relationship with my own parents had become strained when I had come home from Vietnam and ended up in all these scrapes with the law. I was angry all the time, and Dad didn't understand that. My brother Neil did. He saw that I'd remembered what he told me about fighting: *you've got to be angry*. But Dad had no idea that I had that kind of temperament. It seemed to hurt him, and that's not what I wanted. I just didn't know how to control it. Dad told me that I needed to get back into training properly. Training would clear my head, clear my mind. Sport had always helped me, and he knew that, and that was something I took on board when I headed inside.

•

The Bikie

Jail was exactly what you'd imagine it to be like: shithouse. After the sentencing, I was put in a watch cell. They do that to make sure you don't neck yourself before your sentence starts. Then, the next morning, I was sent to the remand wing. That's where they sort you into what area you're going to go to. There's a whole bunch of different ones. More than you'd think. They sort of let you have a say in where you go, depending on whether you know anyone inside.

While they were sorting that out, in walked Johnny Preston. He was an old thug mate of mine from Liverpool. He walked right up to the head screw — that's what we called prison officers — and said, 'I want him in my cell.'

The screw looked at me. 'You all right with that?'

'Yeah, he's a mate of mine.'

'Righto,' the screw said, signing some papers. 'We'll have another bed brought in.'

Johnny was in a single cell because he was serving a life sentence — eighteen years — so I think he wanted some company. They brought in a bed and gave me a jumpsuit and blanket and toiletries.

The next morning, as I stepped out of the cell and hung up our blankets to air them out, Johnny came out, in front of all the other crims, and put his arm around me.

'It was good last night, wasn't it, love?' he purred.

I turned on him and just went, 'Oh, you cunt, you fucking cunt!'

A voice from above us piped in with, 'I know him, he's a *sweetie.*'

I looked up and saw it was Steve 'Dr Dags' Kilby, a bloke I knew who used to hang out with the Finks.

'You arsehole!' I said.

My mates were all like me, always stirring shit.

When we got down to the yard, blokes were coming up and touching my arse. I'd just turn around and punch them in the head and then Johnny would have to come over and cool things off.

'Don't worry, he's only joking,' he said, laughing. 'He's a mate of mine.'

Both Johnny and Steve are out and about now, having served their time.

I got permission to do some work while I was inside. Because I'd been a gyprocker, they figured they could make use of me, and so they got me to fix the prison roof. There was a bunch of old tiles that had had it, so they gave me a big extension ladder and I went up and replaced them. While I was up there, I looked around and saw there weren't any screws in the watchtowers.

'Fuck,' I said. 'Something's going on here.'

I climbed down and saw that there was no one in the yard, either. No crims, no screws, no one. The whole place was empty. I'd been up there busy working away and somehow hadn't noticed it empty out.

'Oh, fuck,' I said.

Something about it made me feel like if I got caught out at that moment, I would've been fucked. Quick as I could, I climbed down, grabbed the ladder and went over to the boiler room. I knew there'd be a screw there. I banged on the door.

This cross-looking screw opened up. 'What are you doing? And where did you get that fucking ladder?'

'I've been up on the roof and youse have just left me up there,' I said. 'I wanna go back to my cell.'

'You're not going to your cell now,' he said. 'You'll get me in the shit. Get in here.'

The Bikie

It was past lock-up time and they'd totally forgotten about me up there on the roof! Instead of taking me back to my cell, the screw took me inside the boiler room and fed me. He let me out later, with the ladder, for roll call. The other screws joked that I could have just put the ladder up against the fence and escaped into the night, but I only had two months to go, I didn't want any more. You got five years' extra jail time if you were caught trying to escape.

When I was up on the roof, I did get to wave at all the ladies over at the girls' prison. That was all right.

The rest of my time in jail went pretty smoothly. Mostly your worst enemy when you're inside is boredom. If you've got friends and a bit of work it's not too bad, especially if you're only doing a few months like I was.

Anyway, that sort of shit is why Patty and I only lasted two years together. We spent most of our second year of marriage drifting as far apart as two people can get. I stepped out on her more than once. There's not a lot more to say. Sometimes in life we fail.

But I got a second chance when I met Lyn.

And that second chance, again, began at a party.

We were hanging out with the Finks at Ralph Rotten's place. We'd been mates for a while; he's a top bloke. Before the Finks became a 1% club, a lot of their parties were just house parties; drinking, hanging out with girls, having a good time. There would always be bands, too, usually a bunch of locals.

Anyway, at this one party, we ran out of grog. What else was there to do but go on a grog run? We'd drink and ride in those days and the cops hardly ever touched you.* But before I got

---

* New South Wales didn't introduce the random breath test or blood alcohol limit for driving until 1968. However, drivers could only be tested after an incident or driving offence. The blood alcohol limit in 1968 was 0.08; this was lowered to 0.05 in 1980.

out the door, these two good-looking sheilas walked down the hall towards me.

I decided to try my luck.

'Oh, got a bottle of cider, eh?' I said, indicating the bottle that one of them was holding.

To my surprise, they didn't run away in fear. We just started chatting.

One of those girls was Lyn. And we've been together now for forty-eight years.

That bottle of cider ruined us!

Lyn liked bikes, so that was a good thing in my book. It was a big contrast to Patty, who didn't like them, even though she had her bike licence. Patty rode a little step-through scooter, but Lyn rode an Indian. An older, vintage one. That was kind of like glue for us, we stuck together because of that.

She was also really good about club life. She got on with everyone, talked to everybody, wasn't a stuck-up snob. She was the perfect fit for me.

I remember a while later we went to a party and Patty was there as well. I introduced them. 'Patty,' I said. 'This is my wife, Lyn.'

They got on well and wandered off into a corner together to chat. Every now and then, I'd look over and they'd be looking at me, laughing or saying something.

'This can't be good,' I said to myself. I went over to them and said, 'What's going on here?'

Lyn turned to me with this big smile on her face and said, 'Piss off. I'm getting info on you.'

We're all still friends to this day. Lyn got on like a house on fire with my folks, which was a blessing. It was beautiful seeing them laughing together and that seemed to help my relationship

The Bikie

with my parents, at least a little bit. As they got older, I helped Dad out with stuff around the house and mowing the lawn, as well as still keeping an eye out for Mum while she was doing her Meals on Wheels.

•

When we started the Jokers, club members were all white. For some it was deliberate, not so much for others. Although, looking back, we did walk around wearing 'white power' T-shirts for a while. I was never really into that because where I grew up, around Fairfield, there were plenty of Aboriginal blokes. A lot of the boxers I went up against and trained with were Aboriginal, so the idea of associating only with white people – and thinking that white people were somehow better – never sat well with me.

One of the blokes I came up with, Freddy Briggs, is now a tribal elder in Campbelltown. We once rode a horse bareback from Fairfield to Cabramatta swimming pool. I had blisters on my arse at the end of it and ended up having to walk back.

Even though I didn't have a 'white power' mindset, because a lot of the other blokes were into it, I didn't put a stop to it. It was easier just to go along with it. At the time, I didn't really see it as doing any harm. Later on, we got in touch with the Outback boys and started to become more affiliated. They had quite a few Aboriginal members, including this bloke Floyd who I'm still good mates with. After meeting them, it was a good reason to finally get rid of all that white power shit. Those Aboriginal members didn't deserve to be disrespected by boofheads wearing silly shirts.

Speaking of Floyd, I think he still wants to bash me.

UGLY

One day he had a bad smash on his bike and was pretty banged up in hospital, so I went to visit him. Floyd was a bantamweight champion fighter, so he and I had a lot of respect for each other. Anyone who could fight like him was okay as far as I was concerned. When I got to the hospital, though, I saw he was stuffed. He was all bandaged up and his feet were sticking out the end of the bed.

'Oh,' I said as I walked in. 'You're helpless and you can't move, eh?'

He just nodded. I walked right up to his feet and just went *ticky, ticky, ticky*. He started screaming and thrashing; he *hated* being tickled.

'I'll kill you, Mawson, you bastard!' he screamed.

I haven't seen him since. But I'm pretty sure he still wants to bash me.

Our brother club, the Fourth Reich, started off wearing the eagle and swastika because they wanted to send a certain message. Over time, they got a lot of Maori members, but they never changed their symbols. I think they like how much it pisses people off – but they're not really as big into the message anymore. They always say they're not the Third Reich, they're the Fourth Reich.

'The Third Reich hated everyone,' Ziggy said. 'Hitler and that. We're the Fourth Reich. We just hate everyone who's not in the club.'

Our two clubs are close. If we go visit them, they always look after us. One time years ago we were at their clubhouse and were getting on the piss. I got drunk and fell asleep in one of the back rooms. When I woke up, all the lights were off and no one was around. I went around banging on doors, but everyone had gone. I finally had to call one of them up to come let me out.

The Bikie

'Oi,' I said. 'You just fucking left me here!'

They had to come and open the gates. When they closed the place up, they'd put a chain around the door to the bar. That's because they have a liquor licence. Whenever the cops tried to raid them they'd find the chain and get confused.

'How come you've got this chain around the bar?' the coppers would ask.

'We've got a liquor licence,' they'd say. 'We can't open it up now, only certain times.'

Well, the coppers didn't like that one bit.

But it always made me laugh.

•

By late 1969, things at the Gypsy Jokers were going pretty smoothly. We had our 1%, we had the name I wanted, we had our rules, and we were separate from the Hells Angels. We had our friends, and we didn't really have any enemies. Jan and the Angels might have been sore, but it wasn't serious. My reputation with the cops was still red hot, they knew me from my charges and the fights I kept getting in — or starting — but things hadn't heated up properly yet, even after the two run-ins with police.

Our first outlaw run had 500 bikes. That's a fuckload of bikes. An outlaw run is basically when a club goes for a long ride in formation, which can take anywhere from one day to a week. All of us lined up, blaring down the motorway. It was like coming home, like being a part of a massive family. All of us coming together just to do what we loved to do: ride our bikes.

If only life was always that simple.

When we weren't doing that, we were doing stuff like the six-hour races. Those are endurance races where companies front the bikes they're going to sell. Riders do six straight hours on the track, and the companies – outfits like Kawasaki, BMW, Triumph, and Honda – get prestige from how well the bikes perform. This is at a proper racetrack.

We were at one of those and this bloke I sort of recognised came up to me. This was around 1970, maybe 1971.

'Hey, Ugly,' he said. 'Remember me?'

Lucky that's my nickname, because a greeting like that, to anyone else, would warrant a smack in the mouth.

'Yeah, I remember you,' I said, and I did, although I couldn't recall his name. 'What are you doing with a Rebel patch on?'

The Rebels were another motorcycle club. They'd started in 1969 up in Brisbane.

'I'm a Griffith Rebel,' he said. 'It's Alex, remember?'

'Alex,' I said, matching the name with the face. It was Alex Vella, a boxer who later became the Rebels' president. 'Right. Of course I remember you, I used to fight your brother Joe.'

'That's right. We met at the fights.' Then he sort of shuffled and said, 'You got any objection to me starting up in Sydney? We're all from Griffith.'

I didn't expect that. Here was someone coming to me the same way I'd come to Jan. There were a few blokes standing around wondering what was going on. Poor Alex, that's when I realised how nervous he looked.

'Not at all,' I said. 'Go for your fucking life. The more clubs the better.'

The truth is, besides the fact that more clubs starting up felt like a bit of a victory, I also had no problems with it because more clubs meant less focus on the Jokers from the coppers. When there's more of us, it's harder to concentrate on any single one of us.

The Bikie

Well, everyone hated me for that. The Outback boys especially. The Rebels were the biggest club going. People figure that more clubs meant slicing up more country, more treaties being made, more enemies; but I was happy to see more people getting into the club life. The Rebels have got something like seventy chapters and more than 2000 members across Australia. The others hounded me, called me a bastard for 'giving them permission'. But they were going to do it anyway. I don't know how much my permission was worth, really.

Unfortunately, the Rebels and the Jokers fell out a few years later, at another six-hour race. It was in the mid-1970s, and us and the Finks had done pretty well. We were celebrating with a couple of kegs of cider down by the track, drinking and having a good time, when Gino and a couple of other Rebels showed up. Quick as you know, they grabbed a couple of our glasses and started drinking. I'd met Gino a few times, at parties. He was a Rebel and he liked people to know it. I think he felt real entitled to everything around him because of it.

'You've gotta pay for that,' I said. 'You can't just walk in like that. You're not invited.'

But a Rebel does whatever he wants. That was their whole guiding philosophy.

Packy, a Jokers club member who's since passed away, walked right up to one of the Rebels. He was already hard on the piss and he probably wasn't making his best diplomatic decisions.

'Wear *this*,' he said, and glassed him.

It was on. Punches flying, a blur of a fight. All of them got punched out, all the Rebels. There weren't many of them compared to us, so it was never a fight they were going to win.

After that, we had our first sort-of enemies. The Rebels blamed us for the fight, even though the Finks attacked them, too.

UGLY

The Finks were like attack dogs that day, they just ran at them and took them out.

I say *sort-of* enemies because Alex and I, as leaders, didn't have any bad blood afterwards. We understood the situation. And we understood each other. We were friends. That wasn't going to change just because of some dumb punch-on. The enmity between the clubs didn't last long, because Alex and I talked it out. We didn't want any kind of war.

Unfortunately, stuff has a habit of not going the way you want it to.

One night, I was with the Jokers and we were hanging out at the Millers Hotel in Brighton-Le-Sands. Every night was a night out, more or less, so nothing felt off or different. I didn't think that stuff from the six-hour race was going to be an issue, at least nothing more than a few punch-ons here and there.

Obviously some of the Rebels had a different idea.

Even though they knew Alex and I were friends, like I said, a Rebel does what he wants.

A couple of Rebels drove past the hotel and took a few shots at us from their car. Up until then it had mostly been fistfights. I hadn't been in a gunfight since Vietnam. But the feeling was the same. The sound, the adrenaline pumping through me. My mind went straight back there.

We ran out and jumped into our car. What else were we supposed to do? You can't let that sort of shit stand. We chased after them and we were just pot-shotting at each other from our cars, like fucking gangsters. We were really trying to hit each other. No one got hit, though, which when I think about it now is pretty lucky. No blood got spilt. If it had, I bet things would have turned out differently. I don't think Alex and I could have remained on good terms. But we have.

The Bikie

As we were driving along, we hit a red light. The Rebels boys sped on through, gunning it down the road. But we got stuck, with all the traffic passing in front of us. Behind us, we could hear sirens. The cops were coming. We got out – there were no other cars behind us – and dumped our guns over the side of a fence into some lady's yard. We figured they'd be safe there.

Of course the cops caught up to us and pulled us over.

'We don't have any guns,' I said, the cops shining their torches in my face. 'We were just chasing after some idiots, you know?'

They bought it and went off after the Rebels.

We figured it was too risky to try getting our arsenal back that night, with the cops out and about. There could have been more Rebels with eyes on us as well. So we decided to head back the next day.

All our guns were gone.

To this day I have no idea who took them. I think kids got in there and found them. There were a lot of people looking for those guns. We ended up having to buy all new stock because of that one night. It really pissed me off!

•

One night – this would have been back sometime in the early 1970s – me and a few of the Jokers were bored and hanging out at the Smithfield Tavern. They've done it up a bit now, but it didn't used to be as fancy. In the olden days it was a regular pub where blokes like me would go to drink. We decided that hanging out at the pub was boring, we were all in the mood to do something, so we headed out to a local Saturday night dance happening at the Smithfield Town Hall. There was a band playing, good music for dancing to.

UGLY

I had Lyn with me, and there were a few other girls as well. This was also the first time I met Packy. At this time he was a young Aboriginal bloke, one of the tough boys around the area, and he was hanging out there with a few of his mates. He was cheeky; he walked right up to Lyn and started trying to chat her up while I was standing around outside having a smoke. His mates walked up to her as well and they were all having a big old fun time, chatting away. Odey, one of the older club members, came outside and told me what was going on.

'He and his mates are trying to have it on with Lyn,' Odey said. 'They must know youse are together, they saw us all come in.'

'Little fucker,' I said. 'We should go and sort out the lot of them.'

We walked inside and Packy, who was being a bit full-on by this stage, grabbed Lyn by the shirt. Now, Lyn, she's the one who always carried the guns for us, because the girls never got searched when we went into clubs and bars. She had on her four .22 cutdowns, about a foot long each, with twenty-round magazines, and I had them double-clipped like we did in the army. She'd keep them under her shirt, across her belly, so she'd look like she was pregnant. When Packy grabbed Lyn's shirt, the only thing you can imagine happened: the guns fell out onto the floor.

And they hit the deck with this almighty *whack*.

Packy and his mates got the bloody shock of their lives when they saw the girl they were chatting up had guns falling out of her shirt. Seconds later there's me and Odey, both of us big blokes, coming up to them, swinging hard. When the other Jokers saw us moving in on this group of fellas, they came charging in as well. That was a club rule; one Joker's in a fight, all of them are in the fight.

The Bikie

Packy was a boxer, so he was ducking and weaving and moving his feet. I was trying to line up a good left hook to his face, but the next thing I know I saw this flash across my face. Odey had taken out a chain and swung it hard at Packy, but he missed and instead managed to wrap it around my head! I don't know if you've ever been chain whipped, but that shit fucking hurts. I saw black for a minute and felt my head explode with pain before it went all tingly and numb.

'Ah, you bastard!' I yelled, holding my head and trying to see straight. 'Hit him, not me!'

'Fuck,' was all I heard Odey say. Then, 'Shit.'

The boys who were with Packy bolted off after a few whacks back and forth. Their hearts weren't in it. As soon as they saw the guns, and the chain Odey was tossing around, they were ready to get out of there. Packy, though, stood his ground. He got in a couple of hits on me while I was wrapped up in Odey's chain, but it was a pretty brief fight. We got him by the shirt and showed him what was what.

After that, he apologised to Lyn and to the club. He said he didn't mean any disrespect. Then, get this, he said he'd love to join. That made me laugh, but after seeing his mates fuck off and leave him alone it made sense to me.

'You really wanna join up?' I said.

'Yeah,' he said. 'You blokes look like you know what you're doing, and you all moved in together. I like that.'

'All right,' I said. 'Come round to the clubhouse and we'll see if you're good enough.'

Standing his ground was a good sign that he at least had a set of fucking balls on him, but we needed to see what he could really do, if he could hack it with the rest of us.

True to his word, he came around a few days later and ended up becoming a full-fledged member. Unfortunately, he only lasted two years with us before being washed away by a grog habit. He's since passed away, cirrhosis of the liver. A bloody shame because he was a top bloke. Good fighter and funny as hell.

Mind you, the entire time I knew him he was still trying to get it on with Lyn. He did it to wind me up; he was a stirrer.

To this day, Odey still laughs about that chain getting wrapped around my head and so do I. I can still remember how much that fucker hurt, though!

Not long after that, I ended up cracking my head again. We were drinking over at my parents' place, having a nice time, and I slipped on the concrete. I went arse over tits and met a concrete flower pot, one of those big round ones, with my forehead. It split my head open. I've hit my head a lot over the years and feel lucky that I've made it to where I am today. They took me to hospital and stitched it up. It left a scar. There's another scar on my cheek, but I don't know where it's from.

•

Browny couldn't handle being a part of the city of Sydney Jokers chapter. He wasn't much for the city life, so I gave him permission to start up the Western Sydney chapter in 1972. He was VP and I figured I could trust him enough to carry on with what we were doing.

Not long after, in 1974, I decided it was time to resign as president. I wanted to marry Lyn and being president of the Gypsy Jokers and a good husband weren't compatible. Your priorities change.

But when I told the fellas about my decision, they didn't want a bar of it.

'I want to get serious with Lyn,' I said. 'So I'm gonna resign.'

The Bikie

'But we don't want you to,' they said. 'You've been leading the club good.'

'How about you let me nominate my successor?' I said.

'All right,' they said. 'Who do you want?'

'Well, I nominate Cowboy. Anyone got any problems with that?'

It still makes me laugh. They did not like that one bit. They ummed and ahhed about it. Cowboy was a maniac. A top bloke, but an absolute loose unit. They didn't love it but, out of respect for me, they allowed it. So, I officially resigned as president, and Cowboy took up the mantle.

Those were some wild years.

I picked Cowboy because he was a nutbag. But so was I. We were tight, real good mates. Every time I was in a blue, he'd be right there alongside me. I'd probably have picked Browny, but he was running the Western Sydney chapter by then. Cowboy loved the noise and the glare and all the fun of city life. He was a happy-go-lucky kind of bloke, a bricklayer by trade.

Unfortunately, Cowboy isn't with us anymore. Cancer got him in the end.

We lost Willie in 1974. We called him 'Willie Bull' and he was a good young bloke. When we went to parties together, he'd get a mouthful of petrol and blow it out onto a flame like he was a circus performer. A real character. The boys made up a song for him to the tune of *Johnny B. Goode*.

Losing Willie Bull was a big loss.

I was living in Fairfield at the time and we were working together. We were at Mum and Dad's place in Cabramatta and I was telling him that the front end of my bike was a spring and it was a bit of a rough ride. I'd already had a spring front

UGLY

end snap on me, so I wasn't too keen on them. Willie said he'd be happy to swap front ends with me because his would suit me more. Problem was, when he swapped them out, his headlight wasn't connected up properly, the wiring was a bit flimsy and it kept flickering out. Wish we'd realised that a bit earlier.

That night, we all went to the Millers Hotel, which was around the block. Everything was fine, we had a few drinks, and then, at some point in the night, Willie said he was going to the Cabramatta pub.

'I wanna show off my new springer to the boys,' he said to me, winking, meaning my old front end. He said goodbye and half the boys went with him and half the boys stayed with me. We kept on drinking.

Up over at Wilga Street, Fairfield, there's a rail crossing and there used to be a couple of boom gates. A car came speeding around into that crossing, swinging around to the right, and, with that jiggly wire, Willie's headlights had gone out.

The car couldn't see him and hit him.

Killed him outright.

One of the boys came racing back and ran into the pub and just said, 'Willie Bull just got wiped out down the road!'

The air froze for a moment and then we all rushed out, jumped on our bikes, and rode down there. I was fuming, dazed. When we arrived, the cops were already there, the flashing lights lighting up the night. I just started shouting.

'Which one of them did it?' I demanded. I couldn't see straight I was so mad.

Someone gestured at a bloke and said, 'That one there.'

They probably shouldn't have, but they did.

I marched right up to the bloke and punched him as hard as I could.

The Bikie

'You cunt!' I yelled. I started in on him with both hands then. He didn't have time to get his hands up, I just kept hitting him.

Then I felt a jerk as the cops grabbed me from behind and pulled me off of him.

'We'll give you a fucking fight,' one of the coppers said.

'Fuckin' oath!' I said, and turned on them with a snarl.

The boys were pulling me back but I was ready to have a go at the cops. They were just an obstacle and I wanted to knock them down. I didn't care. The Jokers dragged me away, which was probably for the best. I would've ended up back in jail. The boys put me on the back of one of their bikes and we rode off back to the pub.

I had to come get my bike later when I'd calmed down and the cops had cleared off. We drank a few for Willie Bull. He swapped that front end from me that day and died that night. I still feel guilty about it. If only we'd gotten those headlights working.* I know it's not my fault, but it was my front end.

After we lost Willie Bull, we lost Bimbo in 1975. He took off on his bike behind a car, went to go around it, and didn't see another car coming the other way. Smash. Dead. There's a lot of people I used to know who aren't around anymore.

●

Sometimes you just meet crazy people and they're forever burnt into your memory. In the early 1980s, a club mate by the name of Norris and I were on a ride. We pulled up in a country town where they had a rodeo going on. Norris decided it would be fun to go and watch. Well, the rodeo people were doing an

---

* The front end of Ugly's bike on the front cover of this book is the front end in question.

UGLY

audience interaction thing where they got a bunch of chairs and put them all in the middle of the ring. Then they got some volunteers to sit on the chairs while they let the wild bull out. If you got up to run – like most sane people would do – you were out. The last one to stay seated got a prize. In this case it was something like $100. Not much.

Norris, being a real character, decided to have a go. He sat there on the chair, waiting for the bull, while all the other blokes around him – and it was only blokes, no sheilas were crazy enough for this nonsense – were shitting themselves. The bull came crashing out of the gate and the audience cheered. It ran back and forth, doing circles around them. Every now and then it would get close and then someone would lose their cool and bolt for safety.

Norris ended up being one of the last men seated.

It was just him and one other bloke.

Rather than just waiting it out, though, Norris got bored. He was watching this bull, pacing back and forth and snarling, and he wasn't impressed.

He just sat there. 'Nah, this bull is shit,' he said eventually.

And then he got what is probably the single dumbest and greatest idea he's ever had. He stood up, picked up his chair, and, when the bull got close enough, slammed it down right on the bull's head. *Bang!*

Obviously, the bull didn't like that. It started snorting. Then it charged at him. Norris ran, zig-zagging, and managed to throw himself over the fence. He barely avoided a horn going right up his arse.

The other bloke ended up winning because he was too scared to move.

•

The Bikie

One thing that a lot of people might not realise is that all the weird nicknames – what we call club names – are given to members on purpose. They usually come from something embarrassing or are a way of giving someone shit. So if you're tall, you'd be called 'Tiny', or if you're short, you might get called 'Big Nuts'. The point of nicknames, back in the old days when we started doing it, was so that you never knew each other's full names. That's why I can usually only think of someone by their club name. We didn't learn our real names on purpose – if you were ever caught by the coppers, you wouldn't be able to give anyone up.

'Who were you with?'

'Don't know.'

And then they'd beat the shit out of you to get you to talk, but you still wouldn't know. You'd only know the club nickname. I learnt that from my army days, in case we ever got captured. No one knew each other's real names unless you knew them personally from before. It was all about protection.

•

I had all kinds of run-ins with cops, but they weren't always fights. One time, not long after I'd got back from Vietnam, I was getting pissed down at a pub in Fairfield. After a few last drinks, I decided to walk to this all-night café not far from there.

Well, who should be there, too? Three coppers parked by the side of the road on their bikes.

I don't know what made me do it, but I just said to myself, 'Ah, I'll give them a fucking race.'

UGLY

I went home and got my bike. Zoomed right past them, revved the engine a few times – *reow, reow* – and then sped off. That got their attention. I led them on a merry chase down West Street, the side street that stretches along the train tracks from Fairfield to Canley Vale, but of course they caught me.

I was wasted.

There was no way they weren't going to catch me.

They rode me to the police station. I had to lean my bike against the wall outside. They took me inside and one of them said, 'Do you want a doctor?'

I slurred back at him, 'Why do I want a doctor for?'

Again, I was gone. Lost my licence for twelve months. Racing the cops didn't work out, but it was fun.

Being a part of a club and not having a licence is like torture. Sure, I rode my bike without my licence. For the most part, nobody checks up on you. Sometimes, though, I had to ride sidecar, which was a bit embarrassing.

Being part of a motorbike club was great fun. You did runs and had kegs and drinks with other clubs. You got respect. And you were free. But by the late 1980s, I was starting to get a bit narky about all these new clubs starting up. I was happy to have more fellas around for a while – they were a good distraction for the coppers – but as the scene grew, it felt like everyone wanted to take a run at each other, which sometimes meant me. Dealing with the politics of it all was becoming a bit of a pain in the arse. Us Jokers had our reputation, but so did all the other clubs.

Around 1989, this club started up in Sydney called the Vietnam Veterans.

'Oh,' I said. 'These are gonna be a bunch of wankers.'

The Bikie

For starters, they had a back patch on, and that wasn't right. Back patches are only for 1% clubs and these blokes *weren't* 1%. They could have just had a front patch, like the Mobbies,* which would have classified them as a social club, but they didn't do that. They wanted the look of the back patch. Back patches were only for clubs who'd been officially sanctioned by leading clubs in the area, which wasn't the case as far as I was aware. It was also something that designated them as more than a social club, if not a fully-fledged outlaw club, so they were walking a fine line there.

I organised a small squad to come with me down to their headquarters in St Mary's and have a little chat. The Vietnam Veterans were renting a bunker at the old army camps. I know a lot of us old-guard bikies were veterans as well, but we didn't associate that with the club life. The two things, while connected, were separate.

'Let's go down and sort these bastards out,' I said to the fellas.

We got down there and we didn't pull any punches. We kicked down the door and barged in on them, right in the middle of them having a meeting.

'What gives you the right to wear a three-piece patch?' I growled.

But before me and the boys could get really started in on them, this bloke jumped up and said, 'Hey, Ugly, it's me!'

It was Carl, an ex-fighter I knew from the 1960s and 70s. That took the wind right out of my sails.

'Carl,' I said. 'How ya going?'

---

* More than likely a reference to the Mobshitters MC, a 1% club that started up in Hurstville, New South Wales, in 1970. Most notable about them is that Angry Anderson, lead vocalist of the band Rose Tattoo, is a friend of the club. Bikie lawyer Justin Birk Hill claimed to be a founding member.

UGLY

'Good, mate. Listen, we don't want any dramas. We're a dying-off club, ya know? We're old, we're all gonna be dead soon.'

That wasn't quite true. A lot of them were still young and fit – well, young enough – but in a sense he was right, they *were* dying. Blokes came back from the war and they died, either in fights or by their own hand. Some of them were older blokes looking to join up with some young blood. Besides, they weren't trying to claim 1% status, so it's not like they were stepping on anyone's toes trying to make a name for themselves.

What could I do? It couldn't hurt to leave them be. I softened up because I knew him. So we let them go and then they went ahead and built up their base. Years later, around 1999, they ended up changing their name from the Vietnam Veterans to just the Veterans because the Vietnam vets were all dying out and blokes who'd served in the forces in other wars and conflicts were joining up to ride with them. I gave them permission to start up in Sydney, just like the Rebels. They're a big club still. We still help them out from time to time.

Sadly, Carl's no longer with us.

Seems to be the way of a lot of the blokes I used to know.

5

The Citizen

In the early 1980s, we sold our war service house in Hurstville, upped sticks and moved to a place in Padstow. I was soon to be juggling kids, so we needed more room. There were a few blokes who wanted to train with me so I decided to start up my own gym – in a garage. I worked with the local council and got it registered. I even had a shower put in at the back. All the mod cons. I had the gym insured for $2 million – a fair amount of money in those days – but I didn't tell anyone because people would have come around to try and burn it down.

A mate of mine, Peter Larkin, helped me build the gym. I trained him from start to finish and he ended up becoming an Australian champion fighter. He died recently of a heart attack. But he was a bloody good fighter in his day. The gym was full of talent, with folks like Jimmy Bowen, the welterweight Australian champion. Phil Kating was an Australian champion as well as a Vanuatu champion. I also had Jim Mawson, an English boxer. I'd put them through a regime I'd come up with which was basically rounds of training and fighting with breaks in between. Simple.

Fox was a trainer from Outback, and a good, tough fighter. He came to Sydney because he wanted to see the gym. He wanted me to put him through some punch work and teach him how to train, and so I outlined the basics.

'If you're fightin' three rounds,' I said, 'you train four rounds.'

He nodded.

'If the fight is two minutes,' I said, 'you train three minutes.'

He nodded again.

It was straightforward; basic stuff, really, but it toughens you up.

Fox took it all in and then went back to Outback. He was one hell of a fighter. But then, more and more – especially when he was drunk – he became like the character Melville from this TV show on the ABC. The show featured a comedy trio, three Pommy blokes, and one of them would always be doing something wrong. Whenever that happened, the others would go, 'Oh, he's turned into Melville.' So Fox got the nickname Melville when he was on the grog, because he'd always be up to something. You'd have to keep your mouthguard in when you were hanging out with him.

One time, I went out to Outback and Fox and I were drinking all the leftover grog in the clubhouse. We were just sitting around, talking, because we were mates. At one point, I saw his eyes go a bit funny. And I just thought, *Uh-oh*.

I said, 'You're not turnin' into Melville, are you?'

'And what if I am?'

'Well, then I'm moving.'

He said, 'Well, take this with ya!'

And he just wound up and whacked me right in the face.

The Citizen

I've taken one or two hits to the face in my time and I didn't stumble. I just acted like it was nothing.

'Oh,' I said. 'That wasn't bad. Let's have another beer.'

'Righto,' he said. 'I'll shout.'

And as soon as he moved, I threw a punch and clocked him right on the side of the head. It was on. We ended up tumbling over and crashing into the coffee urn, hot coffee spilling everywhere. Our drinks smashed on the ground. He punched me and then I punched him. Then I smashed a bottle of beer on his foot to try to stop him.

What I hadn't counted on were the rings he was wearing.

He cut up my nose something fierce.

I had to fly back to Sydney the next day and my face ended up ballooning. By the time I got home, I looked like Mr Melonhead. Lyn took a photo of me and was laughing so hard she was crying.

But it's one of the reasons why people always wanted me in their corner for their fights. I could fight and I could take a punch. People liked having me in their corner because I knew how to encourage them and keep them going, even when things were looking bad.

I helped out Bernie Hall, although he got banned for some fucking thing or another, so he wasn't allowed to be in people's corners. So I took his place. I was in the corner for some redheaded bloke whose name I don't remember who was up against Paul Nassari – he had gyms down at Revesby – and I was supposed to be telling this bloke what to do. But I knew Paul. I liked Paul. So I told this fella a bunch of bullshit, nothing helpful. I was just messing with him. In the end, Paul outdid him without my help. Paul was one hell of a fighter.

UGLY

After the fight was over — and it was still being televised, mind you — Paul went around to shake everybody's hand. Then he went over the ring, leant down and *bang*, clocked me. Oh, that made the crowd roar! That was for being in his opponent's corner. They all knew we were mates. I was laughing and so was he. That was only because he won the fight, though. If he'd lost, I'd have run off.

I used to corner for Peter Larkin all the time, when he was coming up on the boxing scene. I only gave it up because I moved up to where I am now and stopped really dropping by the gym. I've got a pergola out here with heavy bags and gloves and that sort of thing. So I'm all set up.

Peter Larkin died at home of a massive heart attack while he was sleeping. Not a bad way to go. He was a bus driver and I always thought it lucky he didn't die while he was driving. I'm still friends with his brothers and his dad, Greg. Every time I go down to the Padstow RSL, I sit with his dad, who's eighty-five now and was in the Malaya conflict. We give each other plenty of shit. Greg's a good bloke.

•

The Padstow gym was mostly started up for fun. It was never really a full-time gig. We collected dues — five bucks a week for membership — but if people didn't have the money, we didn't really care. It was open every night so that people could come and train after work. Most of the time it was unmanned. Sometimes there was someone sitting in the office but not always.

Throughout the 1980s, I had a bunch of other jobs. I cleaned units down at Caringbah, which was good money and wasn't hard work. Charlie Costa got me a job working for the local

The Citizen

council. He was a garbo and said he could get me a job doing the same.

'I know all the bosses,' he said. 'The money's pretty good.'

'Fuck yeah,' I said. 'That sounds all right.'

I ended up working as a garbo for most of the 1980s.

One shift, Charlie was doing a run down on Elizabeth Drive, heading towards Cabramatta. Usually, you hang onto the back of the garbage truck and, when it slows down, you jump off and collect the bins. Well, the truck slowed down and Charlie jumped off the back but didn't see there was a car coming.

The car didn't slow down.

It slammed right into him and dragged him halfway up the road. A bunch of skin was torn from his arms and legs and back.

The coppers were called and they came down and were holding the driver. Being the rough and tough kind of bloke that he was, Charlie said he didn't want to press charges. 'It's my fault. Don't worry about him. He didn't have time to stop. I didn't look and that's on me.'

Not wanting to do any paperwork, the coppers had Charlie fill out and sign some forms that said that he was in the wrong and that the driver was all right. Silly bastard. The coppers let the driver go and that was that.

Charlie had to give up being a garbo after the accident, but it didn't stop him from hanging out with the Jokers. He was still that same street punk, through and through, and he was always round having beers.

Charlie ended up getting me my other gig as a bouncer, which I did three nights a week. Club members were often hired out as security for clubs and bars and the like, due to our reputation for winning fights. The 1980s were the prime time for that. The underground music scene was huge and they always needed big blokes on hand in case things took a violent turn.

Charlie bounced at the Millers Hotel in Fairfield, and he got me a gig bouncing there, too. It's called the Fairfield Hotel now, but back then it was the Millers. I also worked at the Georges River Sailing Club, which is where Lyn worked one of her two jobs. She was a barmaid and it's where she picked up her real skill: having an answer for everything. She had to in that kind of gig. The other work she did was babysitting for people in the local area.

I also bounced at the rowing club — I think it was called the St George Rowing Club — as well as Shanney's in Hurstville, which is now the Hurstville Ritz, which used to be owned by the former rugby league player Steve Bowden. Another former footballer, a Welsh bloke by the name of Merv Hicks, started up the El Toro in Liverpool, in Sydney's west, and he got me to work with him there, too. He was head bouncer and manager and I was head head-hitter.

It sounds like I didn't have much personal time, but I liked it. I liked working. Doing nothing all day — or worse, sitting at a desk — never suited me. The whole point of club life was rebelling against the idea that, to get ahead, you needed to wear a tie and get a desk job. I didn't want a fucking desk job and I knew plenty of people who didn't, either.

Sadly, Charlie Costa's not with us anymore. He died a few years after his accident while collecting the garbage, sometime in the late 1980s. He was up at Mullumbimby, a country town in Northern New South Wales not far from Byron Bay, working on the railway lines. They found him there on this bush track one day. He was in his work clothes — shorts and a sweatshirt — but nothing seemed to be wrong with him. I don't really know how he died. He was a tough bastard, and I miss him.

It was around this time that I lost my folks. Dad was out in the backyard one day and a neighbour noticed that the lawnmower had been in the same place for a long while. He peered over the fence and saw Dad lying there, dead. He wasn't much older than I am now.

Mum didn't last too long after Dad died.

I think it was a broken heart.

•

Starting a family while still involved with the Gypsy Jokers wasn't as difficult as you might think. Lyn was already deep in it with me; she liked to ride bikes and ride on the back of bikes, and she carried our guns, so it wasn't a problem for her. A lot of the blokes in the club had kids, so whenever I needed time away from the club to deal with family stuff, they were good about it. They understood. It was a better situation than you get in a lot of jobs.

Sometimes, if Lyn was working, I'd take the kids down to the clubhouse with me and we'd hang out there. Those kids had some of the weirdest babysitters you can imagine. And that was pretty common. Lots of blokes took their kids to the clubhouse, especially if their missus couldn't look after them or they didn't have any other place to take them. That was part of being in the club; it was like a family. We looked after each other because no one else did.

If club members were having disagreements, we usually talked it out among ourselves. Diplomacy was always option number one. We'd call a big meeting with all the committee members, in whichever state's turn it was to host the meeting. Everyone would have spoken to their committee members beforehand to let them know how they felt about whatever was going on. Then the committee members would voice their opinions, one by one, and talk it all out until they resolved it as best they could. Then the committee members rode back to their states and let the chapters know what the decision was.

As long as I've been around – which is from the start of the Jokers – no one has tried to kill another member. Jokers stick together, always. It's not like how it is on TV: we might have some fisticuffs every now and then, but we don't try to kill each other.

If we had problems with another club, again, diplomacy came first, and we'd usually just try to avoid each other until things simmered down. Running each other over and shooting each other just wasn't our way. Sure, it happened from time to time, but that wasn't the way we wanted things to go. Clubs fighting with each other gets you too much time in prison and it's just not worth it. That sort of shit brings the heat down on everyone, drawing unwanted attention, when all we wanted was to *not* be noticed. This was understood in the early days, back in the 1970s.

Of course, some people don't want to follow *any* rules, written or unwritten.

And *that* can be a problem.

•

A little while before my marbles came up for the army, I only had two pro fights under my belt; one was a draw, and the

The Citizen

other was a win, which set me up as an amateur lightweight champion. When I got back from Vietnam, I decided to turn pro. I had a few fights with Joe Vella, but he always seemed to win. I always wondered whether or not someone on his team was fixing things in his favour. He was just too lucky!

While training at a gym in Liverpool around 1970, the former champ Frank Bennett came to me with a proposition.

'I've got a bloke by the name of Alipapa Afakasi who's looking to fight his first fight in Australia,' he said. 'Do you want to take him on?'

'Yeah,' I said. How could I refuse? Any fight was good, it would keep my fitness levels up, keep my training up, and keep me in the ring.

Once I'd agreed, Frank went off to sort it all out.

I didn't hear from him for a few days and then he came back to me with the date, 29 October 1970. And wouldn't you know it? That was the same night as a Jokers meeting. So I went and saw my mate Browny and asked him to run the meeting in my absence.

'I have to go out,' I said and left it at that. I didn't tell them that I was going to fight this new boxer. Not that I was hiding it or anything, I just didn't say anything about it. Some stuff is my stuff, and some stuff is club stuff. This was my stuff.

The fight was set to take place at the South Sydney Rugby League Club. A decent-sized venue. I needed to get into the right mindset because the bout was going to be televised. This would be the first time I'd fought on the telly.

Well, little did I know, but Browny and the boys wrapped up the Jokers meeting early and settled in to watch some TV and have a few beers. And what did they turn on?

UGLY

Yeah, you guessed it. The fight at the South Sydney Rugby League Club.

So I was in the ring and the announcer was introducing us. The other bloke was standing in the opposite corner to me, a short, tough-looking Samoan. Compact and wound like a spring. 'In one corner is Ali Afakasi, the New Zealand champion and gold medallist!' yelled the announcer. 'And in the other corner is Phillip Mawson!'

The tone of his voice told me that he thought I was a sucker for going up against this bloke. After the first round, I could see why. Bloody hell, this fella was quick! And his punches landed hard. I was a tough nut, but this bloke came ready.

At the end of the first round, the ref came up to me while I was sitting on my stool.

'You all right?' he said. He obviously thought I looked a little worse for wear, which pissed me off.

'Yeah,' I said. 'I'm fine.'

I ran circles around Afakasi in the second round, each of us taking pot-shots at each other. But by the third round, I'd had enough. I could feel this heat building up behind my eyes.

'All right, mate,' I said to Afakasi. 'Up yours, let's have it out.'

The bell went for the third round and I charged him. He hit me up into the ropes. I used that to my advantage and bounced off, throwing a hook at him. But it just bounced me right into his punch. All I ended up doing was testing the strength of his knuckles. He hit me so hard that it felt like I'd been thumped in the face with a hammer. They told me later that my feet left the ground and I crashed down onto my back.

I had no idea what had happened; I was out cold.

I have no memory of it, but when I came to, my jaw was sore as hell. That fight ended my fledgling professional boxing

The Citizen

career. If they'd told me how good this Afakasi fella was, that he was some kind of proper champion, I think I would've been a bit more serious about my preparation and training.

After I'd recovered – which took about a month – I went back to the gym again. Bennett said it was about time I got back in the ring, and hooked me up to fight with Nino, another boxer who trained at the club. He was also a member of the Jokers. Nino was a number one heavyweight contender, so a different weight class to me, but we were a pretty even match if you just eyeballed us.

Getting back into the mindset to spar wasn't hard. I got my mind right, strapped the gloves on, and that was that, I was back in the saddle.

'You ready?' Nino said.

'Yeah,' I said. 'Ready.'

'Okay,' he said. 'Here we go.'

Bennett started us off and right away Nino got in a straight left jab to my jaw. It was the exact same place Afakasi had hit me! I just let out this little grunt. But then my knees went wobbly, like a cold bucket of water had been thrown over me.

'That's it, mate,' I slurred. 'I'm buggered. I can't do this anymore.'

'Yeah,' Nino said, looking at me. 'Your eyes went funny.'

'And I'm not giving you a chance to get a knockout over me, you bastard,' I said, and we laughed. I took the gloves off and that was that. No more sparring for me.

In his first Australian fight Ali Afakasi had knocked me clean off the circuit. He went on to have a pretty impressive ten-year career with twenty-eight wins, seven losses and only one draw. He was a hell of a fighter.

UGLY

Of course, next time I went to see the Jokers, they gave me hell over it. They'd seen everything on TV. Now, whenever I have a go at the boys, they always say, 'We'll ring Ali to fix you up again.'

That's one I'll never live down; me, the president of the Gypsy Jokers getting tuned up live on TV. Thank Christ my brother Neil didn't come to that fight.

6

The Gypsy Joker

Like I said, most clubs in the 1970s got on with one another. Things were pretty mellow. But everything started to change in the 1980s. Even though I wasn't boxing anymore, I was always fighting. With more clubs starting up, and everyone stepping on everyone else's toes, there seemed to be more and more fights all the time. Everyone wanted to be big dog and not back down. It felt like being a kid again.

When the Bandidos arrived on the scene in 1983, they brought a kind of violence that hadn't really been there before. Not in the same way, anyhow.

One night, two Jokers members were drinking at the Vauxhall Inn at Granville. Also enjoying a couple of beers at the pub were two Bandidos. As you can imagine, words were exchanged, there was a fight, and the Bandidos belted our two members.

Of course, our boys came straight to us and told us what happened.

'All right,' I said. 'We're always drinking there. They know us there. We'll go round now and sort those dickheads out.'

I organised a big group. Everyone got into our cars and we were ready to bloody some noses and crack a few bones. We knew the Bandidos would be there because they were having their meeting night.

We pulled up on both roads that led to the Vauxhall Inn – Parramatta Road and Woodville Road – and we could see all the Bandido bikes lined up out the front. It was clear it wasn't going to be all of us against just two of them, there looked to be about thirty-odd bikes, and there were about thirty of us, too.

The only difference as far as we could tell was that we were armed with bats and clubs.

Once it was all over, our getaway would be waiting to drive us out of there.

As we approached, one of the Bandidos came out of the pub. 'Shit!' he yelled. 'The Jokers are here!'

And he ran back inside. That made me laugh.

One of our blokes – he's since passed away – ran in after that Bandido like a cowboy, throwing fists at everyone. How long do you think that lasted? Not long. He got punched out at the door. We rushed in and started swinging our bats but quickly found ourselves in a stand-off. The Bandidos wouldn't come out because they knew we had weapons, but because there was only one door, we couldn't get more than one or two of our boys inside at a time. Which was a big problem as they'd easily pick us off one by one.

Then, out of nowhere, a Bandido came running out of the hotel doing a high-flying kick – right past my head! My first thought was, *This bloke knows karate.* A part of me was tempted

The Gypsy Joker

to use the moves I'd learnt in karate class, but in a situation like the one we were in, you just do what you need to do to survive.

So I turned around and got him in a headlock.

He was strong, so we were struggling. There I was, trying to eye-gouge him, while he was trying his best to trip me up and get on top of me. He couldn't because I kept moving my feet; even in a tussle like that I was still moving like a boxer.

And then along came our bloke Gummy. Good ol' Gummy.

He ran at us with his bat over his head, yelling, 'I got 'im! I got 'im!'

But instead of clocking the Bandido, the bat came down and smacked *me* right across the fucking head. By sheer luck I kept the Bandido in the headlock, but my vision went all sparkly. If I'd known Gummy was going to be such a bloody pain in the arse, I'd have told him to go help someone else.

'You bastard,' I growled. My jaw hurt from where my teeth had clacked together, and my head hurt from where Gummy had whacked me. 'Him! Hit *him*!' I yelled.

I turned around to face Gummy so he'd get a better shot at the Bandido and *whack*, he knocked me on the head *again*. Christ, let me tell you, I started to feel *really* dizzy then. Two whacks from a bat on your head will do that. I was worried that my grip was going to loosen on the Bandido and then he'd either get away, or hurt one of us.

But Gummy wasn't finished. 'I'll get 'im this time!' he yelled.

You fuckin' better, I thought.

Guess what, though? He didn't. He whacked me a *third* fucking time. What sort of aim did this bloke have? At that point, I sort of detached from myself. Had an out-of-body experience. You try taking three whacks with a bat to the head and see how clearly you think, because it's pretty fucking impressive that I managed to stay standing at all.

UGLY

So I had to let the Bandido go.

Fuck it, he couldn't do more damage to me than Gummy was already doing.

I then reached out and damn near choked Gummy to death. But my grip couldn't have been too good because he squirmed away. The look on his face told me that he knew he'd fucked up pretty bad. He ended up chasing down that Bandido and whacking him with the bat, finally. Then Odey came up behind him and maced him for good measure. Not necessary, but definitely funny.

By that time, I was in Disneyland. When I came back to myself, I was lying on the ground. It was quiet, the air was still.

'Oh, shit,' I said out loud. 'What happened? Where's everyone gone?'

All around me bodies were lying on the ground, in the driveway, everywhere. It was like a warzone. A couple of them were trying to stand up but no one was moving all that fast, me included.

'I've got my gun on me,' I said as I managed to stagger to my feet. I wasn't lying. I pulled out my pistol for emphasis and waved it around. People were too focused on that to realise that I was swaying like a drunkard. In my state, I definitely don't think I could've hit anything. It's lucky for me that people freeze up when they see a gun, and for good reason.

'Anyone move,' I said, 'and I'll shoot yas.'

Everyone got back on the ground again. In that state, it's easier to just do as you're told. Part of you wants to fight, or run, but mostly you just don't want to die. So you freeze. I stumbled over to the carport, gun in my hand, and Nick was still there sitting in the car.

'Get in, get in,' he said.

The Gypsy Joker

I half-fell into the car. It wasn't my most agile moment, but it was the best I could manage given the circumstances. He started up the engine and I just remember thinking how fucking loud it sounded. My head was pounding, like there were knives behind my eyes. I looked down at the gun in my hand and decided it was best to put it away.

'No guns were allowed,' he said, frowning at me.

'It's lucky I had it. I was left there on my own. Everyone bloody forgot me!'

None of us ended up in hospital after that little blue, not that I can remember, anyway. I had a bit of a concussion thanks to Gummy, but I just slept it off.

•

I often think it's amazing I'm still alive and that I survived the things I survived. It feels like more than luck. Funnily enough, it was never the bikes that got me into trouble — there was always human intervention, always someone who wanted to have a go at me and left without finishing the job.

At one point we were organising an outlaw run, which, yes, we did do in between all the fights and parties. It's what we looked forward to the most. The whole point of a club, as far as I'm concerned, is to ride. That's why we got together in the first place. Riding always came first; the violence just came along with it because we didn't take any shit. Later on, newer chapters and other clubs got into it because they wanted to make money, usually selling drugs. A few of the members of the Western Sydney chapter of the Jokers, where Browny was the president, ended up going to jail because of drugs.

That didn't mean we didn't enjoy the partying. Or, if I'm honest, the fighting. But riding was central to who we were and what we were about.

Anyway, after spending some time at a pub in Merrylands organising the run, we headed over to this girl's place. Four or five girls lived there and a few of us used to go back there to, well, party, as they say. But before we had left the pub, one of the Jokers had had an argument with someone. None of us thought anything of it, because it was just a few words.

Next thing we know, a bunch of blokes have jumped the fence into these girls' backyard and they're waving around batons and guns! One of my favourite films is *The Warriors*. It came out in 1979 and is about street gangs in New York. I think that's what led me to say what I said next.

'I'm gonna stick that gun up your arse and turn you into a popsicle!'

Little did this bloke know I had a set of knuckledusters underneath my motorcycle gloves. A lot of these guys who come at you with guns aren't prepared or ready to use them. They think people will see a gun and it's game over. It often is.

But I've been shot at plenty. And this fella wasn't counting on that.

The expression on his face was priceless when I grabbed him and started whacking him in the face with those knuckledusters. The sheer shock. He must have damn near shit himself.

The next thing I remember there was a flash.

He must have tried to shoot me.

Well, he *did* shoot me!

I just don't think he meant to shoot me in the head. There was blood spurting everywhere, people were running around screaming. And those bastards ended up bolting.

The Gypsy Joker

I woke up in Parramatta Hospital. Turned out I got lucky. The bullet had grazed the back of my head, right at the top, which meant no real damage – and only eight stitches. But as the doctors were patching me up, they forgot to take off my gloves for some reason or another.

Just as I came to, a couple of detectives arrived for a chat. All par for the course when someone gets shot in the head but the last thing I needed right then.

I was still wearing my motorcycle gloves.

With the knuckledusters inside.

For those not in the know, knuckledusters aren't exactly fucking legal.

'Here, let us help, I'll take them off for you,' one of the detectives said, all caring like.

'Nah, I'll be right,' I said, trying to slide the knuckledusters off with the gloves. 'I'll get them off myself.' Thinking on my feet after a shot to the head wasn't exactly easy. 'Actually, can you come back and get me in a minute?' I said. I was relying on the fact that they wouldn't consider a bloke lying in a hospital bed with a gunshot wound to the head a flight risk.

It worked a treat.

They left the room.

Quickly as I could, I got out of bed, peeked around the corner, saw the exit was clear and then scarpered. They'd stitched up my head already, it wasn't like I was going to die. Not anymore, anyway.

That night while listening to *Night Watch* – the radio show I'd enjoyed as a kid – I heard about this Gypsy Joker who'd been shot in the head and then escaped from hospital. Now that was one hell of a story!

I often have a chuckle thinking about the talking-to those detectives would have got down at the station after they confessed that a bloke who'd been shot in the head had somehow managed to slip past them.

Oh yeah, and we made sure to go back and sort out those troublemakers from the pub in Merrylands. Armed to the teeth, we went in and made sure they wouldn't dare crash one of our parties again.

Best of all, we wore white T-shirts with 'REBELS FOREVER' written across them!

•

Sometimes my luck manifested in a more normal way, rather than a 'I'm lucky I didn't die' way. For a bit I was a repo man for a bloke named Paul Worth. He was an entrepreneur with a shop down at Arncliffe where he used to loan, sell and do up bikes. He did good work and I liked him.

Anyway, one day Bon Scott walked in.

How about that? It's not every day someone like that comes into the shop where you're working. What are you supposed to say? I just served him like any other customer. He wasn't up his own arse or anything, just a real down-to-earth kind of bloke. I appreciated that.

'I'm a big fan of your band,' I said. 'AC/DC.' As if he didn't know what his own band was called.

'Oh, yeah?' he said. 'You can have my hat.'

And he just took off this Ducati hat that he had on and wrote on it, BON SCOTT, TO PHIL.

I'm still real proud of that.

That night I went home and gave it to my eldest daughter. She was so excited. She's still got it hanging in the garage. I don't know if it's faded, if you can still read the handwriting or not, but it's there. A place of pride. It probably should have

Ugly on his very first bike, a Triumph Thunderbird.

Ugly at twenty years old, in the backyard of his family home, showing off the moves Neil had taught him. He wanted a photo of himself for the boxing ring magazine.

Ugly at twenty-one on one of his early bikes, a 1959 Bonneville.

Ugly (centre) out shooting with mates in Kandos, New South Wales, 1960s.

Ugly in his twenties, out hunting with mate Morris (right). They caught themselves a kangaroo.

On the same trip, they found an injured Australian Raven and nursed it back to health.

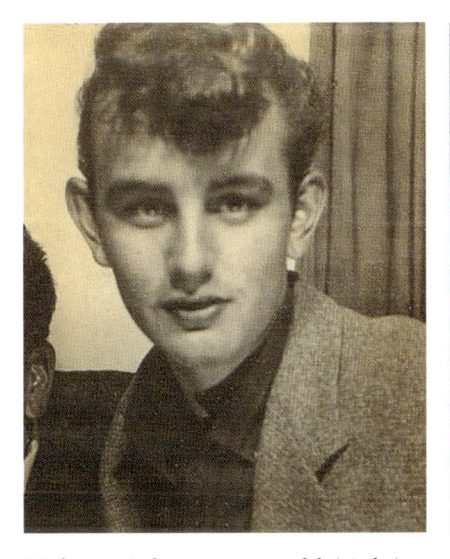

Ugly at eighteen years old (right), out with his mate Billy Burton. He wanted to show off his chic new hair.

At Manly Beach, 1960s, with Ugly doing his best *Singin' in the Rain* impression.

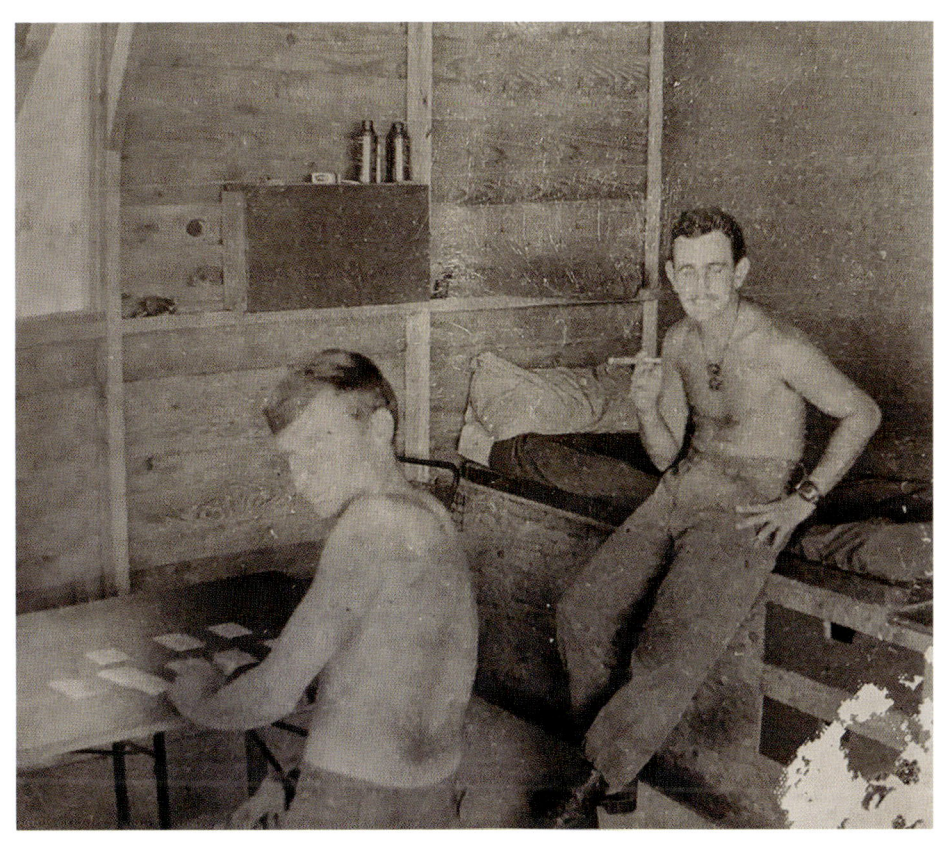

Ugly smoking a cigar at Vung Tau with 'some corporal'.

Private Mawson in his bunk in Vietnam, 1968.

Third Battalion boys back from Balmoral. From left to right: Mick Evans, David Cripps, Brian Rigby and Ugly, who is leaning over, pretending he is carrying a heavy pack.

Double date with Ugly and Patty (left) and Billy Burton and Sharleena (right).

The early days of the Jokers, around 1969. Ugly and Patty (right) along with Charlie and Helen (left).

A cop trying to book a member of the Jokers, as the other members make fun of the whole ordeal.

Group shot of some Jokers boys.

Lined up and ready to ride, 1970.

Ugly (left) and Snotty (right) taking their official Gypsy Jokers Drinking Team photo.

Out front of the Forth & Clyde Hotel, Balmain, 1970. From left to right: Grub, Odey, Ugly, Brutus, Mannix.

Gathering of Jokers at the Millers Hotel, Fairfield. They hung the Gypsy Jokers flag behind them for the photo. Ugly is at centre left, left foot out, in a boxing stance.

Ugly took this picture of Lyn (far left) sitting on Ugly's Triumph with the other Jokers boys at the Crossroads Hotel sometime in the 1970s.

Ugly in his thirties, in the late 1970s, looking suave.

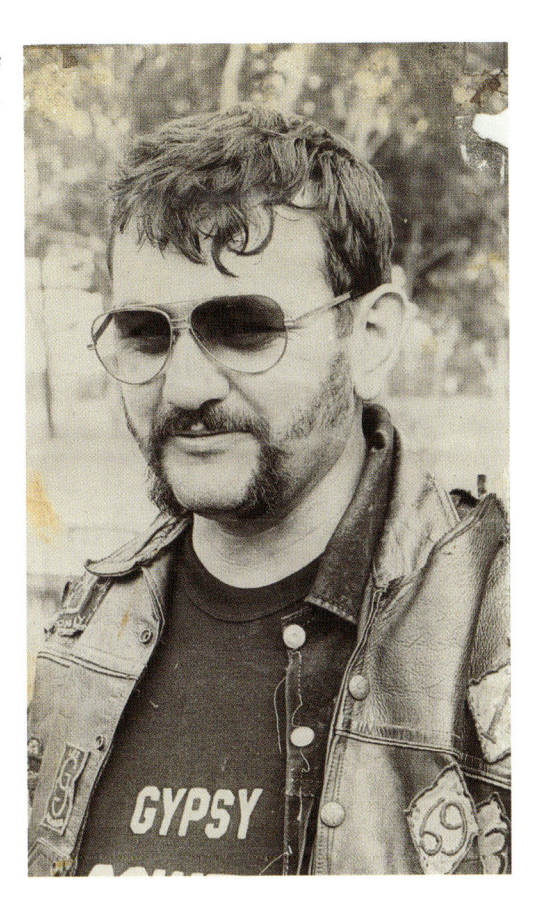

At a Jokers keg party, sometime in the 1970s.

Happy wedding day to Lyn. Lyn is wearing light blue because, in her words, 'I'm a virgin, just been pushed back a bit.'

Lyn and Ugly. Taken at the wedding of Ugly's second-eldest daughter, Bianca.

Ugly (left, with a chain around his neck) at Willie Bull's funeral, 1974. The chain was for his bike, not for cracking skulls.

Haystacks (second from right) and a friend look down in respect at Willie Bull's funeral.

Original Gypsy Jokers patch hanging behind the bike that is pictured on the front cover. The front end of that bike would go on to cause Willie Bull's fatal crash.

Left to right: Bub, Karate, Snotty and Ugly. 'We were being dickheads. Every time a car went past, we would pretend to hump each other!'

Ugly (left) and a fellow karate classmate doing a balancing act for the class.

Ugly in the United States in 1994, standing with the US Jokers' patch at their clubhouse.

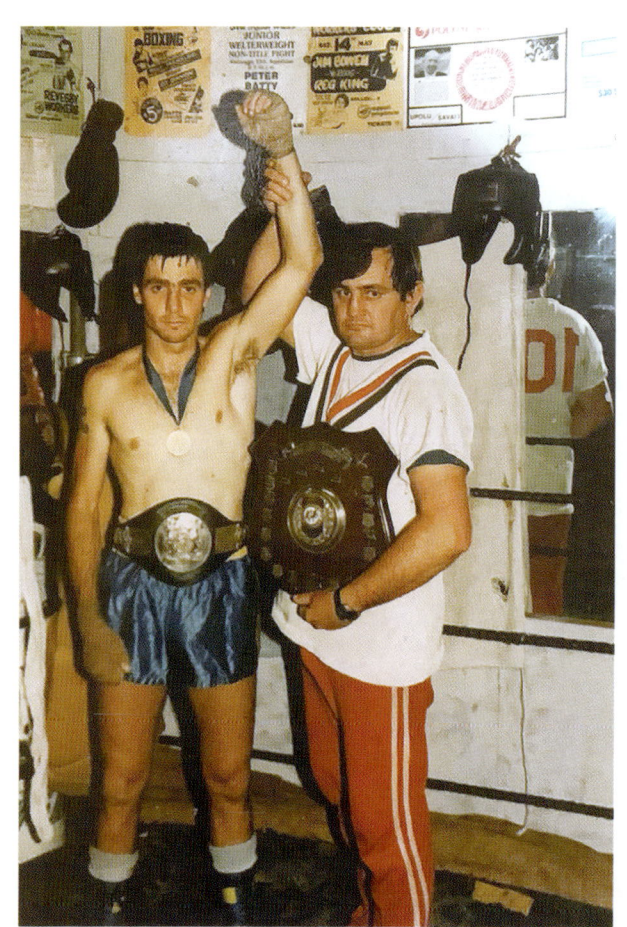

Ugly (right) and Peter Larkin, State Welterweight Champion, in the Hurstville gym. c. 1984.

Ugly (right) with Greg Larkin, Peter's father, at the Padstow RSL, 2020.

On a ferry during a return trip to Vietnam, c. 2000.

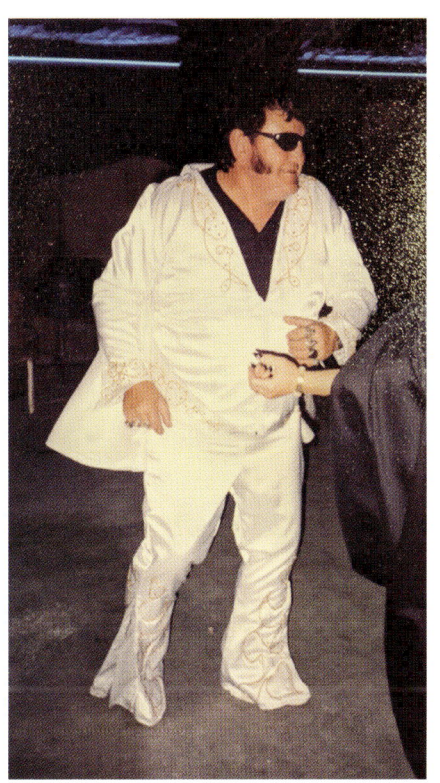

Left: Elvis lives! Ugly as The King at an Elvis Jukebox Night the club held in honour of Elvis Presley's birthday. 'My belt popped off as soon as I jumped on stage!'

Right: The Ugly Stick (2021), commissioned by a prison guard Ugly knows who is in the Veterans MC. It was made by inmates at the prison.

The boxing team at Long Bay Jail, Ugly at centre, c. 2008–2009.

With Bob from the San Francisco Jokers (right), in Norway, c. 2017.

The Gypsy Joker

been in a glass case, especially because it wasn't long after that that Bon ended up OD'ing.

Another piece of good luck came around 1973. Between seasons one and two of the ABC comedy show *Aunty Jack*, they filmed a special called *Aunty Jack Rox On*. Back in the early 1970s, *Aunty Jack* was a big bloody deal, the biggest show on TV and one of the most influential comedies Australia has ever made. One day out of the blue, the director, Maurice Murphy, came down to our local, the Vauxhall Inn in Granville, and asked if we wanted to be involved. He had this idea of Aunty Jack making a grand entrance flanked by bikies wearing the *Aunty Jack* colours.

We all thought that was a fantastic idea. We were big fans of the show so being offered a chance to be in it was something we weren't going to pass up. After promising that we'd behave ourselves, Murphy told us where and when to turn up. One of our members, a bloke we called Haystacks, had this huge grin on his face. He was so excited. He was a big boy, could easily pick anyone up and toss them across the room. Built like a stack of haystacks. And he had this big beard. I suppose you could say he was imposing, but he was a gentle bloke by nature, and a bit of a class clown.

Murphy told us to meet him and the crew at the ABC studios at Gore Hill, just off Pacific Highway near St Leonards on Sydney's north shore. So we rocked up, shook hands with everyone and met Grahame Bond, who played Aunty Jack. He'd be the one riding a Harley-Davidson at the front of the pack of us Gypsy Jokers.

We thought that was so funny. The idea of us being on TV was nuts to us back then, even though these days it might seem pretty normal. There we were, Aunty Jack in the glasses, the big hair, the boxing glove, dress billowing out behind, followed by a bunch of Gypsy Jokers. It was perfect.

The producers had arranged for all these cops to block off the street, which apparently always happened when they had to film something with Aunty Jack on the Harley. When we heard that the coppers had taken a spin on Aunty Jack's motorbike, of course a couple of the Jokers wanted to do the same, especially Haystacks.

Anyway, Murphy told us to ride in formation close to the cameras, making sure we kept the big ABC sign in the background, and then stop at the police line. That was actually the hardest thing. Staying that steady going past these big, delicate cameras was nerve-wracking. Those things cost a lot of money.

The ABC studios car park was on the other side of the road, and between there and where we were was a concrete traffic island. Haystacks told everyone that Murphy wanted us to do a hard right turn *over* the traffic island in the middle of the road and just drive straight into the car park. This, it turned out, was bullshit. We were just supposed to drive straight at the police line and then stop.

But, when we heard the word 'action', we did just what Haystacks had told us to do: cruised down the road and, just before we got to the police line, took a hard right and drove straight over the traffic island and into the car park. I can't remember if Aunty Jack rode with us or stopped and watched as we did it.

Well, everyone lost their shit. Some people were laughing their arses off – Haystacks especially – but the director looked like he was going to pass out. I watched as Murphy tried to play peacekeeper because it was essentially his fault that we were here. The cops looked like they wanted to get into it with us,

The Gypsy Joker

so I went over and had a chat with them about it. There were some arguments about what we were supposed to do, but in the end everyone calmed down.

Grahame Bond wrote about the episode in his book *Jack of All Trades*. He said that I had trouble 'controlling my troops',[*] which wasn't really true. He was right that the shoot was crazy, though. I mean, you put a bunch of boofhead bikies in among professional TV people just trying to do their jobs and you're going to get some weird results.

Then there was our normal banter, but I don't think some of those people knew *how* we bantered. By the looks on their faces, they obviously felt threatened. It was like they all thought they were going to die. They ran off and said they had to set up the next shot, which they said they were shooting from the roof.

That's when Haystacks had his best idea yet. He thought it would be funny to get everyone to ride their bikes *into the ABC foyer*. We couldn't pass up that opportunity. So off the boys went, riding around in circles, gunning their engines and giving everyone a bit of a scare.

Murphy ran up to me in a flap. 'Can't you get them under control?'

I just laughed, 'Yeah, no worries.'

And I rode in after them! After a few circuits, I managed to get everyone back out into the car park so they could finish up the shoot.

A note to Grahame Bond: I don't know why you wrote that I died a few weeks later, but I didn't.

•

---

[*] Bond, Grahame, *Jack of All Trades, Mistress of One*, NewSouth Publishing, 2011, p. 148–9.

Like a lot of people in the late 1970s and early 80s, we spent a bunch of time in pubs and clubs around town. Back then, there was heaps of live music and most of it was hard rock, which suited me just fine. In those days, the gigs were pretty much drug free – there was plenty of beer, and a bit of marijuana here and there, mostly for personal use – but it wasn't like now where there's heavy drugs being dealt left, right and centre everywhere you go.

And, as a rule, Gypsy Jokers didn't deal. That was something I'd laid down pretty early on after we started up. I suspected there were bits and pieces of small-time dealing going on for a while, though. When you are a founding member of the club, information has a way of getting back to you. No one ever owned up to it, though, and I couldn't find any proof. Even if there had been, there wasn't much I could do to stop it.

Then, one of the Jokers came to me and said that he wanted to do it on a bigger scale – and that he wanted to do it for the club.

'I can do it,' he said. 'I've got the access.'

'No,' I said. 'I don't want nothing to do with that.'

I don't know whether he did or he didn't, though I wouldn't be surprised if he had. That particular member ended up going his own way after a while. We always kept him in good standing. Talk continued on and off of some members dealing on the down low, keeping it a secret from me. They all wanted their own stacks of cash and didn't want to give a cut to the club.

Well, I didn't like that. Not at all.

But, again, I could never prove anything. For all I know, it was just shit-slinging, blokes sledging each other to curry favour or something.

I'd never been a fan of marijuana, but each to their own. I tried a joint once and I coughed so hard I nearly died. I thought

The Gypsy Joker

to myself, *How can you smoke that shit?* I don't even like cigarettes. My missus used to smoke, but she ended up stopping. I reckon that's partly because I don't smoke.

The reasons I didn't like club members dealing drugs were twofold: 1) I didn't like the selfish aspect to it, doing something solely for yourself and not for the club; and 2) I knew how severe the penalties were, and I had absolutely no intention of going back to prison as either a dealer or a junkie.

That didn't stop us going out to pubs and clubs, though. Like I said, we liked to party. That was one of the reasons I'd formed the Jokers in the first place. Drugs, on the other hand, just brought you unwanted attention.

But sometimes just *being* somewhere got you the sort of attention you didn't need.

I remember one Friday night we were at a strip club with a bunch of other bikies from all these different clubs. There were ten or twelve Gypsy Jokers sitting on our bikes talking to a couple of the strippers. We were having a good old chat, and I'm pretty sure a couple of the boys thought they were going to get lucky – and I'm pretty sure the sheilas knew that they weren't – but there was that nice party atmosphere you get when people are drinking and having a good time.

Out of nowhere, a group of twenty or so American soldiers appeared. They weren't that much younger than me so some of them might have served in Vietnam. They had decided, it seemed, that they wanted the attention of these particular sheilas, who they probably felt were paying too much attention to us Gypsy Jokers. So they started saying shit like, 'Come here, baby' and 'Come talk to me'.

I just turned to them and said, 'Fuck off.'

Me and my smart fucking mouth.

UGLY

There was a pause while these dipshit soldiers processed what I'd just said. Once they realised, they just went for us. Maybe they weren't looking for sheilas, maybe they were just looking for a fight and figured if they couldn't have one, they could at least have the other. Well, I was happy to oblige. Like I said, I only recruited good fighters and boofheads into the Jokers. Twelve of us against twenty of them? Easy.

I remember kicking one bloke's knee pretty good. When he stopped to scream, I cracked him on the chin and down he went. They were drunk, but so were we, so everyone's blood was up, everyone thought they were invincible. Turned out on the day we were more invincible than them. The sheilas and everyone else watched while we kicked the shit out of those Yanks. I cut my hand punching one fella in the mouth, but I'm pretty sure he lost a tooth, so I wasn't too bothered by it.*

•

When we bought the Jokers clubhouse, in Horsley Park, it was just an old chook shed. We brick veneered it and insulated it – thanks to a building down the road, if you know what I mean – and settled in. We added a dancefloor and a little stage for bands, and a bar, as well as some rooms for members to rest in and sleep. It was the perfect venue for parties, and it was a place we could call our own. We installed this great big jukebox so we could have music when we were drinking at the bar or having parties. It was full of great music.

Along with the regular parties, we'd often have what we called 'Jukebox Saturday' nights. You know, lots of booze,

---

* Campbell, Caesar, *The Outlaw and the Hitman*, Macmillan Australia, 2016, p. 42.

usually a bunch of girls, and plenty of good tunes. We also had Elvis nights and I even went to one of them dressed up in a copy of that flashy jumpsuit The King was so famous for wearing. I jumped up on stage to do an impersonation act, but my belt just went *boing* and flew straight off.

We had a couple of shotguns at the clubhouse, mostly for rabbit shooting, but also of course if any unwelcome intruders wanted to have a go. We also had some rat traps. One day, a couple of young blokes came in and said they'd found a rat stuck in one of the traps.

'Hang on,' I said. 'I'll go get the shotgun.'

I got the shotgun from behind the bar, loaded it with two shots, and went outside.

'All right,' one of the young blokes said. 'Let her go!' He lifted the trap and released the rat.

So I pulled the trigger.

Click.

'Bastard,' I said.

I pulled the trigger again.

Click.

'Bastard!' I repeated.

The gun was stuffed and the bloody rat got away.

I went back inside, cranky as hell. Missing shots I could handle, but when it wasn't my fault and the weapon was buggered, that really pissed me off. I went up to the bar and leant against it.

'This bloody gun's no good,' I said and slammed it down on the floor.

Bang!

The shot took off the peak of my cap and went straight through the roof! The roof was made of timber and it just had this massive hole in it. They left it like that because the story was so good. Talk about a conversation starter. I got through Vietnam and a bunch of other wild bullshit just to almost blow my own face off with a malfunctioning shotgun.

The two young blokes never came back to the clubhouse after that.

•

Up until the 1980s, there really weren't that many motorcycle clubs on the map in Australia. Besides the Gypsy Jokers, you had the Hells Angels, the Rebels, the Finks, and the Gladiators. And we all pretty much got on.

Then in 1982 a new chapter of the Comancheros appeared on the scene. We were down at Parramatta Lakes one day when a few of these new fellas came sniffing around. They thought they were heavies. That did not work out for them. Like I said, I only recruited good fighters and boofheads into the Jokers. We served them their arses on a platter!

Little did we know that the coppers had been keeping a close eye on them.

By this stage, the law was starting to get pretty serious about bikies and their activities.

So they rushed in and started grabbing people left, right and centre. One of the Comancheros' best fighters, one of the Campbell brothers, got grabbed right away. I was eyeing him off to have a go at him, but then they all got distracted trying to pull him away. We served them up and got on our bikes and left. It might have been a different fight if he hadn't been there, so who knows.

That wasn't the only time the Comancheros came looking for trouble. Another time, by chance a couple of them got

The Gypsy Joker

pulled over on their way down to pay us a visit at our clubhouse in Wetherill Park. They had a nice little cache of weapons in the car – and no doubt were intending to use them – but when the cops asked them about it, they just said, 'These guns aren't for us, they're for the Gypsy Jokers!'

They were pretty brazen. You could be in those days. But riding around with a rifle holster on the front of your bike – with a loaded rifle in it – well, that sent a definite message. Those Comanchero boys wanted everyone to know that they weren't to be fucked with.

I thought they were a bunch of bozos.

At the time, I said to anyone who'd listen that half of them didn't even know how to use a shotty. And even if they did, they wouldn't have had the balls to actually fire it. Even so, whenever I got into a fight with them, and their bikes were nearby, the first thing I would do was check the holsters and grab any rifles that might have been stowed.

Unlike in the United States, there weren't many Aussie veterans who came home and joined bike clubs. I wasn't the first person in Australia to return from Vietnam full of hate and anger, but I was one of the first who used it to start a motorcycle club.

Jock Ross did something similar. He was Scottish, ex-British military. He founded the original 'Aussie' Comancheros* in 1966. He tried to run that club like the army. It was all he knew, so why wouldn't he? He had his recruits, I guess you'd call them, doing marching drills behind the house they rented. But a lot of his blokes had never served. And those who had wanted to leave it all behind. They definitely did not want to

---

* *Author's note:* He took the gang's name from the John Wayne film *The Comancheros* and, somehow, they were not related to the American gang of the same name who started in 1965 and were famously chronicled in Hunter S. Thompson's *Hells Angels*.

go and relive the whole thing again. That's one of the reasons why the Campbell brothers ended up splitting from Jock Ross's Comancheros and repatching as the Bandidos.*

And that's when all the drama *really* started.

As you'd imagine, Jock didn't take it too well. It was like a mutiny. He felt like his wings had been clipped.

It ended up leading to the big fight down at Milperra in south-western Sydney.

I barely missed getting involved. It was another stroke of luck. I'd just finished a bouncing shift at Shanney's in Hurstville and was heading in to pick up my pay cheque. I had Lyn and one of the kids with me in the car. When I got to the hotel, a few of the Jokers were inside having a drink.

'Ugly, you goin' down to Milperra for the bike show?' There was a show and swap meet happening in the car park of the Viking Tavern.

'Nah,' I said. 'I've got Lyn and me daughter with me, I just wanna go home. Otherwise, I would.'

And it's true, I liked going to bike shows, but I had other responsibilities.

It was Father's Day, 1984.

Anyway, so the Bandidos were hanging out in the car park. Next thing, the Comancheros arrive, carrying rifles. They were pissed off about the repatching thing and started pushing the Bandidos around. There were lots of words thrown back and forth, and plenty of shirt-fronting.

---

* In 1982 Anthony 'Snoddy' Spencer broke away from Jock's chapter and started his own Comancheros chapter, which Ugly referenced earlier. Spencer went overseas and met with the Texan motorcycle club the Bandidos and the two clubs became allies. Eventually, though, the Bandidos patched over that Comancheros chapter to become the first Bandidos chapter. Patching over is where one club sort of strongarms another club into changing which patch they ride under.

The Gypsy Joker

Then one of the Bandidos went and got a gun. I don't know who fired the first shot, but they ended up in a full-blown shootout.

The press dubbed it the 'Milperra Massacre'.

Four Comancheros and two Bandidos were killed. Jock Ross was hit in the head and the chest but survived. The worst thing was a fourteen-year-old girl was caught in the crossfire and was killed. She was hanging out with the bikies, but she didn't fucking deserve that. Not only that, twenty-eight members of the public were injured as well.

Five Gypsy Jokers happened to be inside the Viking Tavern when it all went down. They were there for the swap meet. When the action kicked off, they barricaded the doors and let the Comancheros and Bandidos go for it. They made sure to keep well away. I'm glad I wasn't there because I know I would have ended up grabbing a gun and showing those blokes how to really shoot. That would have been bad and not something I needed to deal with.

One of the Campbell brothers, Greg, was killed that day, but they ended up charging his own brother, Colin, with the murder, which was crazy. The whole fight was stupid and pointless because it brought the heat down on not only those two clubs, but every other bikie club as well. And it really turned the public against us. Before Milperra, they didn't pay us much attention. 'Oh, they're doing charity rides,' was what a lot of people said.

Suddenly we were all over the news. And the stories weren't pretty.

And suddenly the cops started hassling us, stopping us all the time to check if we had any weapons.

Yep, Milperra fucked it all right up.

UGLY

Jock Ross ended up getting a life sentence, but only served about five years. He got out in 1992. They changed the gun laws after Milperra (and the Port Arthur massacre in 1996), so you couldn't ride with a gun on your bike anymore.* You couldn't even carry a licensed firearm with you on your bike. Your weapons still needed to be licensed, but you weren't allowed to carry them openly, they had to be in a case at home. I used to shoot at the Port Jackson Rifle Club in Moorebank. Before Milperra, I'd stick my shotgun in a pouch and sling it over my shoulder as I rode out there. After the shootout, I couldn't do it because the coppers would grab me every time.

That was the beginning of the end for the old way of doing things. It was all buggered up after that. Same way hard drugs buggered it up. They started letting all these wannabe gangster types into the clubs. The Bandidos, the Rebels, Lone Wolfs, they all wanted to be big-time hard men. I don't know if Jock Ross allowed those types into the Comancheros. The big difference between their way of doing things and ours was that these guys wanted all the money, the flash bikes, flash cars, and all that shit.

And of course to make all that money, they needed to sell a lot of drugs.

And it wasn't just marijuana. They were dealing everything. I heard a rumour from one club that they laced their marijuana with heroin to try to get people hooked. Don't know how true it was, but when I heard about it, I wasn't surprised.

The other difference with these new blokes was that they didn't really care about motorcycles. They owned them because

---

* The New South Wales *Firearms and Dangerous Weapons Act 1973* was amended to require 'a good reason for the issue of' a firearms licence after the Milperra Massacre case. The case was, at the time, one of the largest in Australian history. It was the longest joint criminal trial in New South Wales history.

they could, and they had the backing and protection of a club, but they weren't members because they liked to ride. The bikes were just status symbols.

Even though I didn't have evidence that anyone in the club was dealing, I reminded everyone of the rule that any Jokers who were dealing drugs had to give the club a 15 per cent cut. We never saw any money in the coffers, but the rule was important. I don't know if the other clubs were enforcing rules like that, but they should have been. I think if they had, we wouldn't be in the situation we're in now. There'd be fewer selfish bastards doing it on their own behind their club's back and making a mess of things.

•

In 1999 I met a bloke called Greg King at the Skin and Steel tattoo and motorbike event. Greg had been around the clubs a lot and was a member of the Comancheros before he ended up becoming a full member of the Gypsy Jokers. He's president of the Bankstown Finks now, but he was with us until around 2013. He didn't leave on bad terms. We're all still mates and he's close to the Adelaide Jokers. He's also the godfather to my daughter, Mandy's, kids.

Greg was the only club prospect I never punched, which is probably because he always treated me with respect, and not just because I was a founding member. Vietnam veterans all got respect from Greg. He was angry as hell at the way the then PM Bob Hawke had fucked around with our pensions. He kept an eye on me, even when he didn't need to. I suppose I was a bit of an old bloke to him, and he was always impressed that, even at my age, I would still ride as hard and as long as the other boys, and still sleep beside my bike at night when we were out on a run. He thought that showed character.

One day, Greg and I were up at the clubhouse with our mate Herby. This was around 2003, when Greg was still a nominee. The backyard was full of tall grass, but none of us had a good lawnmower. Herby had a ute, though, and there was an old, rusted gate lying around. Well, they had the bright idea to strap the gate to the back of the ute so that Herby could drive around and, hopefully, cut the grass. He did it for a bit, but of course it didn't work. The grass just sort of folded down under the gate.

'One of youse needs to get onto the gate and weigh it down a bit,' Herby said, pulling up next to Greg.

'Righto,' Greg said and clambered onto the ute.

Herby drove around some more. Even with Greg pushing down on the gate, it wasn't heavy enough. That's when I came back outside after having a piss.

'What's going on here?' I said. 'That looks like fun.'

Herby stopped the ute and I jumped on the back as well. We were both holding onto the top of this gate and pushing down as hard as we could. It was a little rough going, but it was actually working. Then I felt this push against me and I turned to see Greg smiling with this wild man look on his face. I shoved him back, but harder. Of course I did. He stumbled but kept his balance.

Then I heard him say, 'Oh, so it's like that, is it?'

And then we really started in on each other. Herby was driving the ute a hundred miles an hour in circles around the backyard, grass flying up everywhere, and me and Greg were shoving each other with shoulders and elbows like a couple of kids playing 'corners' in the back seat of the car.

The Gypsy Joker

I don't know what finally did it – the speed, Greg's shoving, my knees – but I ended up flying off the back of the ute and landing arse over tea kettle in the grass. It knocked the wind out of me, but I was laughing. Herby slammed on the brakes and Greg jumped down and ran inside to tell the others what had happened. Apparently, he was laughing so hard he could barely speak.

I wandered in after him, still a bit dizzy from the fall, and said, 'All of you bastards, buy him a drink – he just tried to kill me!'

We all had a good laugh at that.

And I knew I'd get him back.

It's important to laugh because life is hard, and sometimes you lose people. And it's not always from a fight, or some random bit of gun violence. Riding a motorcycle can be dangerous and we lost plenty of fellas doing just that. By the time we lost access to the clubhouse, we had a memorial plaque with about thirty names on it.

I knew them all personally.

One weekend in 1994 we were doing a big run up at Ballina with the Outback Jokers. They were riding side-by-side. Usually, you ride staggered, not just because of other drivers, but because the road itself can be dangerous.

There's a big curve in the road outside of Ballina. Trucks would barrel down there all the time and it would get so hot that the tar in the road would become lumpy. When you ride side-by-side, stuff like that is even more dangerous because avoiding obstacles means either ramming into your fellow riders, or careening off into oncoming cars.

Firewood Phil was a founding member of the Outback chapter. A good bloke. We got on like, well, like a house on fire.

As we rode towards this big curve – *pop!* just like that – Phil hit one of the ruts in the road. A family sedan was coming in the other direction. Phil couldn't stop and just went – *boof* – straight into the car, denting the right-hand pillar with his head.

A few boys at the front of the pack went down with him, one after the other. We ended up with about six people crashing and lying sprawled on the ground. I was up the back of the pack and word quickly got to me about what had happened. I sped up there to have a look. Everyone had stopped by this stage. I saw Phil lying there, coughing. I saw where he had hit his head, the dented bit of the car. I knelt down next to him and felt the back of his head.

My stomach sank.

'Oh, fuck,' I said. 'No, he's gonna die.'

And then he did a rough, wet-sounding sort of cough.

It came to me then and I said to myself, 'That's his last breath.'

I got him into position so I could start doing CPR. What else could I do? I wasn't pushing very hard. It was a token effort. But it was too late. He was already dead. He died in my arms. That hurt. It felt like I was back in Vietnam again. I've only ever felt like that twice and this was one of those occasions. The other would come years later.

Even though Phil was gone, I kept performing CPR. I knew that if I didn't, our boys might have killed that family in the car. They would have gone absolutely berserk. And that wouldn't have been fair. It wasn't their fault, it was the road's. There was nothing they could have done to avoid hitting Phil.

A woman came running up. I don't know how long I'd been pushing on Phil's chest, but my arms were getting tired. It's not easy work, CPR. It's hard and you've got to keep doing it until help arrives.

The Gypsy Joker

'I'm a nurse,' the woman said. 'Let me take over for you.' She knelt down next to me.

'He's dead,' I whispered. 'But you need to keep pretending, because otherwise these boys will get the shits, okay?'

'Oh,' was all she said.

But she did as I asked. She didn't have much choice. I felt bad. She must have been scared witless, but I was more concerned about what those Outback boys would do if they saw Phil was gone.

Not long after, the ambos pulled up. 'He's gone,' I told them. 'But you've got to put the mask on his face so they think he's still alive, okay?'

'You sure?' they said.

'Yeah,' I said.

They pretended too and played the game. They put a mask on him and then put him in the ambulance and drove off.

One of the Sydney club members, Shane, and I then had the job of organising all of our blokes who'd also crashed. A lot of them had broken arms, broken legs; it was a fucking mess. There was blood on the road, on them, bones were sticking out in some places. The family in the car were in shock, screaming and crying. You could feel how much pain they were in, too. The poor bastards. It was like a fucking warzone.

But then the boys started taking pictures of the road. At how bad a condition it was in.

'It's not your fault,' one of the Outback boys said to the family. 'It was the road.'

That was good of them. It would have been so much worse if those boys had known that Phil was dead. They might have lashed out. Luckily they didn't and no one else got hurt that day.

UGLY

The founders of the Sydney and Outback chapters diced with death all the time but I just kept making it out alive. I felt lucky. There's no other way to describe it. I came off my bike about five times, but I survived each crash. The last time I came off – which would have been about 2017 – was my last before I gave up riding for good. I fell off a mountain, if you can believe it. Smashed my shoulder pretty badly. The boys had bought me a new tyre because my old back one had gone bald. That new tyre slipped loose and I got tossed.

Another bloke, Dutchy, had something similar happen to him. The bloke riding in front had a tyre blowout and Dutchy swerved hard to avoid him. He was heading straight for a car so was trying to straighten up. He didn't manage to straighten up in time.

The car hit him and killed him.

When that kind of thing is happening all around you, you can't help but feel lucky.

7

The One Percenter

In case it's not obvious yet, getting permission to do stuff from other motorcycle clubs – or members of the club you're a part of – is very important. I always thought that I had permission to start up my chapter of the Jokers back in November 1969 because of that note the American bloke, Fingers, wrote for me in Vietnam.

I honestly didn't think there'd be an issue.

Years later, we found out there was an Outback club also called the Gypsy Jokers who were riding under the same patch as our brother club, the Fourth Reich, whose patch features the German eagle with its wings spread out.

When I found out about those Outback Jokers, I thought, *Oh, that's not good, we've got to get everyone together and try to join up.*

It didn't take long to arrange a meeting. I visited the Outback and told them that we were the first club to start with permission, in 1969. But they had started a year before us, so they felt like they should be the mother club.

'But I've got written permission from the Yanks,' I said.

They didn't like that one bit.

Nope, I held that over them and they fucking hated my guts for it. They felt like I'd stolen the thunder from their being the first club. At the time, though, I thought I was doing the right thing. I thought I'd gone through the proper channels. Iron, the leader over there, was none too pleased with me, but they accepted our patch anyway. They were originally wearing the same patch and colours as the Fourth Reich – green, gold, and black – but they agreed to come under ours, with the Fourth Reich becoming a brother club. That's when we changed our colours to black and white.

After that, I went back to my Fourth Reich mate, Ziggy.

'You should meet the Outback Jokers.'

'Why's that?' he said.

'They were wearing the same patch as you. But they changed when they heard about us being mates and my not wanting to be Fourth Reich.'

He got a kick out of that. The Outback boys changed over to make sure we were all one club, but they're still tight as anything with the Fourth Reich.

I ended up with some really good mates from the Outback chapter, people like Iron. He's been in and out of jail, but he's got his head screwed on. He's a good bloke. We earnt our stripes with them by standing our ground, showing that we weren't going to lie down about this, and that honesty was good. I'm happy we got on with them, too, because Outback are easily the hardest chapter. They've really got their shit together, money-wise and property-wise.

The Wollongong boys like to go out there sometimes when there's a big event on and they get looked after by the

The One Percenter

Outback blokes. They fly, but some of them ride over. That ride takes almost fifty hours. It's hot, it's sweaty, there's dust everywhere. It makes everyone irritable. We do it over three or four days. No matter how far you go, you're always looking forward to the next stop, the next pub.

We've been out there on our Christmas runs. A different state hosts it each year, putting on a big bash. Of course, the coppers try to raid them, but they still happen.

•

By the late 1980s and early 90s, the Gypsy Jokers had really begun to grow. There's a bunch of chapters all over Australia now. Besides us in New South Wales, there's the Queensland boys, and the Outback, then there's the Victorians based out of Melbourne, and two chapters in South Australia, one in Mount Gambier, founded by a fella named Phildo in 1979, and one in Adelaide, started up by a bloke named Stewie.

The Queensland chapter is run by a good mate of mine, Potter, a hard man, ex-truckie. They have to operate undercover because of the laws up there, so they can't wear their patches openly. They're going really well, despite that.

The Queensland chapter started because of Outback. They sent a couple of hard blokes, some nasties, over to Queensland to meet with a club called the Renegades. A bloke named Dirty was the main Outback fella in charge of that expedition. The intent was to patch the Renegades over into a new chapter of the Jokers. There was a bloke called Lofty who was leading the Renegades at the time. They called him that because he was tall. Clever, I know.

UGLY

Anyway, the Outback boys hatched a plan. It took a little bit of time, but eventually they got Lofty when he was alone and pulled guns on him. They tied him up loosely and threw him in the boot of their car then they drove him out to the boondocks. They all got out of the car and walked around to the back, stood in front of the boot and started talking really loudly.

'Right, open it up,' Dirty said. 'And we'll shoot him.'

'Yeah,' the other blokes growled. 'Let's kill the bastard.'

Shit like that. They could hardly stop themselves from laughing. The point of course wasn't to kill him but just to scare the shit out of him. After a minute or so of that sort of carrying on, making sure Lofty was good and riled up, they opened the boot. By this stage Lofty had slipped out of the ropes they'd tied him up with, which was part and parcel of the plan. They *wanted* him to get loose. And as soon as that boot was open, he was up and out of there like a bloody freight train. The Outback boys started laughing and fired their guns in the air. That took care of Lofty.

After they were done, they rode back to the Renegades clubhouse and told them what had happened with Lofty – and that they were being patched over. Dirty told them how it was going to go down; if they didn't want to stay, that was fine, they could just resign from the club. Nothing would happen to them. The Renegades chatted for a bit, and they pretty much all ended up disbanding. Outback are pretty strict and the Renegades weren't, so they weren't too keen on being a part of that, so they just walked away.

All except for one bloke we called Bull.

We called him Bull because he was built like one.

A little while later, when the clubhouse had been patched over and most of the groundwork had been done, the Outback

The One Percenter

boys went home, leaving Bull alone at the clubhouse. Now, that probably wasn't the best idea. Leaving a member alone is against the rules, because if something happens to them there's no backup. But they figured Bull was a big bloke and the odds of someone fucking with him were pretty low.

Not long after everyone left, there was a knock on the back door of the clubhouse.

Bull went and opened it up.

Bang. Bang.

Someone shot Bull and took off.

We reckon it was someone who was pissed because Bull had joined the Jokers, unlike all the other blokes who had quit. We're still looking for whoever it was. It'd be good catch up with Lofty, though. Ask him if he knows anything about it.

Bull survived after a stay in hospital. Outback let him keep his patch, which was good, because again, Bull was all alone. He'd been shot but had survived.

That's when they sent Potter over to look after Queensland, and he's still there now. He's a bit of a legend among us. He's stayed at my place while he's been on runs a bunch of times. We're good mates.

Outback had been on their own with no one really starting any offshoots, but after we started up, the chapters in other states began popping up. The Adelaide chapter was originally called Bandana. They wore red and white patches but no one was allowed to wear that except for the Hells Angels, so they ended up folding in under our patch. We were allowed to wear the red and white, but only because I thought we had permission to do so. I got in touch with the head of that group, one of the hardcore boys up there, Stewie, and they changed over to the Gypsy Jokers. The blokes at Mount Gambier changed over to being Jokers as well after Stewie's club did. The Outback boys even started wearing red and white patches just to piss everyone off, too. Luckily, by that stage, they were all affiliated with us, so it didn't cause as many problems as it could have.

•

In the 1990s, a young bloke by the name of Jimmy had been hanging around with the club for a while and had officially become a member. One night we had a little ceremony and officially presented him with his patch. After that was over, Jimmy wanted to keep the party going, so he went on a night-time ride. And he kept drinking. The way he told it, he was gunning around, speeding while drinking from a bottle. To the surprise of no one the coppers tried to pull him over.

Well, Jimmy wasn't having any of that.

He took a page out of my book and sped off into the night.

He led those coppers on a chase through Fairfield. Luckily he was one hell of a rider. He managed to lose them at some point in the night. Unluckily for him, though, they recognised the patch he was wearing – the patch he'd only had for a night, remember – and decided to wait for him just down the road from our clubhouse.

Sure enough, Jimmy soon came speeding through, intent on getting back to the clubhouse and safely away from the coppers, when they ambushed him. There was no getting away from them this time. They booked him and threw him in the lock-up, and we had to go bail him out. In the end, he got a twelve-month suspension of his licence for DUI.

Now, because he was a new member and couldn't ride, the committee wanted him to turn in his patch for the length of his suspension. Their argument was that, because he couldn't come on the big runs – which is a necessity for new members – he shouldn't be allowed to wear the patch. The committee felt they were 'safekeeping' his patch. Here this poor fella was, just got his patch and he's all excited and now the committee wanted to take it away from him. They had their reasons, but it didn't feel right to me.

'That's bullshit,' I said. 'Yes, he can keep his patch and keep riding – and he can do it on the back of my bike.'

That stumped them. I don't miss a thing. They agreed that it would be fine for him to ride with me, and that way he was allowed to keep his patch. For the next twelve months, I carried Jimmy around on the back of my bike until he got his licence back.

These days he's a bigwig out in the Outback.

And a top bloke.

•

In 1991, I travelled to the United States for the first time to talk with the Gypsy Jokers. We were friendly with the Aussie Bandidos by that stage, and they were friendly with the Jokers in the States. One day, I was talking to one of the Bandidos about the club.

'Have you been to America?' this fella asked.

'Nah,' I said.

'Do you know if you're eligible to wear the patch?'

'Can't see no one taking it off us,' I said. There goes my smart mouth again. But I still had the letter from Fingers, so I thought I was all good.

'No, it's not that,' this Bandido said. 'Look, just go over there and see them.'

'Well, arrange a meeting if you've got any contacts and I will.'

He nodded and we kept on chatting. I didn't really think much of it, until the next time I saw him, a week or so later.

'I arranged a meeting, Ugly,' he said.

That stopped me. I just went, 'Oh, shit. Really?'

'Fucken' oath.'

Right, then. It was settled. We were off to the United States.

First thing was to decide who to take along, because I sure as shit wasn't going by myself. I settled on a couple of blokes from each chapter: two hardcore boys from Queensland, because I wanted to show off what we had going on up there; and three from the Sydney chapter. It made sense to do that, to have a bigger showing from Sydney, because that's where I was based, that's where I started things, and I was the one organising the trip.

We flew into LA and met the Yanks on the top level of the airport. As we were walking towards them, I thought to myself, *It's either gonna be on here, or it's gonna be on somewhere else.* To try and stave that off, we'd brought along gifts with us: nice big bottles of Bundaberg rum.

It was obvious that this was a kind of 'yay or nay' moment. The Yanks would either approve of us and everything would be fine, or they wouldn't and we'd have to fight to get back home alive.

There was no way I was going to give up easy.

Everyone there knew I was a fighting man.

Well, our great idea of bringing gifts went down like a lead balloon. They didn't like the rum. At all. They even knocked the shit out of it.

Fine. In my head I was like, *Strike one.*

The One Percenter

But we didn't start fighting at the airport, so that was something. And they loaned us all bikes, which was another good sign. So we got all our gear, loaded up and set off for their clubhouse in downtown Los Angeles. Of course, by that stage, we'd started sipping that Bundy rum. *And* we were jetlagged. So here we are riding down these long, winding streets *on the wrong side of the fucking road* in a city none of us had ever been to. We kept having to dip around cars to avoid crashing. It was mayhem.

The other thing was they'd loaned us these Harley-Davidson Road Kings, which are massive bikes. This bloke called Kenny was up in front when a sports car came swerving out and cut in front of us; just some prick being a smart-arse. Well, Kenny sped up to this fella, grabbed a shifter – a wrench – from his side pocket and leant over and just went *bam!* Smashed it right through the guy's window! The guy then lost control of the car and swerved off the road and into a fence.

This was our first ride ever with the Yanks.

Somehow we made it to the clubhouse in one piece. As soon as we were inside, I asked them about what Kenny did.

'Oh, that's normal,' they said. 'Kenny'll do that.'

'Fuck me. He lost his shifter, too.'

They told us we were then going to ride up to Seattle. We felt like this was a test – it's about nineteen hours' ride from LA – and they obviously wanted to see how we'd handle it. Well, it just made us angry. We'd been riding for almost thirty years by then!

But we rode up to their Seattle clubhouse without incident. When we got there we found they were hosting all these committees in their cellar. They invited me in. All I thought was, *Oh, here we go.* There were ten people representing the various Jokers chapters in America. I didn't know half of them, but I knew Kenny. And what he was capable of. When we got settled in, they started asking me a bunch of questions. In short, they were pretty dirty that I'd started up a chapter of the Jokers without asking them for permission.

'What gives you the right to start up using our name?' they said.

'I thought I had permission,' I said. 'Here's the letter, check it out.' And I pulled out the letter Fingers gave me back in Vietnam in 1968. It was a bit tattered by then, but still readable. I handed it over to them and they looked at it, made some notes, and talked among themselves. They went and checked these filing cabinets full of documents. It was like a review at a company. They had other members ringing around, asking questions, getting answers, the whole thing.

This went on for I don't know how long, but that's where it all came out: no one had ever fucking heard of a bloke named Fingers! That knocked me for six. Who the fuck did I meet in Vietnam? Just some dickhead who rode with these blokes once and then went around calling himself a Gypsy Joker?

'You started by default,' Kenny said.

I felt weightless, but firm. 'Yeah,' I said. 'And I'm keeping it.'

There was silence and then Kenny laughed. He was a shit-stirrer and so was I, so I suppose we had a similar way of communicating. 'All right,' he said. 'You've proved yourselves, so that's good.'

We were going to be okay.

It also meant I was right about Outback. I had them on a technicality that we were the first to start with permission, even though they started a year before us. It didn't matter that the permission I'd received was from some con artist!

The One Percenter

The Americans ended up keeping the letter from 'Fingers', whoever the hell he was, for their club archives. I never did find out exactly who he was, nor did I ever meet him again. If I had, I would have bashed him. I'm sure the Americans wouldn't have minded a chat with him, too. Despite that, I'm glad I had the letter because it definitely helped our case. If I hadn't been working under the assumption of starting up the chapter with permission, I might still be down in that cellar.

Even though we'd passed another challenge, they weren't finished with us yet. Now they wanted to see if we could fight, which was a test we could pass pretty easily. They took us out to a few bars and basically talked shit. A fight would start and then they'd step back to see how we handled ourselves.

One night while at a Mexican bar, this little skinny bloke called Rudy – a good member – strolled right up to a group of big Mexicans who were clearly ready to go. Rudy just stood there, folded his arms, and growled at them. He was shorter than them all by about a head, so it looked pretty funny. Next minute one of the Mexicans came up behind him and punched him in the head.

We all flew in then and the whole place erupted.

There were grunts and yelling and smashing glass. No plastic cups or cans here; glasses and bottles were thrown and cracked on people's heads. I'm pretty sure that's how I got a cut that bled into my eye, but I didn't pay it too much mind. If I had, I might have taken a heavy swing from one of those giant Mexicans. The energy of fighting, it's honestly the shit I live for. It's not like being shot at – there you're just scared, bullets whizzing past you, thinking you're going to die – that shit's bloody awful. But a big punch-on? Everyone just going mental on each other? That puts the fire in my eyes and in my belly. You ask anyone who's been up against me in a fight. They'll tell you.

One of our members, Paranoid, went up to this big mirrored wall and smashed it with a chair. It was total chaos. The cops were called and we all managed to run off except for one of the Yanks, who was too slow or too hurt to get away.

They had to renovate the bar after that.

It was on this same trip that I found out about not having permission to wear the red and white 1% patch. The Hells Angels in Sydney never had permission to start up, so there was nothing they could do about it, but I didn't know that it was another permission thing. I never got to speak to any Hells Angels in the States because the American Jokers kept steering us away from them. I don't remember how I found out, but we didn't stop wearing the red and white 1% patch. We'd been wearing it for a while already, but they weren't too sure about it. If we didn't earn it, they wouldn't have wanted to know us. Who knows how the trip would have gone if we hadn't shown them what we were made of.

'You're not a one percenter,' Kenny said to me. 'You know that, yeah?'

'Oh? Well, I want it. Proper.'

That was what all the fighting and checking our stamina ended up being about. They were happy to back us after that. They'd walk into bars and start fights and then let me and a couple of the boys finish them off. Wherever we went, they'd look for a reason to start shit. A big part of their scepticism was the fact that the American bikers have this fierce reputation – they're the go-to guys if you need a hitman – but we hadn't adopted that kind of culture in Australia. But after seeing what we were capable of – and I don't think they quite expected how

The One Percenter

gung-ho we were – they eased off and seemed all right with us carrying the same name as them.

'Righto,' Kenny said. 'I'll give you and your two friends a black and white 1%.'

That's what we'd been wanting, because by then we knew about the red and white patch.

'We want to keep the 1% for Australia,' I said to him. Even though we weren't really supposed to be using it, we liked it. It was a part of the club.

'Keep 'em both,' he said. 'Wear the black and white one on the other side.'

So it was official: me, Hoggy and Rick were 1% and the first outside of America to earn black and white patches. It was important for us to have them because without the 1% we would just have been a social club. That's not who we were, not who we wanted to be. We needed the Americans to see that we had the mettle, that we lived and breathed the 1%. Not that I have anything against social clubs, I ride with them every now and then, but the Gypsy Jokers weren't born to be a social club.

'And seeing as you had the balls to speak up like that,' Kenny went on, 'you can have our 1% off the wall, too.' He went over and took it off the wall and presented it to me. It was framed, all hand done. 'You earnt it.'

'You fucking beauty,' I said.

I had a copy made of the original when I got back to Australia and had it put up upstairs in the clubhouse. I didn't want to hang the real one or wear it, just in case it got pinched. The real one stayed home with me and the replica stayed in the clubhouse. No one ever took it.

Part of the agreement with the Americans was that we had to change over to their patch. They didn't like that we were using their name but wore a different patch to them. I was keen on having party unity, so I told them I'd try to change it when I got home.

And honest to God, I did my best.

When we got back to Australia, I told everyone that I wanted us to include a 'Simon' on our patch. Simon is the sinister jester-like figure the American Jokers have on their patches. The idea behind it is 'Simon says' – you should do something, and you do it.

Problem was, Outback weren't having anything to do with it and South Australia weren't too keen, either. To be honest, neither were Sydney or Western Sydney! Nobody wanted to change. They hated this Simon character and wanted to stick with the smiling skull with the earring we'd had from the start. Outback especially didn't want to change because they'd already changed from their original patch, which was similar to the Fourth Reich patch. They also thought Simon looked too much like a fairy or a clown; he wasn't tough enough or dirty enough for them.

We had plenty of votes and arguments and fights, but in the end the only person who was behind me on the patch change was Hoggy. So, we stayed as we were. And the Americans just let it go. They probably figured it was easier to have the Aussies under whatever banner pleased them than to make trouble, which was good. They understood that the skull was part of our original patch, and we were attached to it, just like they were attached to their Simon character. Now that we had a friendly relationship, and they realised we weren't complete dickheads, they started calling our patch 'Simon Skull', which I like.

I got a Gypsy Jokers logo tattooed on my back after meeting the Americans. I stayed at a bloke named Drow's place, and

The One Percenter

he had their big logo tattooed across his back. Unfortunately, Drow's also no longer with us.

'Wow,' I said.

'Yeah,' he said. 'You should get your one!'

I thought, *Yeah, why not?*

I got it done by a bloke named Bear Cameron, who's not in the club anymore but is still good friends with us. While he was doing it, he was smoking and drinking and eating pizza. When he'd been working on it for a while, he said, 'Geez, it's hard to get all the little pom-poms in.'

'What fucking *pom-poms*?' I said.

He said, 'Oh, I'm doing the American Simon design.'

I hollered and leapt out of the chair and rushed to the mirror. He was laughing his arse off behind me. Of course, he'd done the right design. He was just bullshitting me, the bastard.

•

In 1991, at one of our usual meetings, I brought up the rumours about members dealing drugs. I wanted an official resolution from the committee about it, saying it wasn't on, or at least a formal decision one way or the other. This was clearly going to be an ongoing problem and the leadership needed to be united on it. The idea that some of our members might be dealing drugs was too bloody risky, and I wanted it rooted out and stopped. I wanted those who were dealing to be exposed, if the suspicions were true.

At the time Haystacks was working as a truckie, doing lots of interstate deliveries. In order to keep going, he would snort whatever it was he liked. Anyway, he turned up to the meeting late. He'd been at a funeral and was in a bit of a mood.

UGLY

We hadn't actually expected him, but apparently he had a couple of quiet days up his sleeve, and he wanted to discuss something or other. He came storming in around eleven o'clock, maybe a little after.

'So how did it go?' he asked me.

'Half and half,' I said. 'They haven't made up their minds.'

'Oh yeah? Well, I've got something to say.'

'I bet you have, you fucking arsehole,' I said, half-joking but not really, because I knew he was snorting all sorts of shit and he knew I didn't like it.

'Fuck you.' Then he went in to see the committee.

I'm out of here, I thought.

I was pissed off. I just wanted this whole thing sorted out once and for all. It felt like everything was moving so slowly.

Haystacks said his piece to the committee and left not long after. The committee refused to give a yay or nay right then and there. So Haystacks basically got the shits. Around eleven-thirty he jumped on his Harley and sped away from the clubhouse, which was on Elizabeth Street in Smithfield, towards Victoria Street in Wetherill Park. He went up Victoria Street and stopped at a set of traffic lights.

Out of nowhere, someone came up on a bike beside him and shot him in the neck.

Killed him right there in cold blood.

When we found out we were gutted. And angry. But we were stumped as to who could have done it. We didn't think it was a member of another club because we weren't feuding with anyone at the time. If we had been, we wouldn't have let one of our members ride alone. That's just common sense.

We thought it might have been a bloke from a while back who we'd seen manhandling his sheila at a party, and who we'd

The One Percenter

manhandled in return. He could have been that pissed off that he decided to shoot a member of the Gypsy Jokers in the middle of the street. But that would have been a bad move.

I never found out who did it, but if it *was* that fella from the party, it's my deepest hope that a couple of our blokes had a nice little chat with him out in the bush.

Haystacks had been with us for more than twenty years. He'd been sergeant-at-arms at one point. He was family. His death was a massive blow and came as a huge shock to us all. He was a big man, but he was peaceful deep down. He could fight, but he wasn't the first to go fists up. About 200 of us, bikies and truckies, attended his funeral. He's buried out at Pinegrove Memorial Park in Minchinbury in Western Sydney.

Technically, his murder remains unsolved, although the cops announced in 2009 that they were looking into it as part of Strike Force Tuno 2,[*] but fucked if I know why. Tuno 2 was set up originally as Strike Force Tuno in 2001, but evolved over time into Tuno 2 because it had gone on so long and was interconnected with a bunch of other murder cases. It was set up after bits of a bloke named Terry Falconer were found in the Hastings River on the North Coast of New South Wales.[**]

•

---

[*] Tuno 2 became the largest murder investigation in the history of New South Wales. It brought down a major crime syndicate headed up by the Perish brothers, Andrew and Anthony, as well as their associates.

[**] Terry Falconer was a drug dealer and informant who was killed and disposed of by the Perishes and their conspirator, Matthew Lawton. Anthony Perish and Matthew Lawton are currently imprisoned for murder and criminal conspiracy. Andrew Perish was also found guilty of criminal conspiracy.

UGLY

Even when someone's fixing to fight you, you don't always need to fight them. Sometimes, a surprise – something to put them off their guard – will win it for you. Or at least give you a chance to scarper.

That's where my mouthguard comes in.

When someone's itching to have a go, I just pop my mouthguard in and say something like, 'You still wanna talk about it?'

In response, they usually just go, 'Shit.'

The look on their face says it all. It's priceless.

There's a split second where they're caught off balance. It gives you the chance to do one of two things: 1) Hit them as many times as you can while they're surprised; or 2) Run like fucking hell.

I keep a mouthguard on me at all times because you never know when you'll come across somebody with a smart mouth. In my experience, sticking the mouthguard in usually shuts people up. Few expect you to be prepared for a fight like that. When they see the mouthguard, they know they're up against someone with experience.

It allows them to think twice about whether to carry on or quit.

Of course, by the time they've thought things through, it's usually too late.

I was convinced of how effective my little strategy was while on my second trip to the United States.

A bloke called Maynard from White City in Oregon was the Jokers president at the time. When we visited the first time he was stuck in jail, but by our second visit, he was out and about. Along with Kenny and a few other Jokers, naturally enough, Maynard wanted to check us Aussies out. So they took us around to a bunch of bars, as you do.

The One Percenter

The only problem was they were all *wine* bars.

'This is shit,' I said at one point. 'We're just sipping wine.'

'Okay,' Maynard said. He had an intimidating kind of presence. 'We'll go down by the wharf and the river.'

That sounded fine by me. That's where you typically find good places to hang out and shoot the shit. Proper places that serve more than just wine and fucking cheese.

It was me, Hoggy and Rick again. Hoggy and Kenny were close mates. We walked down by the wharf and Kenny waved Hoggy over to have a chat.

At that point, Maynard stopped and turned around. Along with six of his hoons.

Maynard started yelling at Rick, 'You, you fucking cunt! Take my patch without permission? I ought to punch your fucking head in!'

Rick was built a bit smaller, so this wasn't fair at all.

Maynard was about to let fly when I stepped in. 'Nah, nah,' I said. 'He's not the one that done it. *I'm* the founder.' I pushed Rick aside and stared Maynard down. At the same time, I reached into my pocket, grabbed my mouthguard and slammed it in. As soon as big Maynard saw that, he stopped dead in his tracks. He had that look on his face, the one you see every time, like a stunned roo in the headlights.

I took the chance and let him have it.

But just because I got the first punches in didn't mean I was going to win. Like I said, Maynard was a massive bloke and he'd spent a lot of time in prison. He was a hard man. I could throw a good punch, but he knew how to take it. When he got me back – right on the side of my face – I realised he could throw a pretty fucking good punch, too.

UGLY

The others stood back and watched. Out of the corner of my eye, I saw a few of them make a move to break us up, but Kenny stopped them.

'Let this play out,' he said. 'It'll be fine.'

Maynard kicked me in the shin and then swung an elbow. Once again I was glad I'd done plenty of boxing in my time. I dodged the elbow and sunk my fist into his nose, and then brought my other fist up into his gut. That gave me enough time to give him two more quick jabs to the face.

At that point the others came over and broke us up.

They could see I'd won.

It wasn't an easy victory, but surprising him with my mouth-guard definitely helped.

Kenny came over. He was the wizard in charge of everything, the national president. He was a big fella, too, six-foot-four with muscles everywhere. No one fucked with Kenny. He's currently tied up on a racketeering charge, along with some other Jokers. Those same members were also charged with the kidnapping and death of a former club member.[*]

'All right, wrap it up, fellas,' he said. He turned to me. 'He had to get it out of his system, Ugly.'

'Well, he's got it out of him now,' I said. Fucking smart mouth.

Maynard and I eyed each other off for the rest of the night, but nothing started up again.

---

[*] Kenneth 'Kenny' Hause, along with five others, was charged with 'conspiring to conduct and participate in a racketeering enterprise' in 2019, according to the *Statesman Journal* and *The Oregonian*. While Hause was only charged with racketeering, the other five were charged with 'murder in aid of racketeering, kidnapping in aid of racketeering, resulting in death, kidnapping resulting in death and conspiracy to commit kidnapping, resulting in death' for the kidnapping and murder of Robert Huggins, a former Gypsy Jokers member.

The One Percenter

I realised on those trips that there's a difference between American bikies and us Aussies. Although we're both just as rough as each other and we take our clubs pretty seriously, our attitudes are actually poles apart. Say something smart to an American and more often than not they'll just take it on the chin in that laid-back kind of 'Yeah, man, relax' way. That chilled-out vibe rules the roost over there.

Have a go at an Aussie on the other hand and we're like, 'Fuck you!'

Followed by a punch in the face.

•

In 1996 – after the trips to the United States – I decided it was time to go back to Vietnam. It'd be the first time I'd set foot in the place since the war. I went with my mate Eugene and his wife, Angie, as well as two members of the club, Chug and Paranoid.

Eugene was a bouncer at a wine bar up the road from one of the hotels I used to work at in Fairfield. You wouldn't think that a wine bar would need a bouncer, but you'd be wrong. Most Saturday nights, I'd be shooing away all these drunk punters from the hotel, and they'd all end up crowding into Eugene's wine bar. Eugene hung out with the Jokers, but he wasn't a member. He ended up buying my old Harley. Chug was a good bloke, reliable and friendly. And Paranoid was funny as hell and always good for a laugh.

Eugene's wife, Angie, was Vietnamese and her brother had a hire car service over there. Angie, bless her, booked all our hotel rooms for us – in Vietnamese, of course. You can imagine what happened when we arrived. The hotels were expecting a group of Vietnamese locals ... and then we show up! You could just see the proprietors' jaws drop. They'd booked us in under Vietnamese prices, thanks to Angie, not the prices they'd usually charge a bunch of Aussie tourists.

Fuck, there's a whole lot of money gone, they must have thought. *We could have charged them double!*

Angie took us everywhere and was like our in-country guide. I told her that I wanted to go to Da Nang because I had a contact up there. We went and I took a lot of photographs because I'd never really seen the country, certainly not as someone who was there to enjoy it. It was like I was experiencing everything for the first time, but by the same token it was all really familiar. We went to the airport up there and I wanted to take some photos, because I'd been there back in 1968. Well, the guards weren't having a bar of it; they reckoned I was a security risk.

'I used to be on the hill up there,' I said to them, pointing to a hill nearby. 'That's where I watched a jet plane blow up, you know, and two pilots were killed.'

I don't think that endeared me to them. They just shook their heads again and said, 'No photo.'

That wasn't going to stop me.

I pretended to be looking elsewhere, held my camera at waist height and snapped a few shots while they weren't looking.

Going back started off as a good experience for me. We also went to Hue, which is a big city in central Vietnam on the Huong River. That's where the Imperial City is, with all the shrines and palaces. It was nice to feel like a tourist as opposed to a soldier at war.

I found it was easy to hire guns for shooting practice in Vietnam, which I love. The guns are tied to the tables but you

The One Percenter

can swing around with them. I fired an M60 machine gun, an AR-15 ArmaLite, a pistol, and a few other weapons. I ended up spending several hundred bucks on rounds. But it was a great experience and well worth every penny.

Like I said, being back in Vietnam felt familiar, but at the same time completely new. Of course, we went to all the museums and brushed up on the history and culture, but the most memorable experience was visiting the temple in Long Tan. We originally planned to visit the Long Tan Cross memorial, which a lot of veterans make a point of seeing, but you have to hire a police escort because it's in a field outside the city.*

'Fuck that,' I said. 'I'm not hiring some cops to go stand out in the middle of a paddock with a bunch of rubber trees.'

Instead, we went to the Ben Duoc Memorial Temple for the Vietnamese soldiers who'd died. The memorial is housed in a big Buddhist temple where you can burn incense and pray, if that's your thing. There's also a bunch of plaques there with the names of the dead, as well as a large gong. As you'd expect, the atmosphere is pretty solemn. As we were looking at all the names and dates, something occurred to me.

'I think I might have killed that one,' I said. 'I might have killed that one, I might have killed that one . . .'

I was going through all the names and the boys were chuckling along with me. Me running my smart-arse mouth again.

---

* The Long Tan Cross was originally erected in 1969 by the Sixth Battalion, Royal Australian Regiment to mark the site of the Battle of Long Tan, which was fought in 1966. Following the Communist victory in 1975, the Cross was removed and was used to commemorate a priest, but was recovered by the Dong Nai Museum in 1984 and placed on display. A replica cross was erected on the battlefield in 1980s, which is the one that stands today. The original Long Tan Cross was loaned to Australia in 2012, and then officially given to Australia in 2017. It now resides, on permanent display, in the Australian War Memorial in Canberra.

UGLY

Then I walked over to the big gong there and did what you do with a gong: I hit it.

Bong!

Next thing I knew, this big black cloud rolled across the sky, followed by a gale. The temple doors slammed shut and windows started rattling; it felt like a hurricane was brewing. Then this big old painted vase fell over and smashed to smithereens.

'Uh-oh,' I said. 'What happened there?'

Guards appeared out of nowhere, running and pointing up at the sky and shouting. The storm got even more intense so I just said, 'We're getting out of here!'

As we were leaving, Eugene said, 'That only happened when you hit that gong.'

I honestly believe I woke the spirits.

And they weren't happy with me.

Paranoid said, 'You've definitely killed some spirits here.'

I was sure that on those plaques were the names of Viet Cong soldiers I'd shot. There had to be. I'd been to all of the locations where they died and just knew that I was responsible for at least some of their deaths.

This horrible feeling descended upon me, as dark as the storm clouds above.

Being back in Vietnam was a lot to handle. The nightmares I was having were getting intense. It was like all that shit was rising back to the surface. I didn't know what to do with it all. This was the only way I could think of to relieve that tension, to make shitty jokes.

Death had been a huge part of my life in Vietnam. It had shaped how I came back to Australia, and it followed me around for years and years after that.

The One Percenter

A while after the trip to Vietnam, I can't remember when, I was talking to a navy friend of mine, Josh, and he told me that I needed to go and get treatment in order to get a better pension. I'm grateful that he was aware of what the government was offering, because they definitely didn't make it clear. He'd noticed the PTSD, that I was a bit touchy, and that I had a short temper. He was right. I got into a few fights with some of the vets on Anzac Day. I shouldn't have done that.

'You need treatment,' he said, 'not only because of the pension, but because you're fucking mad.'

He told me to go and see a clinical psychologist, a bloke by the name of Cole Collier. He was out at Kogarah in Sydney's south, but ended up moving to Taree on the New South Wales Mid North Coast. I went down to see Collier and he asked me a few questions. I ended up telling him about my first weeks in-country, where I killed that innocent farm girl on the banana plantation. He made a big thing of that. He got in touch with the army, to make sure that I wasn't just some bullshit artist. They can call me a lot of things, but I'm not a bullshitter. When he asked them about me, they just said, 'Yeah, he's mad.'

It was helpful seeing Collier. He pushed me along and I kept seeing him for a while. Talking about it helped get it all out into the open, instead of keeping it in like some dead weight I'd swallowed. He prescribed me some antidepressants, which I took.

Right up until I went to jail again, that is.

•

Around 1995, my old major from Third Battalion, 'Birdy', came to me with a problem. The big, bombastic bugger I remembered had aged, but he still reckoned he could take me in a fight. He also still felt like my commanding officer, and I had a lot of admiration and respect for him. When he called, he told me that he had an issue with his family. He wanted to know if I could get a couple of the boys together to go around with him and sort things out.

'Yeah, no worries,' I said.

I asked a couple of hitters to meet me at the clubhouse. It was probably Odey and Chug, but I don't remember. I gave Birdy the address and he came around, too. When he arrived, I gave him the tour like you would to royalty. As I said, there was a lot of respect for the bloke.

'What's this all about then, Birdy?' I asked him after the tour.

'Well, there's some people that are stealing from me and my family,' he said. You could see on his face that he was angry, but also hurt. 'They're touching up our pensions, our money. I need them to stop.'

'We're on it, Major,' I said. 'Don't you worry.'

We went straight out and got into our cars. Birdy couldn't ride a bike and it was safer for him to just take a car. Besides, this wasn't really club business, it was personal.

When we got to Birdy's place, we wandered around the back of the house. There were three people – two blokes and a sheila – giving Birdy's daughter a hard time. She didn't look like she was taking it too well, which was understandable given the circumstances.

Birdy went over and started trying to comfort her. I think he got a bit of a shock when we walked straight up to these three buggers and started in on them. We picked them right up – their feet were off the ground – and held them up against

The One Percenter

the wall. I made sure we had our mean faces on. We may have been a bit rough with them.

I heard Birdy whisper, 'Oh, shit.'

I don't know what he expected, but I guess it wasn't that!

'That's the way we do it, Birdy,' I said, holding this struggling bloke against the wall. 'We're straight into it. No use mucking around. Now, you tell 'em what's going on, mate.'

He looked at me, then at those three pieces of shit, then back to me. He gave me a nod and came over. Even getting older as he was, he still had that hard-arse attitude about him. That same Big Bad Birdy was still in there.

'You touched my family's pensions,' he said. It was quiet, but it was hard. 'If you take anything else, touch anything else of ours, or mistreat my family in any way, these blokes here will finish you off.'

'Fuckin' A,' I said. The other boys grumbled in agreement.

Birdy put his hand on my shoulder. 'This is my old soldier, "Wrong Way" Mawson. And you can guarantee he'll do to you as he was trained to do.'

Oh, Birdy, I thought. *What'd you have to go and say that 'Wrong Way' stuff in front of the others for?*

The pieces of shit nodded. We let them drop and they ran off. Birdy never heard from them again, so I guess we'd done our job all right. His family was very thankful, but I said it was nothing. It was an order from the major, so how could I refuse?

Afterwards, Birdy came back to the clubhouse for a drink. The boys had been waiting for an opportunity, so one of them just went, 'So, what's this "Wrong Way" business all about?'

Birdy laughed and told them the whole story. He was such a character, knew exactly how to take over a room. Everyone

UGLY

liked him. I think Lyn was there too, because she liked Birdy and made an effort to see him if he was around. I'd never told her the Wrong Way story.

'You bastard, Birdy,' I said, laughing.

No one from the club ever called me Wrong Way – they stuck with Ugly – but they liked hearing that story. Can't blame them, really. If it were my mates, I'd want to know about it and give them shit, too.

●

I've got good mates in all the Aussie chapters, but am really close to the South Australia Jokers. Two of them especially: Stewie, who's still a good mate of mine, and Rhino, who died around 2000 or 2001. Rhino was one of the hardest blokes in the South Australia chapter and was close mates with Stewie, who was one of the top blokes over there. Rhino was our national sergeant for a while. He started off as a debt collector for the BLF,* which are a bike club now.** He was strong as a bull and both he and Stewie were imposing as fuck. Both of them stood at about six-foot-four. Stewie has this big white beard that goes down to his belt. Naturally, I used to give them shit all the time. Everyone was scared of them, but I wasn't.

---

* Builders Labourers Federation.
** The BLF was a trade union from 1911 until 1972, then again from 1978 to 1986. They were permanently deregistered in 1986 by the Hawke Labor government, as well as some state governments. This was as a result of the Royal Commission into corruption within the union. Union secretary Norm Gallagher was jailed for receiving bribes from building companies, the money from which he used to build his beach house. Former members of the BLF formed the Builder Labourers Federation Social Club, as a memorial to the good work the BLF did before it ended, in 1994. It celebrated its twenty-fifth anniversary in 2019. They still use the same slogan as the original BLF, 'Dare to struggle, dare to win', which comes from a saying by Communist leader Mao Zedong.

The One Percenter

One time we were on a run up in Bundaberg in Queensland. We were settling in for the night by the side of the road and getting on the piss a bit. Stewie and Rhino had set up their lean-to – they shared a sleeping space – and were inside getting ready to go to sleep. I wandered by their tent, drunk as, and thought, *Oh, I'm gonna stir these two buggers up.* So I pulled the latches on the tent and just yanked it down. It collapsed on top of them.

Well, they started swearing and carrying on like you wouldn't believe. I took off as fast as I could, laughing all the way like a fucking kid. Behind me, I could hear them coming, those big bloody footsteps just stomping their way towards me. There's a photo of us somewhere, when they'd caught up with me. Rhino has his arm around me, looking like he's going to bash me, and Stewie's on the other side smiling, but it's not a good smile.

'We just wanna talk to you, big man,' Rhino said.

'Yeah,' Stewie said. 'Just have a little chat.'

They dragged me into a tent and just started bashing me – *bang, bang, bang, bang* – all body shots. I was giving it back to them, I wasn't going to just let them work me over. I got Rhino and Stewie both with some hard hits to the body, but they punched the living shit out of me with those body shots.

Back home in Adelaide after the run, Rhino said he had some pain in his back. He said it was sore near his kidneys. We took him to hospital so they could have a look at him. They had to operate, but he ended up bleeding to death on the operating table. It was a burst pancreas. That shocked everybody. Everyone said that I'd done it with my body shots. Even though they were mucking around when they said it, it still hurt. I didn't want that on my conscience.

'You're a murderer,' Stewie said to me.

I ended up being one later on – and I know I'd killed a lot of people in Vietnam – but I didn't want to think that I'd killed my friend.

It had a big effect on me and I felt guilty. After that, I stopped the muck-around friendly fights with the boys, especially because my go-to move was always body shots. I didn't want to risk it. Not again.

We went back to South Australia and had a wake for Rhino. I went up to his missus, Lizzie, and told her how sorry I was. Not that I think I'd done anything wrong, but it was bloody awful losing Rhino. We ended up getting pretty shitfaced and, well, one thing led to another. Nine months later, she had my fifth kid, Victoria. She lives in South Australia with her mum and would be around twenty now. Lyn only found out while I was in jail. I could slap myself.

When Stewie found out he started hitting me with *really* low blows.

'You're nothing but a cunt,' he said. 'First you kill me mate and then you shag his missus.'

'You bastard!' I replied. 'It wasn't like that and you know it.'

Stewie and I are good mates, but he and Rhino were really close. The BLF have a bar called the Rhino Bar, and I've got a shirt made up with that on it. They're allowed to have that name because they're friends with the Jokers.

●

In the early 2000s, we had a club member called Steve Williams. His friends called him 'Horrible', though everyone else called him Mr Williams.

The One Percenter

He got his nickname because, well, he was horrible.

I first met him in Adelaide around 2000, when I convinced a South Australian club – I don't remember which one – to come under the Jokers' patch. Horrible was big, but he had a friendly kind of face. He liked to poke shit, really stir the pot. Soon after I met him, he was teasing people and pushing them around, like he always did. He walked up to me and gave me a shove and said, 'You reckon you're a fighter?'

Then he gave me a whack.

Obviously, I gave him a whack right back.

'Fuck yeah, you got something to say about it?' I said.

'We can keep this going,' he said, jutting his thumb out behind him. 'We can head out the back. There's a spray booth and there's a set of gloves.' A spray booth is a place where they paint cars.

'That'll do me,' I said.

Horrible grabbed two pairs of gloves from behind the bar and I followed him out. We weren't trying to hide or anything, but this wasn't a fight for public show. Of course, everyone was onto us and they followed us out and formed a nice, big circle.

We put the gloves on and faced off.

'You ready?' Horrible asked.

'Fuck yeah!'

And then he was all over me, *whack, whack, whack*. He was big and he was strong, but I was quicker. I'd been training for heaps longer. It took some effort, but I outboxed him. By the end of it, we were both exhausted.

'I'm buggered, mate,' I said. 'Let's call it quits.'

'Yeah,' he said. He put out his hands for us to touch gloves, but as I was reaching out, he dropped them real quick. I had just enough time to think, *Oh, something's up*. Then he gave me a big push and I ended up flying backwards into this cabinet. I crashed through it and brought down all the shelving right on top of me. When I got up, I was covered in white dust. There must have been bits of chalk for writing on blackboards for the pub menus in there. Well, it ended up all over me.

Horrible laughed so hard he was nearly crying. And all the boys watching were cheering their heads off. Horrible helped me up and we went back out to the pub. We must have made a hell of a sight for the other punters.

'You're the only one who's ever given me two black eyes,' Horrible told me afterwards.

I counted that as a win. And I ended up getting off pretty easy.

About a year later, there was this bloke who was always hanging around the club, talking himself up like a big man. We called them hangarounds. It didn't really bother me, but it bloody well ground the gears of some of the other members. One night, we were at the Adelaide clubhouse and Horrible had had enough. He walked over to this hangaround, who was drinking and talking shit. The fella had no idea that Horrible was carrying a hammer and a nail.

Horrible walked right up to this bloke and – *whack!* – nailed his hand to the bar.

'There,' Horrible said, while this fella stared in shock at his hand. 'Now you can hang around even more!'

And then he just walked off.

The other members took a bit of time getting that nail out of the bloke's hand – and the bar – while he was screaming and bleeding everywhere.

•

The One Percenter

In January 2001, a few Jokers and I were down in Beachport, South Australia, hanging out with Horrible and his crew. We were on our Christmas run and planned to stay the night at the Beachport Hotel. We were drinking and pushing each other around, doing what we normally do, when a bunch of coppers arrived and got right up in our faces. They were members of the STAR Force* and they thought they were big and tough.

'What are you doing here?' one of them said. 'Why don't you buggers get out of here?'

'We're just drinking, having a good time,' I said. 'What's the problem?'

'The problem is you're here at all. Now, fuck off.'

Well, Horrible didn't like that one bit. He was such a good street fighter. You didn't want to get on the wrong side of him. He walked right up to that copper and punched him out. It was on! In the blink of an eye a massive brawl started. There were something like forty of them and about fifteen of us. Fists and feet were flying everywhere. I took a couple of decent hits to my head – as usual – but I didn't go down.

I remember grabbing one copper and punching him in the face. His mate came up behind me and got me in a hold and the one I was punching started hitting me in the gut. Luckily I was fat! It didn't hurt too much and I was able to push the one who was holding me backwards until he stumbled over a chair and let me go. I lost him in the tussle.

At the end of it, everyone was a bit beaten up, one of the coppers had a broken jaw, and Horrible had bolted. Of course,

---

* The STAR Force was the Special Tasks and Rescue Force – also referred to as the Special Tactical and Response Force – and was South Australia's answer to a SWAT team in the United States. They have been active since 1978 but are now referred to as the STAR Group.

they wanted him most of all. He was the one who'd started it. A bunch of us ran off, because we knew they were going to try and corner him.

We were right.

Word got back to us that the STAR Force blokes had called for reinforcements. They set up a road block to try and catch Horrible, but they came up empty-handed. And that wasn't just because he was a fast rider. I heard that some of his mates caught up with him down by the river and helped him across by boat. No one expected that, not even me, and least of all the cops. Those coppers didn't check down by the water, so luck was on Horrible's side again.

After the Beachport Brawl,* as it became known, Horrible was elected president of the Gypsy Jokers in South Australia. He wanted to improve the club's image, especially because a lot of people felt that the South Australian coppers were thugs and had goaded us into that brawl. Horrible was president for three years before he was voted out. He also ran a few naughty houses in Adelaide, so he was always busy.

Arthur Veno, a writer from Melbourne, started hanging around the club in 2000 while writing a book about bikies.** He went on a few runs with us and Horrible. He and Horrible actually got to know each other pretty well and became mates. Horrible gave Veno a lot of information, so the book was pretty good.

One day, Veno was on the back of Horrible's bike when we got stopped by the coppers.

Again.

---

* 'SAPOL Defends New Heavily Armed "Security Response Unit" Amid Public Backlash', *SouthAustraliaPolice.com,* 5 July 2020.
** Arthur Veno and Edward Gannon, *The Brotherhoods: Inside the outlaw motorcycle clubs,* Allen & Unwin, 2002.

The One Percenter

'You lot can fuck off, or we'll book you off the road,' the copper said.

Veno tried to explain that we were just out for a ride, and that he was writing a book about bikies – so it was research – but the copper didn't give a shit. He essentially made him leave.

In the early 2000s, Horrible had a little side job on the go. He was totally against child abuse and would get a crew and break into the houses of lawyers and judges who were working on those sorts of cases and steal their computers. Then he'd look for information on paedophiles or child abusers or whatever else and go after them. Not only that, he also made a habit of regularly criticising the police. He was pretty outspoken about the anti-bikie task force in South Australia, which was called Avatar,* following a shootout between the Rebels and the Hells Angels.**

On 14 June 2005, a mate dropped him off at the Gepps Cross Hotel in the north of Adelaide. He was meeting someone there, looking for some information, but no one knows exactly who or what.

He disappeared that afternoon and has never been seen since.

His car was found abandoned in the car park, but there was no blood or signs of a fight.

I reckon he found out something he shouldn't have or ran his mouth about something, and someone got to him. Maybe it had something to do with the debt collecting he was doing. I don't

---

* Operation Avatar was active until 2007, when it was replaced by the Crime Gangs Task Force.
** This is in reference to a shootout that occurred between members of the Rebels and Hells Angels at the 2005 Adelaide Dance Music Awards Night. One member of the Rebels was charged over the shooting in August 2005.

know what to think. Either way, I'm pretty sure someone took him out. Arthur Veno is certain, like the rest of us, that he didn't kill himself.* And I don't believe that bullshit about him being turned into pet food.

Horrible's daughter misses her dad. She was thirteen when he disappeared. She just wanted him home for his thirty-ninth birthday. He was devoted to her and there's no way he would have left her behind, so he has to be dead. But they've never found his body, so whoever did it did not want to send a message.

They just wanted to make sure he was never seen or heard from again.

---

* 'If Steve was going to kill himself,' Arthur Veno is quoted as saying in an article in *The Age* ('Joker feared murdered', 2 July 2005), 'he would have done suicide by cop.'

8

The Killer

In the late 1990s a bloke by the name of Brett Driscoll entered my life. Brett was a teenager at the time, and he took karate classes with my kids. I'd done karate when I was young and I thought it was good, so all my kids – Mandy, Bianca, Brock and Skye – took lessons. Karate teaches you discipline, helps you mentally, and it was something we could bond over. My second-eldest, Bianca, even made it up to black belt. She was bloody good.

My kids had known Brett for a while through karate, but he became especially good friends with Bianca's husband-to-be, Fred. They'd known each other since the start of high school. I remember believing that Brett had the hots for my youngest at the time, Skye. I didn't know that for sure, and I don't know now, but that's what it seemed like to me. It's hard to tell because I was always away on runs or down the clubhouse.

Either way, Skye didn't want anything to do with him.

UGLY

In 2002 Fred got into the scaffolding business. Fred hired Brett to do some scaffolding work, so Brett would stop by the house occasionally to say hello. Nothing out of the ordinary.

Then, around 2004, Fred told me that he thought Brett was fucking mad; he'd do weird shit like lean off the scaffolding, yelling out to God. I think Skye wrote down some of the bizarre stuff he used to say. Turned out he'd done stints at Banks House in Bankstown, which is a mental health facility, and apparently he'd tried to burn down a local church.

As you'd expect, behaving like a crazy person on a building site just wasn't on. The workers didn't feel safe having him on site. He would sometimes go about his work in a dangerous and aggressive way.

'Lord, I'm on my way up to you,' he said one day at work.

'Fuck off, you're sacked,' Fred said. He couldn't take the risk anymore. They were mates, but enough was enough.

Brett went quiet for a little while, but clearly some kind of shit had been building up in his mind. He never got the help he needed.

One afternoon a few weeks later, sometime in June 2004, Brett came round to Bianca's house, where she and Fred lived with their daughter, and started ranting and raving outside. He was yelling and making threats.

'I'll teach you all a lesson,' he was screaming. 'I'll burn the house down!'

Bianca made a police report with the Bankstown cop shop, but by that time Brett had gone away and there wasn't much they could do.

Well, he came back the next day, didn't he? Except this time, Bianca was alone at home with my granddaughter, who was six years old at the time. Brett was screaming again, shouting, cursing the family.

The Killer

'It was all gibberish,' Bianca said. 'It was like he was trying to put a curse on us.'

Once again, Bianca called the Bankstown coppers and made a report. Those weren't the only times Brett came by and harassed them, but that was when she told me about them. She said that six or eight times before this, Brett had come around in the night, yelling outside the house.

'I could hear his voice,' she said. 'But I couldn't see him anywhere.'

Even after she called the cops, he didn't stop. Bianca told me that he came back another six or so times after that, threatening her and Fred and saying he was going to burn the house down.

She would come over to visit pretty frequently and we talked about the Driscoll stuff a lot. It was really bothering her and, naturally, it was bothering the shit out of me. Obviously, because we lived close by, she made sure to keep us in the know, just in case they ever needed any help. Thankfully, it never came to that. Not at her place.

All was quiet from Brett for a little while, then. It wasn't until around the end of 2005 that things picked up again.

Brett came by and delivered Skye a green shopping bag full of papers to give me. He called it his 'book'. When I had a look at it, it was just a random collection of papers, including one twenty-odd-page screed that was full of conspiracy theories that mentioned the army and the navy, and some sort of plan he was trying to lay out. I didn't understand it all. He wanted me to hand the book on to try and sell it. I told him I'd hand it on to someone, but I never did. All I did was show it to Fred to prove that Brett was clearly unwell, and that he might be dangerous.

A couple of weeks later, Brett came to me and demanded the money from the book's sales, which of course didn't exist because there was no book. At this stage it all began to really piss me off, and I was concerned that he might get back up to his old shit. I truly believed he was a danger to my family.

I just didn't think anything would happen so quickly.

In early January 2006, while I was away in Canberra, he showed up at my house.

The way Skye describes it, she was woken up when she heard two loud bangs and a male voice screaming in the night. She couldn't understand anything he was saying. Lyn then went downstairs to investigate what was happening. She looked through the glass panel on the door and saw a small fire in the front yard.

It was raining a bit, and the fire wasn't very close to the house, so Lyn wasn't really worried about it. But when she tried to open the door, she couldn't. It was blocked off. Those were the two bangs that Skye had heard: he had thrown heavy flower pots against the door. Lyn said she heard a voice screaming out, 'I'm gonna kill you fucking women!'

Lyn didn't recognise the voice, but Skye did. She knew Brett Driscoll's voice.

While this was all going down, I was at Summernats with about 120 other Jokers. Summernats is the annual car and bike festival that's been going since 1987. It's a 'by bikies, for bikies' kind of thing. Most years we'd go down and race each other. There wasn't much animosity between club members, a few punch-ups and that, but it's generally a pretty friendly sort of event. Everyone's there to enjoy the atmosphere. Bikies do the security, so a lot of the time we'd be on the lookout for anyone ready to cause trouble.

Little did I know that the trouble wasn't happening in Canberra, but back in Sydney.

The Killer

When Skye called to tell me what Brett had done I just said, 'I'm coming home.'

'No,' she said. 'I'll get Fred and the scaffolding boys to come round.'

They were rough blokes and, because they knew Brett, Skye said they'd sort him out quick smart. She told me not to worry. I wasn't confident though. I had all kinds of shit running through my head about what might happen without me there to help them. I stomped off and went and had a chat with Potter, an old mate of mine. I explained the situation and told him that I was going home right away to fix this Brett Driscoll bloke up good and proper.

'Don't you dare,' he said. 'When we get back to Sydney, we can get some of the boys together and have a chat with him.'

'You know he tried to kill my family?' I said, hot with anger. 'I won't cop that.'

Potter calmed me down. I ended up agreeing that I wouldn't go home right away, that I'd wait for us all to get back up to Sydney before doing anything.

But the next night, the fucker tried to do it again.

Twice in two days he tried to burn my house and my family down!

What was really scary is that no one woke up the second time he came round. When Lyn and Skye woke up the next morning, they came downstairs and found that it was still full of smoke. The front door had been blackened by fire and there was fire damage to the front lawn and the pot plants around there.

This time the neighbours had heard what was going on and came over to tell Lyn what they'd seen. They said Brett had been outside the house screaming threats and yelling abuse, much like the previous night.

By now, my wife was panicking. I was panicking. How could we not? We didn't know if this bastard was going to come back and try it again and again until he got it right. I told myself there was no way I could stay in Canberra; I had to leave. Everyone was telling me not to, that we'd deal with it when we all got back to Sydney, but I hadn't told them about the second attempt to burn my house down. They thought I was just over-thinking it the first time.

My brain was on one track at that point.

So I just started packing all my gear up.

'What are you packing your gear up for?' Potter asked me.

'I always pack it up, just in case the coppers move us on.'

That had the added bonus of being true, because the coppers did usually move us on. So I had my swag rolled up and everything packed away. Then, when no one was paying any attention, I hopped on my bike and took off. I was speeding down the highway, with only one thought in my head: getting home to protect my family.

A while later, I looked behind and noticed the Jokers had sent one of the boys after me. I didn't want them involved. This was personal. This wasn't club business. I know in the clubs, in the brotherhood, you stand by each other, stick up for each other and that, but this was outside the scope.

Eventually the bloke who was tailing me caught up with me. It was a club heavy by the name of Drew. They send Drew to do a job, it gets done right, even if it's nasty.

I couldn't outrun him so I pulled over to the side of the road.

Drew stopped beside me.

'I've been told I have to help you out with this, mate,' he said.

The Killer

'I don't need fuckin' any help,' I said. 'If this fella's coming around, I'll wait for him at home.'

Drew nodded and said that was a good plan, and waited for me to make a move. He said he wasn't going anywhere. He was coming with me no matter what I said.

After a petrol stop, I rode as fast as I could straight back to Sydney.

Somehow Drew managed to keep up with me. It felt like the fastest ride I've ever done. I didn't even feel the pain in my back or shoulders or anything that usually comes with a long ride like that. Everything just went numb. My mind was focused on getting home. I was only thinking of my family.

When we got back, Drew settled in at my place. Lyn showed me the fire trail leading from the lawn to the front door. I remember just seething inside. I couldn't speak.

Drew waited with me all night at my place. I was holding onto a baseball bat. We were sure Brett was going to come back and try it again. But he didn't. The time dragged in that dark silence, knowing any moment we might have to spring into action. I wanted to scare him, to break his legs, to make sure he'd never come near my family again.

In the morning, Drew said he had some business to take care of, some club stuff to do, but he'd be back later that day. I said no worries, and off he went. I fell into bed at about 8 am and slept until midday.

And then I started drinking.

When Lyn got home at about 5.30 that evening, I was still on the piss and she was pissed about it.

At the time I was already on a downward spiral. I was drinking a lot and, on top of that, I was having nonstop nightmares. Lyn and I were arguing all the time. She wanted me to stop the booze and I just wasn't listening to her. I didn't want to hear it. It was the best way to kill the nightmares, or so I thought. Looking back on it, I don't know how much good it really did. Others tried to reason with me and help me, but Lyn just told them not to bother. 'In the end, I just ignore him,' she said. 'I just walk away and leave him instead of arguing with him.'

After we fought for a bit, I said that I was going to the bottle shop to get more grog. She threw her arms up because she knew that there was nothing she could say that would stop me.

I grabbed my .22 Ruger, which was locked and loaded, and put it in a holster I hung around my neck. I figured that if I ran into Brett on the way to the bottle shop, I could stick this under his nose and tell him to fuck off for good, see what he had to say about that. I knew he sometimes drank in the hotel next to the bottle shop. He could kick the shit out of me in hand to hand, so I wanted any advantage I could get.

I didn't want anyone else involved. This was my business and mine alone. I was so full of rage. Something I hadn't felt in a very long time. It was almost like I was outside of myself, operating on autopilot. Greg King later said that he wished he'd known what was happening. He said he could have stayed with my family and helped out.

But I would have waited until he left or sent him away, same way I did with Drew.

I left home and walked up the street towards the bottle shop. Round and round in my head all I could think about was Brett Driscoll and the shit he was pulling, the danger my family was in. I didn't want to hurt him too badly, I knew his parents and they're good people. My intention was just to scare him off. I didn't want him coming back a third time. Skye was just about

The Killer

to have her baby, little Beau, and there was no fucking way I was going to let what Brett had done slide. If he'd killed her, I'd have lost not only Skye, but also my grandson.

That was all going through my head as Brett reversed his car out of the driveway. Where he was living was on the way to the bottle shop.

Seeing him filled me with rage. He'd tried to kill my fucking family.

I ran over to his window and I leant in.

'Remember me, arsehole?' I said. 'I told you not to fuck with me.'

'Oh, shit,' he said.

I could see there was a woman sitting beside him in the passenger seat. She looked scared but, in that moment, I didn't care. All my focus was on Brett.

I pulled out my Ruger and pointed it at him. He must have tried to drive off, but it all happened so fast. The car kangaroo hopped. The gun went off. I shot him – *bang, bang* – either side of his chest. The woman in the car opened her door and ran off when she heard the gun.

That smell of gunpowder. It made my mind hazy.

Bang! Bang!

I shot him twice more. It was an eight-shot revolver. He staggered back.

'Gotta put the enemy down,' I said, I think out loud, but it could have been in my head.

I pulled the gun up and aimed it carefully and fired twice more. He went down.

Something came over me, then. And a really dark feeling crept into my mind.

What the fuck have I done? Where am I?

UGLY

I was back in Vietnam. It was the same feeling. I didn't know where I was. Neighbours said I was screaming Vietnamese at him. It was apparently something like, 'You fucking *kakadao*!'*

Bang! Bang!

I put two more in his head. It was instinct, the way I used to deal with Viet Cong back in the army. I looked down at him and he had that sign of the cross on him in bullet holes, like we used to do.

I shouldn't have done that.

But I've already done it.

The gun was going *click, click, click* in my hand. Empty.

I reached into my pocket for more ammo – which I didn't have – and that's when I came to. I looked around and realised all the neighbours were standing there staring at me, terrified. Then the garbage truck pulled up.

'Fuck off!' I screamed, lifting the gun and pointing it at the driver. It sounded like I was yelling at him from underwater.**

That was the first time I'd ever seen a garbage truck screech its brakes going backwards, like it was running away.

I shouldn't have done that.

I was standing there holding the empty gun. I'd never had a flashback like this. As soon as Brett went down, I just had to finish him off. It was like my body was running on automatic. Which, in a way, I guess it was. But my actions brought with them a feeling of overwhelming grief and sadness. Later, the lawyers said that if I'd waited for him to return for a third time and killed him while he was actually attacking my home, they could have at least

---

* This is a roughly transliterated bastardisation of the Vietnamese word for 'kill' or 'dead'.
** The sentencing judgment makes note that, at this time, Ugly had a blood alcohol level of 0.118. The legal driving limit is 0.05. The judgment also makes note that there was no dothiepin in Ugly's system, which is the drug he had been taking for many years to relieve the symptoms of his PTSD.

The Killer

made an argument for self-defence. But as it was, I went over to his place. I confronted him. I couldn't just sit around. And then, in the middle of all that, my brain just went its own way.

I waited with the body. It made sense to me to defuse the hunt. It wasn't like I was going to get away with it.

'Call the cops if you want to,' I yelled at the neighbours watching. 'I'm sick of him threatening my family.'

Five or ten minutes later the cops pulled up with their high beams and sirens on. A female officer got out of the car and just started yelling at me.

'Drop the fucking, fucking,' she was stuttering. 'Drop the, the, the fucking, fucking gun, now!'

Oh, she's shitting herself, I thought.

The gun was empty and I wasn't going anywhere, so I said, 'All right.'

I wound up like I was about to throw a baseball and threw the gun. The cop sort of let out a squeal and I thought that she was going to shoot me. Next thing I knew this other copper came running up behind me. He grabbed me and pushed me to the ground and started trying to get the handcuffs on me behind my back.

'Mate,' I said. 'My shoulder's not real good. Can you cuff me from the front?'

'Yeah,' he said. 'Righto.'

And he did.

'I'm not goin' nowhere,' I said. 'I was waiting for youse.'

He knew it was true. I could have tried to run, but there was no point.

They pulled me up. As I was being walked to the police cruiser, I had a word with the body on the ground.

'Payback's a bitch,' I growled.

As they drove me to the station, they tried to question me. All I said was, 'I've got nothing to say.'

Club rules are club rules. You say nothing. You shut your mouth until the solicitor comes and gets you. We had a club solicitor and I called him when the coppers got me to Bankstown Police Station. They kept trying to question me and I just kept saying that I had nothing to say. Finally they left me alone with the solicitor.

'I can't get you out of this one,' he said.

'I haven't said nothing,' I said, pacing the room. 'And I won't sign a statement.'

'Sign a statement,' he said.

'Get fucked. I won't sign nothing.' I sat down then, and said, 'That cunt tried to kill my family.'

'So you admit to the killing?'

'Oh, no, Jack Robinson did it,' I said. 'Fucking idiot.'

I was caught red-handed standing over Brett Driscoll with a smouldering gun. What kind of a question was that?

The solicitor was silent for a moment. 'This is too big for me,' he said eventually.

That's not exactly encouraging, coming from your lawyer. '*What?*' I practically yelled.

'You'll need to get someone else,' he said. 'I'm sorry.'

The club brought in the big guns. They got in touch with the well-known Sydney lawyer, Chris Murphy.

I said I'd confessed not just because it was obvious, but because if I didn't, they'd pull my home apart and harass my family. That's why I just stood there and waited for the coppers to arrive. I felt like running home, that's all I wanted to do.

It made no difference in the end. They ended up pulling my place apart anyway. They even dragged me in there with them,

The Killer

pointing stuff out. The .32 was still on top of the fridge and one of the coppers looked up and said, 'What's that in the bum bag?'

'That's my .32 revolver.'

Not great.

Even worse, Driscoll's brother was an ex-copper.

They took me straight to Silverwater Correctional Centre and put me in the remand section. As soon as I got out of the paddy wagon, a female copper came up to me and said, 'You've been refused bail.'

'No kidding,' I said, and laughed at her.

'Are you under treatment for anything right now?' she said.

I told them about the antidepressants that Collier had prescribed me.

'Were you on them when you shot the bloke?'

'No,' I said. 'And I'd still fucking shoot him.'

They told me to fuck off and I didn't get any medication while I was inside. After processing me, they put me on suicide watch, just to make sure I didn't off myself. They do that with everyone; it's not like I was in any special danger. When they asked me what section I wanted, I knew I had to do something while I was inside.

'I want a working wing,' I said.

'What do you want a working wing for?' the female warden asked.

'Time goes quicker. I can get my mind off things and I can settle in and do some courses.'

'Oh,' she said. 'You want to do courses?'

'Yeah,' I said. 'I want to do courses.'

'Right.' And she put me in the working wing.

I ended up making earphones for Qantas, if you can believe it. And I spent time training at the gym. We had the afternoons to ourselves and all there really was to do was go to the gym.

UGLY

While doing my old boxing training, this big Indian bloke, Gunda Singh, noticed that I knew how to fight. He was in remand at Silverwater before being sent up to Long Bay. He was in for drugs, which I guess is what most sportspeople end up in jail for.

'You want to train with me?' he said.

Other blokes had already been saying to me, 'Get him to train you, get him to train you.'

'Yeah, I'll train with you,' I said.

'I'm the head sweeper on your wing,' he said, meaning that he was in charge of the inmates who had floor-cleaning duty on the wing.

'Oh, right.'

'Want to lose more weight?' he asked.

'Fuck yeah,' I said.

'Righto. I'll get you in as a sweeper with me.'

Next thing I knew I was out of the earphones manufacturing business and in as a sweeper. And fucking hell, that Singh bloke trained me. He was good. Not surprising, seeing as he was an Olympic wrestler for Australia.*

He had me running up and down the stairs, doing squats, running on the spot, running here, running there; he had me fucking working hard. The thing is, it did the trick. I went into jail weighing 140 kg, and I was 110 kg when I was transferred out of Silverwater. He trained the arse off of me, literally.

---

* It's hard to find any information on this person, although cursory research shows that only two Indian–Australian men have represented Australia at the Olympics: Sandeep Kumar appears to be the first, competing in the 2008 Beijing Summer Olympics; and Vinod Kumar Dahiya was the second, qualifying in the 2016 Rio de Janeiro Summer Olympics. Dahiya failed his Olympic qualification doping test in April 2016 and was subsequently removed from the Australian team and banned from competing for four years. The only Australian wrestler I could find who spent time in prison was Bruce Akers, who competed in the 1972 and 1976 Summer Olympics. He spent six months in jail after twenty-two horses were found dead on his property from neglect.

The Killer

Although, it didn't stick; I ended up finding that 30 kg I lost in prison all over again. I've shed a bit of it now, but it stuck around for a while.

•

Also in Silverwater at the same time as me was the notorious Neddy Smith.* Over the years, he'd gotten a tough cunt rep for getting into brawls and street fights, and plenty of stand-over stuff around Kings Cross. He was a tall fucker who people described as menacing, but I wasn't scared of him.

When I first walked into 17 Wing, there was Neddy. I'd been moved from 16 Wing, which was a pretty hard wing, to 17 because that was the workers' wing. I'd heard a couple of Maori boys were looking after Neddy. They got him his meals and everything. They looked after him because he was King of the Streets and they respected that.

Neddy got caught on tape admitting to some murders and ended up testifying against the ex-detective Roger Rogerson and a bunch of other dirty coppers in exchange for immunity for all his crimes except the murders.** My cell was a little further down than his, so I walked into the wing and went upstairs.

Neddy was there, but I didn't see him at first.

'Hey, Mawson,' he said. 'I got a good book here for ya.'

I'd talked to someone who was going to do a book on Neddy while he was in jail. The way I'd heard it, he'd raped a girl's mother – right in front of the kid – while some other bastards

---

* Australian crime boss Arthur 'Neddy' Smith has been in prison since 1988. Although he has been accused of eight murders, he has only been convicted of those of brothel owner Harvey Jones and tow-truck driver Ronnie Flavell during a road rage incident in 1987.
** Smith was the star witness for the Independent Commission Against Corruption (ICAC) in the early 1990s, and the Wood Royal Commission (1995–7). Smith alleged that he was given the 'green light' from several police officers to commit crimes and make money, which allowed him to pay off officers in order to avoid criminal charges.

held her down, and I believed it. That shit's not on. It's disgusting, especially in front of her kid. The book never ended up happening, but I knew the stories from other books that I'd read that had quotes from people who were in the know, as well as newspaper clippings.

I spun around and just shouted at him, 'You, you fucking rapist! You fucking weak cunt, raping a woman in front of her fucking child, that's fucking low!'

Suffice to say, the Maori boys were shocked. I just heard them go like, 'Woah.' Neddy himself went white as anything. I don't think he could believe that someone would dare talk to him like that. He left after that exchange. He knew I wasn't going to bow and scrape or take any of his bullshit.

He had a cell to himself. He had this typewriter and he'd pump out these memos. I always wondered if he was writing about me, about some cheeky little prick who was giving him shit. I hope so. I wouldn't cop a bit of him.

The next morning, after breakfast, the Maori boys came down to my cell.

'What are you having a go at Neddy for?' they asked.

'What are you, his minders?' I said.

'Yeah, we look after him.'

'You fucking know what he's done,' I said to them. 'And if youse go for him, you're no good, too.'

That's when I saw it on their faces: they had no fucking idea. They didn't know all the shit I knew about him. So, instead of sniping at them, I sat them down and told them what had happened, that I wasn't just slinging shit. They deserved to know the kind of low-life bastard they were protecting.

'Oh, right,' they said. They were stunned. They didn't like what they heard one bit.

The Killer

'But don't worry,' I said. 'I'm not gonna touch your boy.'

The day after that, I had a visit from my son-in-law, Dion, who's a Maori. Neddy's fellas watched Dion come and go and then came to talk to me again.

'Who was that?' they asked.

'Me son-in-law,' I said.

'Oh,' they said. They looked impressed by that. They knew then that I wasn't a racist. Soon after they started putting some distance between themselves and Neddy.

The Maoris would often work out in the gym in a clique. They had the run of the place at certain times. When they were done, they'd go outside and spend some time on the running oval. That's when I'd go into the gym and start doing some bag work. I didn't want to work out in front of anyone else. There was the risk that they might have go at me, test me out. I also didn't want to intrude on what was clearly their time. That was a good way of starting shit I didn't need. I didn't want to fight them, I had nothing against them.

It felt good to be training, though. I wasn't as fit as I was when I was younger, but I was getting back into shape. I was back to working the bags the way that I used to, just putting big heaves into them.

One day I had a funny feeling on the back of my neck. When I turned around, all the Maori blokes had lined up at the back wall and were watching me.

'The white boy's done a bit of fighting, eh,' they said.

I said, 'Yeah, I used to be a trainer as well.'

'Want to train with us?'

'Fuckin' oath, I do.'

That's when I started training with them, catching punches left and right. I actually had a good boxing troupe in there.

UGLY

If anyone in the 17 or 16 Wing wanted to have a blue, they could come and see me and I'd arrange it for them. It was like having the 17 Wing Championships.

Soon after, Neddy Smith was diagnosed with Parkinson's, and they transferred him over to the hospital wing. That wing was covered in tiles from floor to ceiling, just in case you vomited or shat yourself. Fortune smiled on me, then, just as it cast its shadow over Neddy. Because I was a worker, they got me to help pile up all his gear and bring it over to the new wing. I told them it would be my absolute pleasure.

It's no surprise I had no time for Neddy Smith. He might have been a big gangster and a hard fighter back in the day, but I don't sit with the shit he did. Who necks a mother in front of their own kid? Fucking savage.

I'm glad he lost everything and that he'll die in jail.

•

I was on remand for a year and a half before the trial. A lot of that I ended up doing by video link to save Chris Murphy from wasting money on transportation costs. I was already pleading guilty. The trial wasn't for murder, it was for murder with 'disresponsibility',* because of the mitigating factors. They had to get psychiatrists, one for and one against, to check me out and make a decision.

I think I freaked them all out.

---

* The legal term that Ugly is referring to is most likely the 'defence of diminished responsibility', which essentially lowers the charge from murder to manslaughter. This can be applied in circumstances relating to mental disorders (like PTSD), or any other 'mental impairment' that the offender may be suffering. According to the sentencing judgment from Ugly's trial, he was found guilty of 'Manslaughter – Diminished Responsibility'.

The Killer

I didn't give a shit, I told them whatever they wanted to know. I'm no bullshitter and brute honesty has always been my way.

The case was heard in the Supreme Court of New South Wales. They called in a bunch of people from the army, including Colonel Rothwell from the SAS. He knew Birdy and Jock, my mates from Vietnam, who actually ended up in the SAS. Rothwell and I knew each other because he would sometimes be there when I was hanging out with the boys from Vietnam. He used to always have a dig at me – in a friendly way – saying shit like, 'You wouldn't have made it in the SAS.' He was funny in a stern sort of way.

Birdy came down to Sydney one time and needed someone to drive him around. He was staying with Rothwell, but was getting gout and his feet were swelling up really bad. I showed up to take him somewhere and he asked me for help getting his boots on. Next thing, Rothwell walked in and saw me there on the floor, trying to carefully get Birdy's boots on.

'It's nice to see a subordinate looking after their major,' he said. 'Even after all this time.'

Rothwell appeared in a book called *The Team** about Aussie soldiers in Vietnam. It described how he was cutting down vines to help get the boys out of some shit because one of them got shot in the arse. Rothwell was firing his M16 with one hand and chopping down vines with a machete with the other hand so that the helicopter could come and pick up the wounded. Proper hero stuff.

Rothwell ended up taking over at court instead of Birdy.

Reason being that Birdy up and died on me, the bastard, while I was in jail on remand.

---

* Ian G. McNeill, *The Team: Australian Army Advisers in Vietnam, 1962–1972*, University of Queensland Press in association with the Australian War Memorial, 1984.

UGLY

The major was going to stand up for me, but because he couldn't, the colonel stepped up instead.

Birdy had called Lyn as soon as he'd heard about me being involved in Driscoll's death.

'Tell me,' he said. 'Did he shoot that bloke in the head?'

'Yeah,' Lyn said. 'He did.'

'That's my boy!'

When she spoke to me next, she was like, 'What does he mean, *that's my boy*? What's all this "shoot him in the head" business?'

'Well,' I said, 'I forgot to tell you, but I used to do that in Vietnam.' She was shocked. I'd never told her about all that before. 'I was trained to do it,' I added. A lot of things made sense to her after she found out about that.

When I learnt that Rothwell was going to testify for me instead of Birdy, I was worried. It was important that the court knew about the PTSD and the flashbacks – about the trauma that occurred while I was over there, and the repercussions when I got back home. Rothwell didn't know me nearly as well as Birdy, but he ended up describing my mental state perfectly. I needn't have been worried. As soon as he took the stand, he had a lot of authority behind him. He took over the whole court, the way he spoke. Just as bombastic as Birdy. He talked and everybody listened.

'One day, that bloke there,' Rothwell said, pointing at me, 'was a young soldier, fighting battles on seek-and-destroy missions. The next day he's sitting down with Mum and Dad for breakfast. How do you think he is? No detoxing, no nothing. He's still in the Vietnam frame of mind.'

He talked about how we didn't get any help when we came back, which was true. I was thankful he was able to put it into

The Killer

words like that. It was good that he was able to show that side of it because I didn't – and still don't, really – know how to talk about that stuff. I can give you the vagaries, but not the full picture.

'Did you serve with Mawson in Vietnam?' the prosecutor asked him. Not Private Mawson, just 'Mawson'.

'We served in the same regiment and performed similar operations,' Rothwell said. 'But I can't say whether we did or didn't, as that information is top secret.'

That made me smile. Imagine that! In an open court, he was pretty much saying, 'I can't tell you the stuff you want to know.' It wasn't a military trial, it wasn't some big treason trial or anything, it was a civilian criminal trial, so a lot of stuff that they wanted to know he simply couldn't say. Rothwell helped me a lot. He sounded really good up there and I owe him.

The main defence was PTSD, which played into a kind of self-defence argument. They said that the thought of my family almost being killed triggered my flashback. My brain basically reset to Vietnam. I lost the plot. When I took the stand I explained about the dark cloud descending upon me and how I ended up speaking in Vietnamese. The neighbours heard that, which made them think, *Fuck, he thinks he's back in Vietnam.*

When Driscoll hit the ground, I just went over him and did what I was trained to do in Vietnam.

It was my job.

They weren't allowed to bring up my history with the Gypsy Jokers at the trial. That was suppressed. They also didn't charge me for having guns. I thought that was odd. It was just a stroke of good fortune that I had given my 7.62 target rifle to Paranoid beforehand, because he wanted to take up shooting. I was lucky they never put a gun order on me. When you're slapped with one of those, the coppers can enter your house whenever they want. I still get coppers coming around for a visit every now and then, with Raptor.* They try to warn me off doing runs ever again and threaten me, saying they'll lock me up and all that sort of shit.

I didn't like facing down Driscoll's family in court. I had no beef with them, but they sure as hell had a beef with me, which I suppose they had a right to. Each day, sitting on the other side of the courtroom, it felt like they were eyeing me off. Some of the boys and my family would come and sit with me on my side, which was more to calm me down than anything else.

Thank Christ the boys got Chris Murphy on board. He's a top lawyer and worked wonders. He cost a pretty penny, though. The Outback chapter put up a bunch of money, thanks to all the gold mines out there. The Sydney and Western Sydney boys held a fundraiser and made up some 'FREE THE JOKER' T-shirts to sell. They had raffles and parties, as did Lyn and the kids; anything they could think of to foot the bill. Greg King took parts off of his motorcycle to auction off, too. They all came together for me, every single one of them. All up, I think it cost us nearly half a million dollars.

In the end, I got a seven-year sentence, with four of those to be served in jail. I'd expected to be looking down the barrel of twenty years. The army had saved me again. I think Rothwell's dead now, but he really helped me out.

---

* Strike Force Raptor is a special police task force that focuses on Outlaw Motorcycle Gang (OMCG) activity. It was established in 2009 after the Hells Angels and Comancheros brawled at Sydney Airport on 22 March and one man was killed, and also after the bombing of the Hells Angels clubhouse in Petersham in February. Former detective Mike Kennedy said in an interview with Radio New Zealand that New Zealand was considering a similar program, but that it was 'a disaster' and had only driven gangs 'underground'.

The Killer

So there I was, a sixty-year-old heading inside again, this time for a four-year stretch. But I could handle it. I'm sorry that the shooting happened. It shouldn't have. I caused everyone, my family and Driscoll's family, a lot of pain. I can't imagine what it must be like for his parents to lose a son. But in the end, my family came first. Always has, always will. It didn't matter that I was sent to jail, I honestly didn't care. I just wanted all this to be over.

I'd been there before. And I knew how to look after myself.

•

Civil ward was no picnic, but I had Singh training me even harder, and I got right back into boxing with those Maori boys. I made sure I kept myself distracted. And fit. We made catch mitts for boxing out of toilet rolls stuffed in shoes. We worked out a system where, instead of calling out left, right, left hook, we only called out numbers, 'One, two, three, four, five, six.' It worked better.

Most people would say four years in jail is pretty bad. But Singh saved my life. He got me back in shape and helped me lose weight. I'm still a bit round now, but not as much as I was before I went back inside. I met Singh again after he got out of jail.

'I was a big keg,' I said. 'And you got me down to a nine keg.'

'I diluted you,' he said, which I thought was funny.

The Outback boys wrote to me while I was in jail, which was nice. They're our hardest chapter, but they're a top bunch of blokes. I'd write back saying shit like, 'You're my favourite chapter because none of youse know how to fight.'

The letters I'd get in return! I was the most popular kid in school. The replies were filled with words like 'hate' and 'kill' and 'get you by the balls when you get out'. It was all in good fun, they didn't really mean any of it. I pushed their buttons and they responded the way I expected them to.

Apart from the training, I also did some anger management courses while I was inside, which helped me deal with my temper. The Maori blokes and Singh told me that when I came up for parole, it would look good if I had a few courses under my belt. I did a drug and alcohol course as well, because alcohol was a problem. I'm still against drugs.

When my parole review finally came up, the screws said, 'You've got to do a couple of courses.'

'Already done 'em,' I said.

'What?'

I showed them the paperwork and the certificates.

So after four years inside, they let me out. I was then to serve the remaining three years on parole. A free man? Not by a long shot.

•

When I got out of jail, I started the 1% clothing label. The coppers didn't like that at all. It was kind of a little 'fuck you', capitalising on the whole 1% thing, just to stick it to them. The Americans sent me an Iraqi war medal for being a good boy in prison, which I have hanging on my wall.

Unfortunately, while I was inside, Lyn developed polycystic kidneys. One of them started playing up really bad and she ended up having to have tubes shoved in through her guts to purify her blood on a dialysis machine.

It didn't help.

She got so crook that they had to take one of her kidneys out. Not long after that, the other one died, so then she was left

The Killer

with no kidney function at all. I don't know why, but they left the dead one in there. She had to be transferred to the Royal North Shore Hospital to do a course on their big dialysis machine. Now she's got an egg-like thing on her arm and she puts all the needles in there and does all the blood transfusions. Skye makes sure that everything's done right.

But sometimes, it doesn't go right and things blow out a bit. When that happens, I take her over to St George Hospital in Kogarah, and she spends a couple of days going back and forth doing the courses on the machine there. They're very good at looking after her at St George, that's been her hospital ever since this all started. Otherwise, she does the dialysis at home on a machine herself. I don't know how she manages it. She's been on that thing for at least four years now.[*]

On top of all that, she had to have some gallstones removed. She must feel completely hollow. But she's one tough rooster. I love her. I killed for her and my family and I'd do it again at the drop of a hat. Like I said: family is important to me.

Naturally, I was glad to be out of jail and on parole, but the big problem was I wasn't actually allowed to go home. The judge ruled that because Driscoll's family lived one street over, it would be too distressing for them for me to live nearby. They were frightened that I was going to go over there and kill the rest of them.

As a result, a condition of my parole was that I couldn't go home. That broke my heart. There's nothing harder than being a 'free' man, but not being able to go home. In fact, I wasn't allowed to be in Padstow at all. The whole fucking suburb was off limits.

---

[*] Four years since interview date, December 2019.

UGLY

I snuck over a few times, especially with Lyn being crook. And I hadn't had sex with my wife for six years because of prison and her kidneys, so let's just say we had some 'unlicensed' conjugal visits.

On top of that, Driscoll's family got victim compensation. They each got about ten grand, for about a fifty grand total, that I had to then pay back to the government! I was livid. So I went to Chris Murphy to see what we could do.

'I can't pay this,' I said. 'Do I look like I have fifty grand? I'll have nothing left.'

'Let me talk to them,' he said.

He took it to the tribunal and told them that I could only afford twenty dollars a week. So that's what I do. I'll be paying twenty dollars a week, essentially forever, to the Driscolls.

Not being allowed to go home really hit me hard. I felt alone. My eldest daughter, Mandy, put me up for a bit in one her kids' rooms, which was so good of her. But after a year or so, I ended up having an argument with her de facto and I thought, *Better get out, or I'm gonna do something wrong to him and it'll do me parole in.*

Then my mate Paranoid, the one I had lent my rifle to, decked out his garage shed like a little granny flat with some bedding, but that was only meant to be temporary, so I only spent a few months there.

Then my mate Vince Caballeri – he races Ducatis – put me up in a campervan with a tent that folds out for a bit. I had a TV and a bed. But the cops came around to breathalyse me. They just wouldn't leave me alone!

Vince and I got on really well. Still do, even though his wife won't have anything to do with me. She's Vietnamese and she must know about some of the stuff I did during the war.

The Killer

That, or she just isn't keen on anyone who was in the army at that time.

I have no qualms with the Vietnamese people, but some of them – I guess understandably – have qualms with me. I have some Vietnamese neighbours now in Padstow and I surprise them sometimes by saying *chào anh* (hello) when we pass each other. I spent two years over there, so I picked up some words here and there.

Not being able to see Lyn much during my parole was the reason I got one of my tattoos.

At my review, this young, snotty-nosed parole officer told me that I couldn't go home. I think she was enjoying it.

'I fuckin' own my house,' I said. 'Driscoll's not there anymore, there's no more danger.'

'Yeah,' she said, in that really dry *listen, fuckhead* tone of voice, 'but his family don't want you around them.'

'Well, they shouldn't have attacked me then,' I said, getting a bit worked up. 'I didn't attack them, I defended myself.'

'Yeah, but Brett Driscoll's dead,' she said, as if that ended the matter.

'Yeah, I defended myself real well, then, didn't I? He fucking attacked me, coming round to my house, tried to kill my fucking family, and I'm the one that's not allowed to go home? I've got a sick wife and you're telling me I can't go and see her?'

'Oh, right,' she said. 'Well, you can go on weekends to see her.'

'Whoopdi-fuckin'-doo,' I said. 'What about when she's on the dialysis machine and I'm not there?'

'You'll have to make other arrangements.'

I didn't tell that parole officer Skye was living with Lyn, helping to look after her. I just wanted to make them let me go home. None of it mattered. They didn't budge.

UGLY

I was so pissed. I didn't know what to do with myself. I wasn't allowed to drink and I couldn't go home, so I ended up hanging out with a bunch of Vietnam vets up at Murrurundi in the New South Wales Hunter region. I could drink up there because no one was around, and the boys would always know when the local cops were stopping by for a sticky-beak. They'd tell me when they were on their way and I'd go off and hide in the bush. Those boys looked after me.

While I was up in Murrurundi, I ran into an old mate of mine, Aldo, who's a veteran, too. He's also a tattooist and inks folks out of Penrith usually.

I was in a state when I caught up with him, filled with frustration.

'Listen, mate, I want to get a hate tattoo just to piss these parole people off,' I said. 'A few blokes in jail had barbed wire right on their eyebrow, to show that they were in the murder club.'

As the name says, these Long Bay fellas all had barbed-wire tattoos on their faces that showed they'd murdered people. I was good mates with some of them, and I told Aldo that I wanted to get one as well. The Americans have something similar – a black teardrop. Aldo agreed and did the tattoo right above my eyebrow, which made me even more pissed off. It was supposed to be right on the eyebrow, so I could shave off the hair and show the barbed wire, and then grow out the eyebrow again if I wanted to.

'Fucking hell,' I said, looking at it in the mirror.

'What? I thought that's what you wanted?'

'It's all right, mate,' I said. 'It'll still piss the parole people off.'

We both had a good laugh about that.

When I went in next to the parole board, I wore my hat, which mostly covered the tattoo. I sat down in front of them

The Killer

and after a few questions, I asked, 'Any chance of me getting back home?'

'No,' they said. 'You can't go home yet.'

'You bastards,' I said and slammed my hat onto the floor. You should have seen their faces when they saw my tattoo.

'You can't do that!'

'You can't tell me what to do with my own body!' I yelled. 'You're telling me I can't go home even though I'm not in jail anymore. I still feel like I'm behind barbed wire. This is my own form of protest.'

I didn't tell them that it was also the symbol for the murder club.

I got the tattoo done outside of jail because you do not want to get one done inside. You run the risk of catching all sorts of diseases from the unclean tools. Later on, I added 'VIETNAM' beneath the barbed wire, to kind of take it away from the murder club, and then 'LYN' on the side as well. I then got 'GYPSY' down my neck. I've got a mate who has tattoos all over his head and he said to me that I needed a few more. I've joked about getting some more barbed wire above the other eye, just for the symmetry.

Being on parole was fucking awful. I wasn't allowed to see the Jokers and didn't get to hang around with them legally until 2013. It was murderous to not be able to see my mates. Not only was I cut off from my wife and kids in a way that I hadn't really been before, but I was also cut off from my biggest social circle of friends.

Understandably, it fucked me up a bit.

I wasn't allowed to associate and I wasn't allowed to drink. So I used to go up to Murrurundi. What else could I do? That went on for three long years. In the end, the Murrurundi boys

UGLY

and I had a few arguments, and that was kind of it. We just lie low now and pretty much avoid each other.

When my parole was finally over, the Jokers held a big party – I have the poster hanging on the inside of my toilet door – that they called the 'Ugly's Right to Associate' party. There were bands and beers and everything.

I was a free man again, more or less.

9

Strike Force Raptor

Policing has changed a lot in my lifetime. Back when I was first arrested, I got three months and a pretend slapping. Then it was all over with and forgotten. Nowadays, *nothing*'s forgotten. Once you've been inside – especially if you're 'associated', like I am – you can expect to be under their thumb for the rest of your fucking days.

Strike Force Raptor began in 2009 after those Comancheros killed that Hells Angel bloke at Sydney Airport. They did it right there in front of everybody. Bikies attack each other in public – they always have – but this was different. This was like a second Milperra. Raptor was formed to target us specifically, as well as other 'outlaw groups', with 'high-impact and proactive' policing. That basically means they're all over your shit, all the time, busting down your door and turning your life upside down for stuff they'd otherwise let go.

Around 2017 or 2018, four heavily armed Raptor coppers pulled up on my front lawn and got out of their car. Two stood back, while the other two barrelled up to my front door and told me that I had to get them a photograph of at least six of my brothers in the club.

Remember, I'd served my time by this stage and was a 'free man'.

Well, not according to Raptor.

'You're not allowed to associate with those fellas,' they said. 'They're all in the club.'

I'd known these blokes for forty-odd years, and now I was being told I wasn't allowed to see them. The coppers said that if I was caught associating with any one of them twice after the warning, I'd be sent straight back to jail for three years.

'That's bullshit,' I said. 'That's communist!'

'That's Raptor. We can do what we want.'

Oh, Christ, I thought.

This Raptor business was serious. It was going to come down like a hammer on our lives. I thought, *Bugger it, I'm going on a run anyway*. And so we did a ride down to Melbourne, even after that warning from the coppers. What were they going to do? They couldn't track us all the time.

Defiance is the only stance to have in the face of shit like that.

So we rode down to Melbourne, and the Melbourne coppers didn't say a thing.

Because that went okay, we decided to do another run. We thought we'd keep pushing, see how far we could go. This time, though, the coppers found out about it. They rocked up at my house again and warned me not to go. This was in 2020.

'As soon as you're back in New South Wales,' they said, 'you'll get hit with consorting and we'll red card your bike.'

'What do you mean you'll red card my bike?' I'd never heard of that before.

'We'll put a defect notice on it,' they said. 'You won't be able to ride it, and you won't be allowed to move it from where it is.'

'I'll call a tow truck,' I said.

'If a tow truck shows up,' they said, 'we'll red card that, too.'

Lyn had been listening from the other room and came up behind me. 'Well, I've got a brand-new car,' she said. 'I'll just come and pick him up.'

'We're Raptor,' they said. 'We'll defect the car, and then we'll defect *you*.'

'Fuck youse,' I said, and slammed the door. I stood back, waiting for him to bash it down, but he didn't. He knew – I know he knew – that I was standing there just waiting for him to have a crack.

They'd threatened my fucking wife. Older coppers wouldn't have done that sort of shit. But these coppers were different. They were out of control with all these new powers. What do you think happens when you give people like that total power to do whatever they want? They're going to use it and it's going to be ugly. I was in my late sixties at this point. A Vietnam vet on a pension with a wife, kids and grandkids. It's not right to come around to my place and talk to me and my family like that. I'm no angel – none of us are – but that kind of shit? That's not right.

•

Ever since I started up the Jokers, there was always something going on between us bikies and the coppers. They treated us with disrespect and so we gave it right back to them. But mostly, the old guard had their heads screwed on.

Not always, though. Sometimes things turned more violent than we intended.

UGLY

In 2000, the former police chief at Perth CIB, Don Hancock, was running the Ora Banda Hotel just north of Kalgoorlie. The Jokers were on a run and stopped in at the pub to have a few drinks. One of our boys, Billy Grierson, started flirting with Hancock's daughter,* who was working behind the bar. From what I hear, she was flirting right back. Well, that didn't go down well with big daddy Hancock. He got mighty pissed off and quick as you like threw Billy and the Jokers out.

He basically told them to fuck off and that they were never allowed back.

The boys didn't really want any trouble; they were tired after the run, they just wanted to have a drink, and this sort of aggro wasn't really worth it.

So they left and went out into the bush, made up a little camp fire, and got back on the piss. It's just as good drinking under the stars as it is in any old pub. Might even be better. They were all just minding their own business, knocking back a few longnecks and chatting away, when two big shots** rang out.

Bang! Bang!

One shot hit the camp fire where the boys were sitting.

The other went right through Billy Grierson's back.***

Billy dropped to the ground and everyone scattered.

The coppers arrived at the scene not long after. All the Jokers were saying, 'Hancock done it! He done it!'

One of the crime scene guys said, 'We're gonna have to do ballistics.'

---

* According to *The West Australian*, Grierson and the others were using 'crude language' directed at barmaid Alison Hancock, Don Hancock's daughter, so he kicked them out.
** They were fired from a sniper rifle.
*** Police were 'unsure' whether the bullets were meant to strike anyone, or were only used as warnings against the bikies.

Hancock had also arrived. One of the Jokers looked at his arms and his face, had a sniff and said, 'You've had a lemon wash.'

You wash yourself with lemon juice after you've fired a gun to get rid of the gunpowder residue. That way, if the coppers swab you, they'll get a negative result.

This was what told us that Hancock had done it. Why else would he have washed himself in lemon juice?

'It's only some lemon wash,' said one of the cops there. 'You're being rude, mate.'

I thought the coppers were being slack, which made me angry. It was like they believed every word he said because he used to be in the force, and our boys were only bikies. My gut told me Hancock was going to get a free pass.*

The cops said nothing could be proved.

Eleven months went by and very little happened. Hancock wasn't arrested. The authorities reckoned his involvement was all hearsay.**

But then in September 2001, Hancock and his bookie mate Lou Lewis went for a little drive to the racetrack in Perth. While they were at the races, a bomb was slipped under the bonnet of Hancock's car, near the driver's side. As he was pulling into his driveway at home, it was set off with a remote-control phone.

---

* Hancock was long considered the prime suspect, although no one has ever been charged for Grierson's murder. The head cook at the pub testified she saw Hancock rev his car and race off after the bikies, and that Elizabeth Hancock, Don Hancock's wife, told her that he had gone to get his gun from Grant's Patch, Hancock's mining lease. Hancock did not actively cooperate with police.

** In 2006, at an inquest into Grierson's death, the coroner stated that there was a body of evidence to indicate Hancock 'may have been the shooter', although the Gypsy Jokers had 'a large number of enemies'. He said he was unable to determine the identity of the shooter as the police had not conducted routine forensic tests, nor searched Hancock's home.

UGLY

Boom.

It killed them both outright.

They later found both Hancock and Lewis were armed. At this point, Hancock had been retired from the force for a very long time. And that's when they uncovered just how corrupt he was. He stitched up the Mickelberg brothers, dumped them for some gold bullion.* And there was plenty more. I wish I could have done Hancock in myself. I feel bad about Lou Lewis, though. He didn't deserve it.

Sid Reid, or 'Snot',** as we knew him, rolled over when the cops questioned him. The little dickhead. He said Graham 'Slim' Slater was the mastermind behind the bombing. The cops said they'd keep Snot out of jail if he rolled over, but they still threw him behind bars. He pleaded guilty to the murders of Hancock and Lewis in the end. He also pointed the finger at another club member – Gary – for the killing of some drug dealer,† and he's serving time in prison now. He'll be out in the next couple of years. His lawyer reckons he was wrongly convicted because Snot lied. An investigation suggested Snot might have been the one who killed the drug dealer and set Gary up to take the fall.‡

---

* Ugly is referring to the Perth Mint Swindle from 1982, where it was found that Hancock and his colleague Tony Lewandowski fabricated evidence against the three Mickelberg brothers. After Hancock died, Lewandowski admitted to the fabrication. Subsequently, all three Mickelberg brothers had their convictions overturned. Lewandowski committed suicide in 2004 pending trial for perjury and other crimes.

** Sidney 'Snot' Reid had the dubious honour of being labelled 'Australia's Most Protected Prisoner' after testifying.

† While in custody, Reid accused Gypsy Jokers associate Gary White of the murder of drug dealer Anthony Tapley in August 2001. White ended up sentenced to twenty-two years' prison time. However, Reid's testimony is considered to be unreliable and there is fresh evidence from others who served time with Reid that may discount it.

‡ Operation Stirling was a 2012 top-secret investigation into the claims that Reid had set up White for the murder. There have been calls, since 2015, to reopen the investigation into whether Reid may have been lying in his testimony about White to get the three-year sentence reduction he received while in prison.

Snot ended up serving fifteen years.* And that was the reduced sentence he bargained for! Slim was found not guilty. Clearly nobody believed Snot in court. He sold out a fellow Joker for prison perks like a PlayStation and visits from his girlfriend. I'm sure fifteen years doesn't feel like a reduced sentence when you're in there.

To top it all off, someone firebombed the Ora Banda Hotel in 2019 and it burnt down. I don't know who did that. If it was anyone from the club, no one's told me about it and I haven't heard any rumours. I'm bloody curious, though.

•

In the middle all of this, around 2013, we gave our patch to the Gypsy Jokers in Norway. They were newly founded and had got in touch with other chapters with the intent of joining up officially. Travelling to Norway was one of the first big things I did once my parole was over.

We'd heard there were Gypsy Jokers in Scandinavia, but the Americans didn't want anything to do with them because there was some bad blood between the Norwegians and the Angels. At the time, Norway wore a patch of a skull wearing a three-pronged jester hat. I said that we should unite with them, got in touch and invited them out to Australia for one of our Christmas runs.

I could see some advantages in a union. Expanding the Joker family had always been a goal of mine and this was a chance to take it across the water into Europe. When they arrived, we

---

* As of April 2018, it was reported that Reid had been released from prison. His whereabouts are unknown and it is believed that he and his girlfriend have assumed new identities and are in the Witness Protection Program.

gave them bikes to ride. You've got to feel people out, give them space to breathe. Turned out they were top blokes. Everyone learns English in school over there, so we could all talk and laugh without any language barriers. We got on real well. After that, they said that were going to change over to our patch. They didn't have any problems with changing over, just as long as they were officially affiliated with the Gypsy Joker network.

'We've got to tell America,' I said.

They did that pretty quick. America then wanted to send over some people to Oslo in order to induct them in an official ceremony.

'I'll go,' said the American president, a bloke called Bob, 'and represent us.'

In that case, the boys said that I had to go as well. It made sense. I'd met everyone before and I was the boss here in Sydney. I was no longer the president, but I was still looked up to as an important figurehead. That's the respect given to old-timers. At least, that's the way it's supposed to be. Either way, it wouldn't have looked good if I didn't go in person.

The club wanted to pay for me, but I told them that I'd pay my own way. I wasn't getting the PTSD pension anymore, just the regular army pension, but I'd saved some money. At that stage, the club really needed every single cent, what with all the shit they had going on with Strike Force Raptor.

It took me two days to get there. I didn't know it was going to take so bloody long. When I arrived, exhausted, I was supposed to meet my mate Granno from the Outback chapter. He's another top member, trustworthy, a real good bloke. But I couldn't find him, so I went to the information desk. They told me his flight had to turn around.

'Why?' I asked.

Strike Force Raptor

Apparently, somebody had died on board. The plane had to turn around and take the body back. As a result, Granno was running about eighteen hours behind schedule. Not ideal. On top of that, I missed my flight from Oslo to Stavanger in the south-west of the country because the customs line was too long. I went to the Emirates desk and they got me on another flight later in the day.

By the time I eventually got to Stavanger, I was seven hours late and didn't have any phone numbers. I also couldn't get in touch with Granno at this point; he was stuck in the air somewhere. So there I was, hanging around the airport at Stavanger, and of course it was freezing. Six degrees below zero, and snowing! It wasn't a heavy downfall, just these little flakes, but I'd never felt cold like that. I thought, *Okay, I'll stay inside the airport. I'm not going out there in that.*

So I just sat there at the exit where all the arrivals come out, folded my arms and went to sleep. I figured if the Norwegians showed up, they'd see me right away, asleep on the bench, and it'd all be fine.

Next thing I know, a bloke kicked my leg.

'You Ugly?' he asked.

'Fucking oath, I am,' I said, still foggy.

'I'm Erik, from the Stavanger chapter,' he said. 'You're seven hours late.'

I told him I'd missed my flight. He took me back to the clubhouse, fed me some Maccas and a Coke, and gave me the lounge to sleep on.

'I'll be back tomorrow,' he said.

It was pitch dark. So with nothing else to do, I went to sleep.

They came back the next day and I explained what had happened. They were all apologies. Then Granno showed up, and everything was sweet as. Once all three of us – Granno, Bob and me – were there, we wheeled their new patches in on a trolley. The Norwegian blokes lined up.

'Righto, fellas,' Bob said. 'Who wants a patch?'

They all had their individual names on their patches. It was like we were the motorcycle club Santa Clauses. They didn't have a proper patch before we got there and gave them ours. It was a really good feeling. They put on food and drinks, but it was a closed party, so no girls, no hangarounds, just club members. We had a proper feast that night. As gifts, they gave us all patches for our vests, too. Granno and I got silver ones and Bob, the cunt, got a gold one, because he's from the foundational American chapter.

The next day, one of the Norway boys took me for a drive up the mountains in a Jeep. We flew down these winding roads at crazy speeds. The Scandinavians are rally champs and are used to it. Big chunks of frozen ice were tumbling onto the road. That's what I call cold.

'Fuck!' I yelled. 'What about all the ice on the roads?'

'Don't worry,' he said. 'We've got studs on our tyres.'

They don't use chains over there, they have special snow tyres with spikes on them. I'd never seen that before.

I wasn't in Norway long enough to work out if any of those fellas were good fighters, but they sure were all big enough. I invited them out to Australia again. We went on another ride and that was where I fell and broke my shoulder. As a joke, I dobbed them into their chapter. We laughed our arses off about that.

Travelling to the other side of the world for just two days is insane when I think about it now because it's such an endless trek to get there. When I arrived home, the customs bloke

Strike Force Raptor

looked at me and said, 'Why did you go all that way and only stay two days?'

I smiled at him and said, 'I was there for a christening.'

Which was true, in a roundabout sort of way, when you think about it.

•

Thanks to Strike Force Raptor, you can't really exist as a bikie in New South Wales anymore. If you're wearing a patch, the cops will pull you over and try to take it off you. If you give them any cheek, they'll red card your bike and then you can't get home. When that happens, you pretty much have to wait around until the coppers knock off shift and then you can get someone – a friend or a family member – to come and pick up your bike. They've made it so that you can't go anywhere, even if you aren't doing anything wrong. If they get wind of you turning up somewhere, they just show up and destroy everything.

Like Moudi Tajjour from the Nomads said, bikies are being forced to live in isolation because of these new laws. It's fucking wrong. Isolating people can kill them. I went over to Vietnam to fight for our so-called freedom from oppressive communism only to find we've got another version of it here now. I'm not allowed to associate with blokes I've known for forty-five years? They're good mates – my brothers – and now we're completely cut off from one another. What good does that do? What good does taking away people's social network do?

The coppers are currently trying to bring in a 'drink order', which basically means you won't be allowed to go to certain pubs if you're a bikie or if you're wearing any sort of bikie gear. It won't be the pub owner's fault – you can't blame them, really. If they let us in, they'll get fined up the arse. It won't be long until you're banned from going anywhere if you're caught wearing your bikie gear. If they catch you socialising with other bikies they'll send you to jail. Even a bottle-o like Dan Murphy's won't let you in if you're wearing club stuff. It's wrong. You can wear Harley-Davidson or Ducati gear, but if you've got anything to do with Gypsy Jokers or Hells Angels, you're screwed. That sounds like a communist attitude to me. The politicians have got their heads stuck up their arses with that sort of thinking. It only forces us underground, which is ultimately more dangerous.

Most people in bike clubs aren't doing anything illegal. They just like to go out riding their bikes. Enjoying the mateship and the freedom of the road. That's why we formed the clubs. Yeah, with the 1% stuff we live outside the social norm – we want to be able to say 'fuck you' if we feel like it – but really we just want to ride. Working on our bikes, getting in fights, drinking, shooting guns, that's all we want to do.

But riding bikes is what brought us all together in the first place.

We didn't bond over fixing them up. Being a mechanic was never really a part of it. Come to think of it, we didn't have any mechanics in the club, but we all knew how to look after our bikes. That was a must. The only time I can remember someone building a bike was Rick Pittard in 2018. He's dead now; got cancer, poor bugger. He wanted to do up an old Triumph, but he didn't have the right tools. He brought it round to my place and I said he could work on it as long as he covered it up at night so no one would try and nick any parts. He built that whole bike up. It was an absolute beauty.

Strike Force Raptor

But, like I said, being in a motorcycle club meant riding. Most of our runs were up and down the coast, or through the mountains, just enjoying being out in nature. We'd pull up, have a beer or three, camp overnight, then ride back. It's that simple. Not everyone's into nasty business. The ones who are into that are the ones who are getting us all in the shit.

I used to love riding. But not anymore. How can I? Every time I pull on my gloves and helmet I'm worried I'm going to get knocked over by some bastard copper from Raptor. A few years back I was shooting some TV stuff out on the highway with Paul Fenech, and I had on my patches and I thought, *Oh, fuck me, I'm gonna get pulled up.* Luckily a big truck was riding up my arse. *Good,* I thought, *no one will be able to see what I've got on!*

I know this makes me sound like a cranky old man, but it's true.

It's also true that I'm an old man, but that doesn't stop me being right!

•

Even at my age,[*] I'm still up for a fight if some dickhead wants to have a go. A while back, my son-in-law, Dion, and I were down the pub, sitting at a table outside, enjoying a few cold ones. It was a nice day, sun out and everything. There were some non-locals hanging around. Usually that's not an issue, but one of these blokes stumbled over and started talking shit and kind of dribbling – he was absolutely munted – before picking up Dion's beer and trying to walk off with it. Just like that.

'Oi,' I said. 'You can't fucking do that.'

---

[*] At the time of writing, Ugly was seventy-six.

UGLY

'So what?' he said back to me. Arrogant little shit.

He was half my age or less, in his thirties, I reckon, but I just got up and gave him one, two, three right there. All his mates jumped on me to stop me. Didn't matter. The little prick was already knocked out and on the floor. I wasn't going to go any further than that.

It probably shocked a few people that day; not everyone goes to the pub and expects to see a fight. And of course I don't advertise the fact that I used to box, so it's bound to be a bit of a surprise when this old fella gets up and knocks some dickhead out.

Yep, I've still got a nasty streak. But I never beat my missus.

10

The Jaded Old-Timer

The 1970s and 80s were good years to be in a motorcycle club. It wasn't until Milperra that it all got fucked up. Jock Ross and his shootout with the Bandidos changed everything. The police suddenly became very interested in what we were doing. Of course they did. Before that, we'd been a bit of a nuisance, but they more or less let us be. The public mostly thought we were all about charity runs and that sort of thing. But with bullets flying around pub car parks, blood being spilt and innocent people getting killed and injured, what else were the coppers going to do?

The Sydney Airport brawl between the Comancheros and Hells Angels was something else again. Bikies had never done that kind of thing in public before. We'd always tried to keep civilians well out of it. We wanted to keep that dark shit hidden away because it's no one's business. When you carry on in broad daylight in public, you make it *everyone's* business. But you're not some big-time gangster like on TV.

UGLY

You can't go and do that kind of shit and expect to get away with it.

In reality, you just go to jail. End of story.

It's not glamorous or cool, it's just ugly and the prize is a stretch inside.

Club life is essentially ruined. The way we used to just hang out and ride is over.

And it's not just in New South Wales. Nationally, it's not much better. In Queensland, our chapter can't ride with patches at all, and can only ride in threes or fours. In Adelaide, you can only ride around in twos. Any more than that and they'll pull you over. At least over there you're allowed to wear your patch. Melbourne's a bit better and you can ride down there without being constantly hassled. We had a poker run in Victoria not long ago which was good. The Melbourne coppers don't seem to have their heads up their arses quite so much. They're strict, but they're not stupid. They get that this type of Raptor shit just turns people into nasties; it pushes them underground and forces them into street gangs.

These days in New South Wales, the scene is all about street gangs with no patches. No traditions. The cops – and they've done this to themselves – have no idea who they should be keeping an eye on. And it's not just bikies, the coppers have used their powers to stop Islander rappers from performing because they had criminal records.[*] The cops said they'd pull venue licences if they didn't cancel shows, just like they do with pubs for bikies.

---

[*] This is in reference to the Western Sydney rap group OneFour who, in 2019, were forced to cancel their tour shows in Melbourne and Adelaide 'at the request of NSW Police' because 'the group's lyrics incite violence', as reported by Osman Faruqi for ABC News.

The Jaded Old-Timer

It's fucking communism.

And I shot communists.

That's the only thing I'm really dirty about when I look back on my life. Raptor has taken away our freedoms. If you ride down to Wollongong wearing a bike club patch, you're going to get pulled over and booked. You're stuck there on the side of the road with your bike. They'll even try to take your patch from you. That's not on. It feels like I'm unwelcome in my own country. It's the second time in my life I've been made to feel that way. Being told not to wear your patch in public was like being told not wear your uniform when I returned from Vietnam.

I've had coppers barge into my house, spot some piece of Gypsy Jokers memorabilia and then just nick it. Just like that! I'm not breaking the law by possessing club mementoes, but they'll make some excuse about it being 'illegal paraphernalia' and swipe it. And why? What purpose does that serve? It's exactly what it was like being in prison. You're stripped of your identity. Stripped of your possessions. I think they want us to feel like we're already in prison.

'What else?' I want to scream at them. 'Are you going to take the shirt off my fucking back, too?'

They would if they could. Cops these days are ruthless. They lie, cheat and steal worse than we ever did. Their powers are unchecked. And the law protects them.

I saw a Facebook post the other day showing a bunch of Raptor coppers standing in a line proudly displaying all the Hells Angels patches they'd pinched. What right do they have to take those? It's not a crime to own a patch. They're just pieces of material! The coppers think they're doing the public a favour, but they're not. They haven't got a clue how these new fellas operate and how this kind of thing will force them to behave.

UGLY

If they want to drive us underground, then what they're doing is perfect. There'll be no more uniforms, no patches, no nothing.

Everything will be done in secret.

But they don't really care about that. Not so long as they can have their little photo-ops and bust a few heads, throw a few low-level dickheads in prison after a different low-level dickhead snitches on them. They'll drive a wedge between us, sure, but all it's likely to do is make everyone less trusting. And more violent.

•

One of the best things about the Gypsy Jokers was the respect we had for each other. You stuck by your brothers no matter what. We'd fight by each other's side and would always try to break up a fight – unless someone was being an arsehole, and then they deserved what they got. It's just my old boxing way. Just put 'em up and get in there. That's what real friends do; they stick by you. The Gypsy Jokers were like family to me. It was like having bodyguards for brothers; they'd always go to bat for you, and you'd always go to bat for them.

There's a bloke out of Outback who's teaching young ones how to box. One of the girls he's teaching won a gold title in Australia. A real big award. He's got lots of kids training with him now, and that's important to me. It all started with boxing, and it's nice to see that tradition being carried on. He got his training regime off me, back from when I used to have the gym. Boxing was a big part of my life and I'm glad others are taking it up, because it really does help develop your brain as well as your body.

Boxing helped me and I'm glad it's helping other people, too.

The Jaded Old-Timer

That said, I don't train much now. I've got a fridge too nearby, and it calls out to me: 'Phil! Phil!' That's my trouble; alcohol and food. You won't find much of a six-pack on me anymore, but who needs abs? I prefer a different kind of six-pack these days.

The problem with a lot of modern clubs is that these young blokes are only interested in acting like gangsters, selling drugs and making money – and it's all for themselves. I've always been against that. Back in the old days, we'd just get a few longnecks, ride out to the boondocks and shoot the shit. Now it's selfish. All these guys are fighting over drug money. I don't like that one bit. I'm an old pisshead, but I'm not a junkie.

A young member called me that once, 'an old pisshead', after I'd had a go at him.

'Yeah, I like that,' I said. 'I am a pisshead, but at least I'm not a cokehead!'

I'm pretty sure there are some blokes who have brought hard drugs into the Jokers now. I don't know if it's all the chapters, so I can only talk about mine. And I'll tell anyone who'll listen that I hate that shit. I'm sure they're sick and tired of hearing it, but that doesn't stop me. There have been a fair few arguments about it.

I'm disappointed my legacy has come to that. The Lebanese gangs deal big time and buy all these fancy motorbikes and cars with their drug money. I never wanted us to be like that. We weren't into that shit. We liked the bikes for the bikes, for the sake of riding them, the machinery, not because of how much they cost. Not because they were some sort of status symbol. When I started up the club, half, or more than half, of the Jokers put their bikes together themselves. These new guys join because they want the protection of the name – which they get – but they don't really give two shits about the bikes.

UGLY

Even though I'm no fan of some of the younger types joining the club, I do get on well with a lot of the members, like my mate Tubbs. He got his nickname because he's a big bloke. He plays the mouth organ in a band, and he's got a real set of lungs. They'd use the clubhouse to rehearse in, and we'd always try and get them to practise on a Friday night so we could have a party as well.

But, like I said, there are members I have no time for.

One of them is a former president, Lucky. Back when he was in charge, he and an ex-member, Fruit – short for Fruitcake, who was a sergeant at the time – sent me down for a meeting with the Bandidos. I knew the Bandido boys and the Jokers were on pretty good terms. This was around 2014 or 2015.

'I need you to go meet them,' Lucky said. 'They've got some turbos for sale and we wanna buy some.'

I knew exactly what he meant by 'turbos'.

So I drove down to the Bandido tattoo parlour in Parramatta and parked around the back. Next thing I knew, everyone started running around in a panic. I got out of the car and they came up to me, not exactly friendly-like, and gestured for me to go inside.

'Have a seat in there, Ugly,' one of them said.

It wasn't really a question, but it was fine with me. This was their place. I sat down and waited. I didn't have to wait long. In came the president and stood in front of me. He was surrounded by his fellow members, who all had guns poking out of their belts.

Well, that was a surprise.

'What's going on?' I said, pointing at them.

'What are you doing here?' the president asked.

The Jaded Old-Timer

'Lucky and Fruit sent me down here to buy some turbos.'

He stared at me for a minute. He looked me up and down, then said, 'Don't you know what happened the other night at our clubhouse?'

'No. What happened?'

'Fruit and Drew punched the shit out of the whole bar. *Our* bar.'

Well, this was news to me. Not that they *wouldn't* do something like that – remember, this was the same Drew who the fellas had sent up with me from Summernats to deal with Brett Driscoll – but I was surprised Lucky and Fruit hadn't said anything about it when they sent me over.

I started thinking that they'd set me up.

'I wouldn't be sitting here like this if I'd known about any of that,' I said. 'Do you think I'm that dumb?'

They searched me, just to make sure, but I was clean – no weapon, no recorder, nothing. After that it was like everyone let out a collective breath.

'Christ Almighty,' the president said. 'Your club's got to get communications going.'

Too fucking right, I thought.

I left there none the worse for wear and drove straight back to our clubhouse. I was in a state. That sort of 'communication breakdown' gets people fucking killed. It's no laughing matter. It had honestly never occurred to me to play the game like that. I've always been straight up with people if I have a problem with them. Sending me in hoping someone else takes care of your problem? That's weak shit.

I told Fruit what had happened and he just laughed. Lucky wasn't there, he'd gone away to some drag racing event.

UGLY

Not content with Fruit's response, I brought it up at the next club meeting. Unfortunately, because Lucky and Fruit had a lot of allies, they all laughed it off, like it was no big deal.

'You shouldn't have gone in the first place,' Paranoid said. 'You should have had more fucking sense.'

'But what about what they've done?' I growled. 'Starting shit, messing up their bar, then sending me in like that.'

They didn't see it as a problem. That told me a lot about some of the blokes in the club then. The vibe had definitely changed.

I stayed a member of the Jokers, but after that I pulled back a bit. It hurt.

That lack of respect, that lack of caring, felt like a punch in the face.

Walking away from this thing I'd built, that had been my whole life for forty-odd years, was bloody hard. It's *still* hard. It was like leaving behind family. Me, Browny and Wally, the old sergeant-at-arms, we're all old pissheads. We're not used to how drugs make people act. And we were never in it for the money. We didn't play games like some of these younger blokes do. We'd just go out and party, no animosity among us, and just have a good time.

It doesn't happen so much now. They're young and we're old, that's all they see. They've pushed us out, pushed us around, because they're the new crop and they think their way is best, even if it isn't.

There's nothing else to do but let it go, really.

•

For ages after the incident at the Bandidos' tattoo parlour, I kept trying to think of why Lucky would have done it. What had

The Jaded Old-Timer

I done that struck him as so wrong that he wanted to pull that kind of shit on me? Why would he send me into something that could have been really bad, not just for me, but for the whole club? It could have brought us a lot of unwanted attention and heat.

Then it hit me.

A few months earlier, before all that shit went down, we'd got a few new hangarounds – six young blokes – who were keen on joining the club. What they weren't keen on was the drag racing that Lucky kept making everyone watch. Most of us weren't that interested. Watching drag racing ended up feeling like one of those office bonding exercises that bosses make their employees do!

A few of these young blokes were a bit more like me. They didn't want to go to the drag racing, they wanted to go out partying, go for a ride, maybe sit by a fire, talk shit and knock back a few longnecks. I thought to myself, *Well, why don't I just take them to do that instead?*

I went to see Lucky the next day. 'If it's all right, Lucky, I might start up a little chapter over in Fairfield. I've got a house and we can go there on Saturday nights and get a bit of a fire going.'

Well, he did not like that one bit.

'No!' he yelled. 'You're not gonna start up another chapter! I'm the only president here and I don't need another.'

'I'm not gonna be a president,' I said to him. 'I'm just gonna be, like, a manager. Something like that. We'll go out on a Saturday night, ride out into the bush or whatever, you know, do a bit more outdoorsy kind of stuff.'

'No fucking way. That'll split the club.'

'No, it won't,' I said, but I knew it was over. Lucky was an autocratic sort of leader and thought I was trying to start a splinter group to drive a wedge into his power and authority over the club. It probably didn't help that, when he was campaigning for president, I supported someone else.

Lucky was arrested by Raptor a few years ago, but he didn't end up going to jail. It looked like he was set to do some serious time, but somehow he got off. One good thing that came out of it was that he stopped being president and now someone else is in charge.

After the Bandidos incident at the tattoo parlour, I only wished Lucky bad luck. And it looked like I got my wish when, not long ago, he ran into a tree in his car. I don't know if it was by accident or on purpose, but it doesn't bother me one bit.

•

Just because I'm out of prison, it doesn't mean I'm free of my association order. The anti-bikie laws mean I'm still not supposed to hang out with people from the club scene. Years and years on, the coppers still think they have the right to keep me apart from people I've known the longest in my life. When I go to see the boys for rides – which I still do – I get warnings from little birdies that the coppers know we're about to associate and so I head off and hide for a bit until they fuck off. It's good to have a little menagerie of birds; you never know when one might come in handy.

If only one had let us know what was going to happen in 2017.

No one likes it when the cops are called to a party, especially the Gypsy Jokers. We were all lined up to have a shindig – we had about fifty blokes come over on a ride from the Outback and we were in the mood to celebrate – when somehow the cops got wind of it. It's not like we were planning anything

The Jaded Old-Timer

illegal, but because of the way Raptor works, they knew they could swoop in and do whatever they wanted. We don't have the resources to take them to court. And what judge in this country is going to say, 'Yeah, you did this big group of bikies wrong'? Not a single one.

Anyway, we were getting ready for the party when someone went outside to grab another case of beer from the truck. He immediately came running back inside.

'Cops!' he yelled.

I was with Lyn at home at the time because she was having a bit of a day on the dialysis machine. Skye and her husband, Dion, had left the kids with us, so we were swamped, otherwise I would have been at the clubhouse helping the boys get ready for the party. Once again, my luck served me well.

After that, from what I heard, everyone just waited for the cops to enter. They knew it was pointless to try to run off or fight them. There was nothing they could really do at that point, surrounded as they were. So they waited until the cops came barging in, looking like a military squad – which is what they pretend to be, because that's how we treat them, how we arm them – yelling and screaming and waving their guns.

In the end, four Jokers were arrested and charged with possessing an unspecified quantity of drugs and ammunition. They took two of our antique rifles. Mostly, though, all they got was a shitload of booze. They found very little drugs, probably a couple of blokes with a few joints and some meth for themselves and mates at the party – no more than you'd find at any uni student piss-up – but we had a lot of alcohol on hand, because, as I've said, that's my poison and we were having a party.

I bet those coppers had themselves a nice little time afterwards, the bastards.

They also issued some defect notices and traffic infringements, which meant that a few of those Outback blokes were fucked. Some of their bikes were stuck, and the bloke with the beer truck got fined for not having a valid licence, which was bullshit.

This is what a lot of cops spend their time – and taxpayer money – doing these days. They get paid to run around and play nanny to a bunch of old mates who just want to have a party. Think of that time you were out and someone had a joint, or a couple of pills. The cops aren't going to show up and bust you. It's a thin line.

After that raid, some of the Outback boys stopped by my place. We bought some grog and were sitting round the side of the house having a nice old chat, when Lyn came home with my daughters after doing the shopping. She looked at us sitting there and had a go at me.

'Look at you, sitting around getting on the piss,' she said. 'And he won't give me money for shopping!'

She was joking of course, so I had a good laugh, and so did some of the Sydney boys, but one of the Outback blokes reached into his wallet!

'Here you are, love,' he said, and handed her a hundred dollars, just like that.

'You can't do that,' I said. 'Take it back.'

'No, no,' he said. 'I'm happy to fix that up.'

They take money seriously in Outback, like I said before, because they're so well set up. They always have cash on hand, and they're keen on helping out other club members. Otherwise, what's the point in having the money? My legacy is being upheld by the Outback boys, which makes me feel good, but it's sad that my home club in Sydney isn't really doing the same.

The Jaded Old-Timer

There's some distance between me and the Sydney blokes compared to the closeness and unity of the Outback boys.

That brings me down a little bit, because the brotherhood was the whole point.

•

In 2017, while on a ride at Mt Hotham in Victoria, I came off my bike and did my shoulder in. That was the beginning of the end of me on two wheels.

Not long after, we were riding along the motorway in St Marys. A club member named Chad Hogg had been up all night doing who-knows-what and was totally off his face. He rammed right up the back of my bike and sent me sprawling onto the road. It knocked me out cold – as well as knocking out my front teeth. I had my helmet on, but I still cut up the top of my head. I spent the night in St George Hospital getting X-rayed. Luckily, I have the army pension, so they took care of all the bills.

'Nothing's wrong with you,' the doctor said. 'But you are full of arthritis.'

'Well, I know that!'

After that accident, I couldn't really ride anymore. That cut me pretty hard. My bones just can't take it. And I started getting dizzy spells. To cheer me up, the club pooled some money and got me a trike. That's what I ride now. A big, black 2018 Harley-Davidson that lives in the shed behind my place. Rob, a mate of mine who runs a bottle shop, was one of the donors. The Outback chapter put up a chunk of money, too. Unfortunately, I can't really ride the trike with the boys – thanks to the association order – and have to arrive half an hour before everyone else.

UGLY

The year after Chad Hogg sent me sprawling onto the highway at St Marys, he kidnapped his girlfriend and took her back to the clubhouse. He tied her up and proceeded to shave off her hair and slap her around a bit.

He kept her there for two fucking days.

Eventually she managed to escape and call the cops. When they found out she'd been held captive at the Gypsy Jokers clubhouse, they immediately sent in their armed squad and arrested him. The place became an official crime scene, and then they made it a restricted premises. No one with a criminal record could go there, and the cops didn't need a warrant to search the place for drugs, alcohol or weapons. They could just waltz in and turn the joint upside down as they pleased. It was like they owned it.

After that, I couldn't go anywhere near the place. Half the members couldn't go down there. A record hangs over you like that. Even though it's been years since I was in jail, I still have a consorting order dangling over my head. It basically means I'm not allowed to associate with known criminals.

It was the excuse that the Raptor bastards were looking for.

They'd raided us a few times but all they ever found was a few drugs and a boatload of booze. But now, thanks to Chad's dumb stunt, they had a reason to restrict entry to the clubhouse. They even made it so that they could seize anything that could *store* alcohol. No more parties, then.

We don't have a new clubhouse and so we just meet at different people's houses now. We rent out the old clubhouse because we still officially own it, but we no longer use it for club stuff. We can't. A waste disposal person is making use of it at the moment. It's not much, but it helps pay the mortgage. I don't know what the future holds on that front, but it won't be something that I'll be dealing with.

The Jaded Old-Timer

Chad's in remand at Parramatta Jail and I'd say he'll be there for a little while yet before his trial comes up.* We were in the middle of taking Raptor to court over that raid where they took all of our grog when he kidnapped his girlfriend. The booze wasn't even in the clubhouse, it was in a van out the front. It was for a party but they just came up and nicked it. They had no right. We took them to court and filed a harassment claim because there was nothing to justify the raid.

But it was over in seconds. The magistrate just said, 'Raptor's favour.'

'There's no use doing any more,' I said to the boys after that. 'It's not gonna work.'

So that was that. We never got anything back.

But at least we tried.

•

Despite being on good terms with the Veterans up at Murrurundi, there was a time, a couple of years ago, when things turned sour. I'd served in Vietnam with the president, a bloke named Tower, so called because he's fucking seven feet tall. When I left the army, he stayed on and became an MP. We always had that kind of friendship where you joke with each other and talk shit.

One time, me and a couple of Jokers went up to Murrurundi to have a drink at the Veterans clubhouse. It was just before

---

* Chad Hogg was officially sentenced in February 2021 over the kidnapping and assault of his girlfriend. He was due to stand trial in November 2020, but it was halted after Hogg entered a guilty plea. He read a letter to the court, apologising for his 'foolish and cowardly' behaviour during his sentencing, although the Crown Prosecutor argued there was no insight to the apology, and that it was purely derived from 'being caught'. He has been jailed for a minimum of four years and will be eligible for parole in 2022.

their annual general meeting where they were holding a vote for president. We walked in and sat down at the bar. Tower was there, too, and I leant over and said with a smile, 'You've got a few against you out there.'

'Oh, yeah?' he said. 'Who?'

'Top secret,' I said, still smiling. I was just fucking with him, so I kept on drinking. And smiling.

Anyway, they had their meeting and Tower was elected as president by one single vote. The bloke he was running against was a mate of mine, and, after Tower won, he had this fella walking around picking up ashtrays and doing all sorts of menial shit.

Then Tower came up to me and got real serious.

'Right,' he said. 'Now tell me, who were the people who were against me?'

'I can't tell you that. What do you want to know for, anyway?'

'I wanna give 'em shit jobs!'

'What you should do is be making friends with 'em. Not turning them against you.'

The truth was I didn't know anyone who voted against him, I was just stirring him up. But after the vote, because he didn't glide into office on a landslide, he figured there really were some rats in the ranks.

'Righto,' he said to me. 'You've lost all your privileges up here. You're not welcome. You stay outside the wire from now on.'

He was referring to the fencing outside the clubhouse. But the military implication was not lost on me. As you can imagine, I was stunned. We'd been mates for so long, and the clubs were so close, that it felt mad.

'Oh, really?' I said. 'You can go fuck yourself.'

The Jaded Old-Timer

I walked out and told myself I'd never go back again. And I haven't. Treating me like that, after everything, was just not on. Just because of some dumb bit of fun, Tower decided that I was banned. I was only giving him shit the same way he gives it to everyone else, but he took it way too seriously. He took himself way too seriously. And he was the president, so he could do as he wanted. He's still the president now.

He's since tried to invite me back, pretending like nothing ever happened, but I told him I wouldn't be going, and reminded him of what he'd done. He's sent apologies, and photographs of us together, but I'm not having a bar of it. It was an over-the-top reaction. There was no need.

I've scrubbed him from my life.

I haven't scrubbed the Veterans, mind you, but I've decided that while Tower's president, I'll never go back to Murrurundi.

For Vietnam Veterans Day, I usually present a regiment book to the local library in Murrurundi, through the Veterans club, because I was in a regiment. We do it up at the memorial there. But after our fallout, Tower got Rusty from the Gladiators to present it. Rusty knew full well that this was my tradition.

'Sorry, mate,' Rusty said to me. 'I got no say in it.'

'No worries, mate. Not you. It was him.'

I don't forgive easily. You want to shit on me? I'll keep it in mind. I've got other friends who are nice to me.

I wrote Tower a note that just said, 'Once a copper, always a copper'. It felt like shit, like he'd pretended to be my friend.

•

Sometime around 2011, Greg King introduced me to Pauly Fenech. Pauly was shooting a show called *Housos* and Greg said that he needed a bunch of real bikies to act as a fake club, the Sunnyvale Hunters MC. I thought that'd be fun, especially after the time I had doing *Aunty Jack*. There was a casting session and Greg brought me in and I met Pauly. We chatted and I guess he liked the look of me because he ended up casting me as one of the recurring bikies throughout the series and movie. That was fun, just hanging out with my mates, being on TV and making a little bit of cash. And it was easy playing the role; I just stared at people and growled. Occasionally, I got in a fake punch-on. I may or may not have slipped a couple of real punches in there, just to keep the others on their toes.

At one point, Pauly said he needed a big crew of bikies for a scene.

'Probably something like fifteen. Can you help me out?'

'Yeah,' Greg said. 'I can arrange something.'

Well, Greg, the cheeky bastard that he is, said to me fifteen wasn't enough.

'He wants bikies,' he said. 'I'll give him bikies.'

Greg made two phone calls and over a hundred bikies showed up the next day. Pauly arrived in his car and you could just see his face through the driver's-side window. His jaw was on the floor.

A mate of Greg's got busted under Raptor, and this newbie cop who clearly hadn't seen the show came running out holding up two patches. One was the Finks and the other was the Hunters MC.

'This bloke's in *two* clubs!' he said.

•

The Jaded Old-Timer

I don't want anyone thinking that just because I'm old now – and made it further than most of the blokes who came up alongside me – I don't have any fight left in me. If someone wants to start some shit, I'm ready to give it right back to them. As ready as I ever was when I was a young bastard. I long for the old days sometimes, to go out on rides, get out into the scrub and go to a country pub. Half the country pubs won't let us in anymore, because of the patch. We have to buy all the bottles we can and sit in a park. Sitting or lying in the bush or in a park is a bit more difficult for me now. My knees are buggered. I keep a cane attached to the trike because I need it to help me stand up when I'm down.

A little while back, the boys and I were on a country run, heading north, when we stopped off in Cowra in the Central West of New South Wales for a beer at the local. I don't remember if it was the Australian, the Imperial or the Cowra. Because it had been a long ride, I wasn't in the best mood, and my limp was aggravated by it. I needed my stick to walk.

Well, some would-be, could-be local who was hanging around the bar decided, after seeing me come in with the boys, limping on my cane, that he'd be a smart guy.

'Looking strong there, mate,' he said, laughing and turning to the barman. 'Can you even ride straight?'

Like I said, I was in no mood for this. I walked up to him and whacked him as hard as I could over the head with my stick. He tumbled to the floor, grabbing his head, but my cane had split in two.

'Fuck,' I said. 'Now what?'

One of the boys, I don't remember who – might have been Tubbs or Chug – walked me over to the Chinese restaurant across the road. He asked them for some chopsticks. We put them either side of the snap in the cane – like a splint – and used some gaffer tape to keep it all together. It's just like new.*

And ready to wrap around the skull of the next dickhead who wants to be a smart-arse!

It makes me feel old, that sort of shit. Body breaking down, needing a cane. Not a lot of my mates made it to my age. I didn't think I'd make it this far. Pretty sure there were a few hoping I wouldn't, either, but I showed them. The only other one is Stewie, who's a year older than me. He'll turn seventy-seven in March 2021. I was going to send him a card, but I think I might give him a call instead and give him some shit.

The only other fellas who are my age either left the club or died. People can leave the club if they want to. If they leave on good terms, as friends, they're still allowed to stop by for a drink, or come on runs, but they can't hang around all the time. If they do, we kind of put the bounce on them.

What's the point of leaving if you're going to be hanging around all the time? If you are, you might as well be a dues-paying member. Some leave on bad terms, but not that often. If that happens, it's more like, 'Get the fuck out of here and, if we see you again, we'll bash you.' Usually, it's for stealing.

We had a problem a little while ago with that. There was a jukebox up at the clubhouse. You had to put coins into it to make it play a song. It was just another way to get a bit of cash for the club funds. Problem was, the count on the money was always coming up short. So we set a trap. We painted some of the coins on one side and put them in the jukebox, that way

---

* *Author's note:* During the writing of this book, Ugly sent me a text message with a photo of a new cane a friend of his had made for him in jail. It is jet black, with a hammer head as the handle, and it has the words 'UGLY STICK' written down the side.

The Jaded Old-Timer

if anyone came into the clubhouse with any of those painted coins, we'd know who was stealing.

Not long after we had this young member pay for a couple of beers. Can you guess with what? Painted coins. He was pinching money from the jukebox when he was alone in the clubhouse. He was stealing from the club. That's breaking rule number one.

As soon as we saw the painted coins on the bar, we jumped him.

We gave him a good thumping and one of the boys – I ain't saying who – grabbed a ball pein hammer and smashed up his knuckles, right there on the floor of the clubhouse. After he'd had his knuckles broken, and we'd given him a few clips over the ears, we tossed him out the front gate. We took his bike off of him, too, just for good measure.

He was lucky to get out alive.

People could be killed for stealing from the club – remember Guitar Zaan – but usually they end up getting bashed. In South Australia you might end up down a mineshaft. In Outback you end up going fishing. I haven't heard of anyone ever getting killed lately, but it's a risk. Why do jail time over a thief? A hammer to the knuckles does the job.

If a member does something like that, we're done with them. We don't go after them anymore. That thief got a pretty bad bashing, so he's not likely to come back for more. His father got upset and wanted to call the coppers on the club. A couple of blokes went round to his place and told him what had happened, what his son had done. They said that if he was going to stick up for him after that, then he was going to cop the same. Old mate said he was disappointed in his son.

'How about we say he fell off a bike?' one of our blokes said.

'Yeah,' the father replied. 'He fell off a bike.'

Good thing he agreed, because otherwise he would have fallen off the same fucking bike.

•

Strike Force Raptor coppers raided the clubhouse a few weeks into 2021, but they didn't find anything besides some old rubbish bins and storage containers. There's no Joker stuff there anymore. And they haven't been around to my place for almost a year now.* Last time they paid me a visit – there were two of them, one older and one younger – they gave me that same song and dance about red carding the bike, and the tow truck and our car. It all took place at the front door because I wouldn't let them in. They could have forced it, but they didn't. They don't even need a warrant to enter your house if you've got a criminal record. It's bloody authoritarian.

'What are you coming round to see me for?' I asked them.

'We're coming to see you because you're a habitual criminal,' said the older copper.

I just smiled at him, slowly. That kind of thing makes me feel rebellious, makes me want to spit in the face of authority. But I was in no mood to get arrested.

The young copper, wanting to show off that he was tough, went, 'If I catch you on the road wearing your patch, I'll pull you over and take it off you.'

I turned to him. I could see by the old copper's face that he knew what I was going to say. 'Well, then you'll have two fights on your hands. One to try and take me patch, and the other in court.'

---

* Correct at the time of writing, in March 2021.

The Jaded Old-Timer

I'm sure they have it in for me because I killed a copper's brother. They're just the Big Blue Gang, as Arthur Veno called them.* Biggest gang in the country.

•

Despite my complaints, life is all right now. I have Lyn and the kids. I have my memories. We lived big, the Jokers and me. I won't lie, it hurts how much the old ways have been corrupted, not just by the cops, but by all the young dickheads who want to be big-time gangsters like on TV. Real life isn't like that. The way we did things? It wasn't fucking *Sons of Anarchy*. That show is full of shit. All that killing each other and other people. We tried to avoid that at all costs. Getting involved in that kind of palaver just draws attention to you; look at what happened after the incidents at Milperra and Sydney Airport.

Sons of Anarchy is fake. We don't do those big drugs and guns runs. They might think the Americans are like that, but the American Jokers aren't. It's sensationalised. It's mostly just a bunch of normal blokes who don't want desk jobs, don't want to conform to society, who work in trades and pay their dues that way. Chug's a carpenter, does mostly wood flooring now. A top bloke from the club, Dwarf – tough little bastard – took up hot air balloon hiring up in Newcastle. Weird, right? But hey, it's work!

That even went for the coppers. They used to leave us alone – except when they got a bug up their arse about us, for one reason or another – and we could just do our own thing,

---

* Arthur Veno had a chapter in his book *The Brotherhoods* that was titled 'The Big Blue Gang' and was about how bikies see the police.

UGLY

fighting and partying and riding our bikes. Until Avatar and Raptor and all those squads, the cops and the clubs tolerated each other.

We just wanted to be left alone to ride our bikes.

And of course that's what really started it all: the bikes.

Since I was a kid, all there was – besides boxing – was motorbikes. The freedom of riding down the road, the wind on your face. It was also about living outside of everyone else's bullshit. They didn't want anything to do with us vets when we got back from Vietnam, so I didn't want anything to do with them – or the army for that matter. Why would I want to fit into their mould when, after all I'd fucking been through, they wanted me to hide the fact that I'd served? That I'd fought off communism, fought for my country and come back in one piece; that I'd done it all for Australia.

So I built my own civilian army. If I had to do it all over again, I wouldn't change a thing. I'd try and stop a few folks from dying, but can you ever really do that? Happens all the time. I went to places, met people, I never would have if it hadn't been for the Jokers. I lived the way I wanted to. How many people can say that?

Knowing what I know now, I'd probably have been smarter about a few things, but, if I had my way, things wouldn't have been much different than they were. Like I said, I never got into this for the money, or the drugs, or whatever it is the young blokes are after these days. I just wanted something, somewhere, that was mine.

It took them fifty years, but the army finally gave me a Gallantry Citation for the things I'd done in Vietnam. It's hanging on my wall now, and I look at it every time I go to sleep. My dog tags hang inside the frame as well. Vietnam wasn't the easiest time,

The Jaded Old-Timer

but the recognition is important to me. I fought and bled for my country and I deserved my citation, just like everybody else. And just like every other time in my life, I had to fight for it. But I got it. I was even on the front page of the *Canberra Times* carrying the Third Battalion flag in 2019.

Despite everything that happened with Major Martin, I liked my time in the army. The mates I made there were mates for life and they're still good mates now. We still go to the Civic Hotel, near Central Station, and have a few beers and talk about old times. Pauly Fenech has met them, too, and they all get along well. Barclay is still around, but he's going blind, the poor bugger. He's around eighty or eighty-one now.

It feels like the meaning behind being 1% has changed. That's rotten. The drugs are a real problem. I was always against it but it felt like I couldn't do anything to stop it coming in and taking over. It seems to me that, for a lot of blokes these days, wearing the 1% patch only means being a crim, selling drugs and making a profit. The part I hate most is that us old blokes are tarred with the same brush. But most of us aren't into drugs.

Back when we started, if we needed to make some money for the club, we'd just throw a keg party, charge everyone five or six dollars for entry, and that was it. Any profits after paying off the kegs went into the club coffers. Now, it's like all I hear about is blokes wanting to sell as many drugs as possible. Such-and-such might be dealing, such-and-such got arrested for it, such-and-such is on the news for it. And I feel guilty that that's where it's all led to, that it's happened that way. The young blokes have come in and gangsterised it. It's turned me right away, driven me and the club apart, especially after the Lucky and Fruit bullshit. When I told the South Australian blokes about it, they were shocked. They couldn't bloody believe it. Jokers stick together, always. Or so I thought.

There are reasons to have hope, though.

Some of the young blokes, like Tubbs, give me hope. The new president gives me hope too. He's a good bloke and he's running the club well. It makes me think that maybe the kind of club that I started, the life that I lived and loved, still has a place in the future. He's a younger type, not one of us oldies, but he gets it. Even though we're not supposed to be doing anything official, he's still holding meetings. We've gone underground because of the coppers. They don't want us to run at all, but we are. Things are moving forward more or less as normal. We still wear patches when we're in twos and threes, but bigger groups attract too much attention. I reckon I couldn't do any better a job than the current president. He's doing the best he can, and that's good enough for me.

Of all the things in my life, I'm probably most proud of starting the Gypsy Jokers. Even though I technically started the club without permission – unbeknown to me – I went over to America and sorted that out and now we're a part of an international brotherhood. Without the Gypsy Jokers, I can't imagine what my life would have been like. What would I have done with myself? Would I still be making fucking shoes, like I was before the army? Would I be training boxers? Or would I have just been some crim, some bloke with anger issues beating up his wife?

The Jokers gave my life structure. And they gave me respect.

As weird as it might seem to some people, they also gave me purpose. We all look for something like that, don't we? Some find it in normal society, in following the letter of the law and getting a white-collar job, going up the pub with your mates on

The Jaded Old-Timer

Friday nights, and spending the weekend with the family. Well, the Jokers and I had way more in common with them than those people like to think. We just went about it all a different way.

Like I said to Major Gary Martin just before finishing my tour of Vietnam, I'd start my own army.

And I did.

Afterword

Being immersed in Ugly's world for so long was fascinating. I hope the stories in this book have helped people understand a different point of view on life, even if they don't necessarily agree with the choices made or the opinions expressed. Everyone's experience of life is different.

Since I started writing this book, Strike Force Raptor has been in the news again. Greens New South Wales MP David Shoebridge called elements of the New South Wales Police Force 'lawless' after it was found out that a Strike Force Raptor senior officer ordered two police to intimidate a solicitor. The solicitor in question was to represent a client who was involved in a case against Raptor.

The events were summarised in a series of tweets:

> The police waited outside the solicitor's home early in the morning then twice stopped his car, issued infringement notices and defects, as he drove to town. He took his car

home and caught a taxi. The police followed and stopped the taxi too.

They then waited on the street outside his office before the hearing and followed him to court. He was so shaken he told the magistrate what happened and had the case adjourned. None of this is disputed [by the way].

As he left the court between five and ten Strike Force Raptor officers were outside and he was so intimidated he went back inside and asked the magistrate if he could exit [by] the rear door. The magistrate let him. He told his client he better not act for him because of this.

Police then defected his motorcycle the next day (he was riding his bike because his car was off the road due to earlier police action). Did I mention this was all intentional intimidation directed by a senior (now retired apparently) police officer[?]

End result is no one has been charged with attempting to pervert the course of justice, intimidation or anything (other than the solicitor who paid one of the fines). This is seriously lawless behaviour by a number of police acting in concert and it's close to unbelievable.

This was all detailed in a recent report by the Law Enforcement Conduct Commission (LECC) in March 2021. This story lends credence to the behaviour previously ascribed by Ugly to officers from Strike Force Raptor. It is worth having a look at the report for further information.

Afterword

Following this afterword is a series of articles and books that were either referenced by Ugly, or used by me as research. A lot of the things Ugly discusses are matters of public record, so it may be of interest to others to seek out more detailed information on these events. Obviously, while I was able to relay some information regarding Ugly's personal experience, or second-hand tales from friends, there is information that is beyond the scope of Ugly's knowledge, and therefore beyond the scope of this book.

I hope you all enjoyed this read and thank you for coming on this journey with me through Ugly's life. And remember, always carry a mouthguard!

Jordan King-Lacroix, March 2021

Acknowledgements

Paul Fenech

Thanks to Mathew Bowie and Andrew Taylor for their help in making this book happen.

Jordan King-Lacroix

I'd like to thank Paul Fenech first of all for bringing me this fascinating project. It's not every day that something like this falls into your lap. I'd like to thank Lauren Finger, who did the initial edits and structural report on this book, without whom it would not be nearly as neat and tidy as it is now. Your notes were not nearly as annoying as you were worried they might be. Huge thanks to Rod Morrison, who tightened up this read and made it hit with a punch. Thanks to Kathryn Knight and Alison Urquhart for helping me so much with this book and for being so patient with my initial bombardment of questions. You helped bring this thing to life and I'll always be thankful. An enormous thanks to Phil 'Ugly' Mawson, obviously, who welcomed me into his home multiple times while I sifted through his life for stories with a fine-toothed comb. And, of course, thanks to Lyn and Skye and Dion and the kids for letting me take up their time with him. I must thank Jannali Jones, who helped prepare me for what I had in store when writing a book and going through the editing process. Her experience made me ready and I thank her for sharing it with me. I want to thank my parents, Melanie and Serge, who've been extremely supportive and wonderful, as well as my amazing wife Alex, without whom I wouldn't have had the courage to do this. Finally, I want to thank Dinah and Morgan, who told me I was being dumb when I needed it the most.

Bibliography and Further Reading

ABC News, 'Bikie gang charged over May shooting', 17 August 2005.

ABC News, 'OMCG bikie clubhouse raided after violence between rival gangs', Chloe Hart and Jessica Clifford, 11 August 2018.

ABC News, 'Gypsy Joker bikie charged with allegedly holding ex-girlfriend captive at clubhouse', Mark Reddie and Antonette Collins, 19 September 2018.

ABC News, 'Popular YouTube rappers OneFour forced to cancel first national tour dates following police pressure', Osman Faruqi, 25 November 2019.

Adelaide Now, 'Anzac Day: Vietnam War veteran Robin Carbins talks about the battle of Coral-Balmoral in which 26 Anzacs were killed', Craig Cook, 23 April 2018.

The Age, 'Joker feared murdered', 2 July 2005.

Australian Missing Persons Register, 'Steven Charles Williams', 18 June 2005.

UGLY

Boxing Records (BoxRec.com) for Ali Afakasi, Charlie Costa and Phil Mawson.

Daily Mail Australia, 'Do you know your hangaround from your patch-over? Top-secret bikie dictionary is revealed as police try to put an end to the deadly turf war between Nomads and Finks gangs', Brianne Tolj and Charlie Moore, 20 April 2018.

Daily Mail Australia, 'Tough anti-bikie cop reveals how she made former Nomads boss back down and beg her to forgive him for insulting Instagram post about her appearance', Charlie Moore, 18 November 2019.

Daily Mail Australia, 'Feared Comanchero boss who was shot in the head and sentenced to life in prison for his role in the infamous Milperra Massacre now serves the community as a local firefighter', Zoe Zaczek, 26 April 2019.

Daily Mail Australia, '"Walk tall and f*** 'em all": Notorious crime boss Neddy Smith is refusing medication and just days away from death – a shadow of the 6'6" killer who was once the most feared criminal in the land', Stephen Gibbs, 9 October 2019.

Daily Mail Australia, 'Comanchero jailed for life over the infamous Milperra massacre "runs down a motorcyclist after five-minute road rage chase"', Stephen Gibbs, 1 June 2020.

Daily Mail Australia, 'Gypsy Joker bikie who taped a woman to a pole, choked her, shaved her head and taunted "I'm going to make you look ugly" is jailed after last-minute guilty plea', Kylie Stevens, 28 February 2021.

Daily Telegraph, 'Former Fourth Reich bikie and notorious paedophile Lester Mills claims Strike Force Raptor police stitched him up', 1 October 2017.

DinosMc.com, 'News Archives'; various news clippings on bikie cases.

Bibliography and Further Reading

FindAGrave.com, 'Gregory John "Haystacks" McDonald (1948–1991)', updated 27 March 2012.

The Herald Sun, 'Old-time bikies angry over public war', Arthur Veno, 16 April 2009.

HotCars.com, '24 things to know before joining a motorcycle club', 5 August 2018.

The Independent, 'Biker gang chief cleared in police murder case', Kathy Marks, 30 October 2003.

Law Enforcement Conduct Commission (LECC), 'Operation Monza: Report to parliament pursuant to section 132 Law Enforcement Conduct Commission Act 2016', March 2021.

New South Wales Supreme Court, REGINA v MAWSON [2007] NSWSC 1473, 14 December 2007.

New South Wales Police Force website description of Strike Force Raptor ('Reporting bikie gang activity').

The Oregonian, '"Star witness" in Gypsy Jokers Motorcycle Club racketeering, murder case is man who dealt fatal blow, lawyer says', Maxine Bernstein, 11 April 2019.

The Oregonian, 'Ex-Gypsy Joker motorcycle club member accused of racketeering fears retaliation in custody, testimony reveals', Maxine Bernstein, 9 September 2019.

OzBike.com.au, 'Builders Labourers Federation Social Club 25th Anniversary', 2019.

PerthNow, 'Don Hancock car-bomb supergrass Sidney John "Snot" Reid freed', Tony Barrass, 22 April 2018.

The Public Defenders, 'Partial defences to murder, provocation and diminished responsibility', Peter Zahra SC.

Radio New Zealand (RNZ), 'Australian ex-cop blasts National's "Strike Force Raptor" plan', 27 November 2019.

SAPOL – South Australia Police Corruption (blog, SouthAustraliaPolice.com), 'SAPOL defends new heavily armed "Security Response Unit" amid public backlash', 5 July 2020.

Seven News, 'Strike Force Raptor: Behind the specialist police taskforce busting outlaw bikie gangs', Duncan McNab, 1 December 2019.

Solidarity.net.au, 'Deregistration – union busting the BLF', 16 August 2019.

SpiritofEureka.org, 'The Builders Labourers Federation "Never Powerless" – lessons for the 21st century', 14 September 2013.

Statesman Journal, 'Gypsy Joker gang members charged with murder, racketeering, kidnapping', Whitney Woodworth, 31 January 2019.

Sunshine Coast Daily, 'Jokers keep police at bay', 14 January 2012.

Sydney Morning Herald, 'A long and bumpy road to RBT', Andrew Stevenson, 17 December 2002.

Sydney Morning Herald, 'Fatal Sydney shooting: Man refused bail', 13 January 2006.

Sydney Morning Herald, 'Gypsy Joker sniper shooting mystery', 22 April 2006.

Sydney Morning Herald, 'Don't outlaw bikie gangs', Georgina Robinson, 23 March 2009.

Sydney Morning Herald, 'Tattooist dies after suspected bikie gang shooting', Vanda Carson, 28 March 2011.

Sydney Morning Herald, 'How a murderous empire was brought down', 18 December 2011.

Sydney Morning Herald, 'Brutal facts of a seedy underworld', Malcolm Brown (reviewer), 8 September 2012.

Sydney Morning Herald, 'Gypsy Jokers clubhouse declared "restricted premises" after court hears alpaca allegations', Georgina Mitchell, 8 December 2018.

Bibliography and Further Reading

West Australian, 'Violent times in reign of bikie gangs', Sean Cowan and Gary Adshead, 1 June 2010.

West Australian, 'Reopen murder case: Former cop', Colleen Egan, 30 August 2015.

West Australian, 'Gypsy Jokers, Don Hancock, murder, mayhem and a suburban car bombing. What happened at the Ora Banda Inn?', Luke Eliot, 18 May 2019.

West Australian, 'Historic Goldfields pub Ora Banda Inn destroyed in fire north of Kalgoorlie', Jason Mennell, 18 May 2019.

ThrillingDetective.com, 'Larry Kent'.

Who.com.au, 'Australian outlaw motorcycle clubs & their territories', Rhys McKay, 27 March 2019.

Bond, Grahame, *Jack of All Trades, Mistress of One*, NewSouth Publishing, 2011.

English, Michael C., *Brave Lads: 3RAR in South Vietnam 1967–1968*, Australian Military History Publications, 2008.

Lovell, Avon, *Litany of Lies: A true story of gold heists, bombings, feral cops, greed, murder & revenge*, Bookscope, 2010.

McNeill, Ian G., *The Team: Australian Army advisers in Vietnam, 1962–1972*, University of Queensland Press in association with the Australian War Memorial, 1984.

Schwenkel, Christina, *The American War in Contemporary Vietnam: Transnational remembrance and representation*, Indiana University Press, 2009.

Scott, Stuart, *Charlie Don't Surf but Aussies Do: Taking time out from the Vietnam War*, 2009.

Thompson, Hunter S., *Hell's Angels: A strange and terrible saga*, Modern Library, 1999.

Veno, Arthur and Gannon, Edward, *The Brotherhoods: Inside the outlaw motorcycle clubs*, Allen & Unwin, 2002.

About the Authors

Paul Fenech is the brains behind the incredibly successful brand that is Fat Pizza. He plays the main character, Pauly, writes the scripts and directs the shows and films. He *is* Fat Pizza! When not working away at making Fat Pizza even more of a household name than it already is, Paul is a fully sick car hoon with an impressive line in tracksuits and an enviable police record.

Jordan King-Lacroix is a writer and musician from Sydney, Australia by way of Montreal, Canada. He wrote regularly for current affairs website The Big Smoke and has had short stories and poetry published in a handful of journals. He can be seen gigging around Sydney with political punk band The Limited, as well as on Twitter at @jaklacroix. *Ugly* is his first book.

Discover a new favourite

Visit **penguin.com.au/readmore**